SPIRITUAL LIVES

General Editor
Timothy Larsen

SPIRITUAL LIVES

General Editor
Timothy Larsen

The *Spiritual Lives* series features biographies of prominent men and women whose eminence is not primarily based on a specifically religious contribution. Each volume provides a general account of the figure's life and thought, while giving special attention to his or her religious contexts, convictions, doubts, objections, ideas, and actions. Many leading politicians, writers, musicians, philosophers, and scientists have engaged deeply with religion in significant and resonant ways that have often been overlooked or underexplored. Some of the volumes will even focus on men and women who were lifelong unbelievers, attending to how they navigated and resisted religious questions, assumptions, and settings. The books in this series will therefore recast important figures in fresh and thought-provoking ways.

Titles in the series include:

Woodrow Wilson
Ruling Elder, Spiritual President
Barry Hankins

John Stuart Mill
A Secular Life
Timothy Larsen

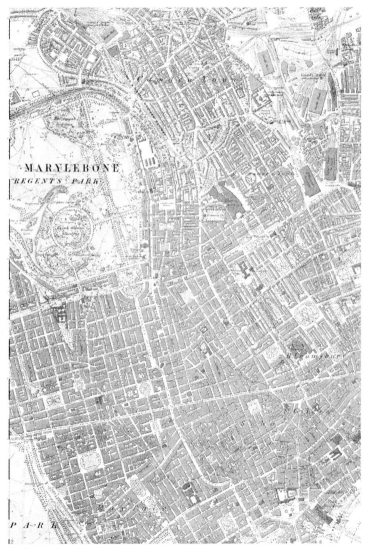

Rossetti's neighbourhood from an Ordnance Survey Map of London, 1880–1882, National Library of Scotland.

Christina Rossetti

Poetry, Ecology, Faith

EMMA MASON

OXFORD
UNIVERSITY PRESS

OXFORD
UNIVERSITY PRESS

Great Clarendon Street, Oxford, OX2 6DP,
United Kingdom

Oxford University Press is a department of the University of Oxford.
It furthers the University's objective of excellence in research, scholarship,
and education by publishing worldwide. Oxford is a registered trade mark of
Oxford University Press in the UK and in certain other countries

Published in the United States of America by Oxford University Press
198 Madison Avenue, New York, NY 10016, United States of America

British Library Cataloguing in Publication Data
Data available

Library of Congress Control Number: 2017964280

ISBN 978–0–19–872369–1

Printed and bound by
CPI Group (UK) Ltd, Croydon, CR0 4YY

Links to third party websites are provided by Oxford in good faith and
for information only. Oxford disclaims any responsibility for the materials
contained in any third party website referenced in this work.

♪♫
with love

Acknowledgements

Several colleagues have contributed to this book with an intellectual generosity for which I am extraordinarily grateful. Many thanks to the series editor, Timothy Larsen, for his enthusiasm and support; to Tom Perridge and Karen Raith at Oxford University Press for their guidance with the project; and to the book's anonymous reviewers and copy-editor, Dorothy McCarthy. I am indebted to both the kindness and exceptional scholarship of those who work on Rossetti, especially Diane D'Amico, Anthony Harrison, Lorraine Janzen Kooistra, Lizzie Ludlow, Jan Marsh, Dinah Roe, and William Whitla. Thanks also to those who invited me to speak on this book, and shared with me their own perspectives on Rossetti: Matthew Bradley and Louisa Yates at Gladstone's Library, Hawarden; Lizzie Ludlow and Kirsty Harris at Anglia Ruskin's Nineteenth-Century Studies research unit; Tessa Whitehouse at the Queen Mary Centre for Religion and Literature in English; Jan-Melissa Schramm at the Nineteenth-Century Seminar, University of Cambridge; Rebecca Styler at the Midlands Interdisciplinary Victorian Studies Seminar; and members of the Victorian Seminar, University of Oxford.

For assistance with archival research, thanks to Mark Aitken, the Master of St Katharine's, London; Nicola Allen at Woburn Abbey; Diana Coulter at ChurchCare; Kate Courage at the University of Warwick; Colin Harris at the Bodleian Libraries, University of Oxford; Anna James and Benjamin Arnold at Pusey House, Oxford; Alison Leslie at the National Library of Scotland; Claire Nicholas-Walker at the Humanities Reference Service at the British Library; Lyn Rees at the Central Archive, British Museum; Emma Robinson, Chair of Frome Museum; Andrew Wilson at the Torrington Square Chaplaincy, University of London; and Michael Woods at the British Library. Thanks also to Colin Cruise and Liz Prettejohn for helping me source images; Liese Perrin at Research Services, University of Warwick; and the staff at All Saints, Margaret Street, the Bodleian Upper Reading Room, and University of Warwick Library. I am also grateful to Chris Fletcher, keeper of Special Collections, at the

Bodleian Libraries, University of Oxford; Chelsea Shriver at Rare Books and Special Collections, University of British Columbia Library; and Craig Statham at the National Library of Scotland for quotation and image permissions.

Many conversations and correspondences helped me to think about this project, for which thanks to Isobel Armstrong, Grover J. Askins, Richard Capobianco, Jo Carruthers, Graham Davidson, Jane Dowson, Maureen Freely, Peter Galison, Dana Greene, John Holmes, Eileen John, Mark Knight, Simon Kövesi, Peter Larkin, Ayla Lepine, Jeanne Marie Missud, Ralph Norman, Tracey Potts, Jon Roberts, Michael Robson, Christopher Rowland, Jason Rudy, Matthew Rumbold, Robin Schofield, Ryan Service, Joanne Shattock, Jonathan Skinner, Elena Spandri, Jane Treglown, Camil Ungureanu, Rhian Williams, and Santiago Zabala. Finally, thanks to the Leverhulme Trust and the University of Warwick for time to write this book, and to family and friends, nonhuman and human, for encouragement and support.

Contents

Note on Names

I refer to Christina Rossetti as 'Rossetti' throughout this book, unless it is necessary to use her first name to distinguish her from family members in the same sentence. I refer to other members of her direct family using their first names: her mother and father, Gabriele and Frances, and her siblings, Maria, Gabriel, and William. Other familial Rossettis are introduced with reference to their full names.

Rossetti believed the same author wrote both the Gospel of John and the Book of Revelation. While the distinction between John the Evangelist and John of Patmos dates back to the early Church, many Victorians followed Christopher Wordsworth's suggestion that after his discipleship, John, Son of Zebedee, was banished by the Emperor Domitian to the island of Patmos where he wrote Revelation. The references to John in this book thus follow Rossetti's belief in the equivalence of the Apostle John and the visionary author of Revelation.

Note on Text

All references to Christina Rossetti's poetry are to Rebecca Crump's three-volume *The Complete Poems of Christina Rossetti: A Variorum Edition* (Baton Rouge and London: Louisiana State University Press, 1979, 1986, 1990). Dates of composition are given in the text; publication details are given for undated poems. References to her prose and letters are given in the notes. References to the Bible are from the King James Bible and Book of Common Prayer.

Introduction

Poetry, Ecology, Faith

In July 1890, Christina Rossetti wrote a short 'Memoranda for my Executor' in which she outlined a series of instructions to be fulfilled following her death. Her first request was for what would now be called a 'green' funeral: 'I wish to be buried in the nearest approach convenient to a *perishable* coffin'.[1] Perishable coffins were introduced in the late nineteenth century as part of a wave of environmental thinking. Wicker coffins, in which the deceased was shrouded in herbs and flowers, catered to those who, like Rossetti, wished to opt for a 'natural' burial. The request was important to her, one of only a few details in her will and listed alongside instructions that her executor (her brother, William) deposit a copy of one of her father's books in the Oxford Movement archive in Pusey House Library, and donate her rings to 'a Church Offertory'.[2] Her material bequests confirm her intention to be remembered as both a devout Anglo-Catholic and as a member of a universal Catholic Church that she believed embodied all Christians. Rossetti's desire that her body disintegrate into the earth, however, intimates a belief in the cyclical interdependence of life until restored in the 'new' creation, or New Jerusalem, at the end of time.[3] Her practical appeal for a biodegradable coffin alongside her doctrinal belief in death as renewed life reveals a poet who was keen to live collectively with creation both in this life and the next. Rossetti longed for the Second Advent and the end of this time because it constituted a material transformation of a creation she saw scarred by the priorities of industrialization, consumerism, imperialism, slavery, war, poverty, and the exploitation of the nonhuman for human gain. Such uneven and unequal thinking would not bring on the apocalypse, she argued, but block it from unfolding. She believed that the

new creation was the old transfigured through a graced and loving
knowing and being free of judgement and sin, and was thus dependent
on the lived realization of communion and interrelationship in this
world. Much of Rossetti's life and work was dedicated to preparing
herself and her readers for the transition into the new creation by
endorsing a way of living harmoniously with other humans and nonhumans. Her writing revealed faith as the ability to recognize one's
collective being in grace with others and God, part of a divine body in
which the Christian was moved into an environmental and ethical
relationship with creation in which all things are gathered through
grace: 'and all the members of that one body, being many, are one body:
so also is Christ' (1 Corinthians 12. 12).

It is sometimes a surprise to modern readers that many Victorian
proto-environmentalists were Christian. This is in no small part due to
a mainstream critical refusal to attend to the specifics of the history of
Christianity and ecology. Some ecocritics even deem Christianity the
'cause' of the modern ecological crisis, and align themselves with Lynn
White's much-quoted 1967 article that blamed a Western dualistic
thinking for the production of a worldview that wire-cuts the human
from nature.[4] But even White concluded his analysis with a discussion
of the patron saint of ecology, Francis of Assisi, a major influence on
Rossetti, as Chapter 3 suggests, but currently popular with thinkers
like Michael Hardt, Antonio Negri, and Giorgio Agamben for offer-
ing a spirituality that counters capitalism, consumption, and power.[5]
Pope Francis's 2015 encyclical 'Laudato Si': On Care for Our Common Home', is also resolute that human beings 'must respect the laws
of nature and the delicate equilibria existing between the creatures
of this world'; while the Eastern Orthodox Bartholomew rules that
to 'commit a crime against the natural world is a sin', to 'destroy the
biological diversity of God's creation' and 'degrade the integrity of
the Earth by causing changes in its climate' or 'contaminate the
Earth's waters, its land, air, and its life with poisonous substances—
these are sins'.[6] These pronouncements, however timely they appear
in a twenty-first-century context of environmental crisis, emerge directly from a Christian tradition in which love of creation and one's
neighbour has always been paramount. To read Rossetti's faith as
ecological is not presentist, then, but historical; her dedication to
Anglo-Catholicism was one in which she committed herself to a

series of doctrinal and moral statements about the incorporation of nonhuman, human, and divine in the figure of Christ. Through an affectionate relationship to the sea, woods, parks, stars, galaxies, and the creatures and life forms that dwelled therein, she developed her Tractarian faith into the foundation for an ecological spirituality in which all things are united in God's love.

This spiritual life of Rossetti traces an ecological love command in her writing—poetry, prose, and letters—from her early involvement in Tractarianism (Chapter 1) and the Pre-Raphaelite Brotherhood (Chapter 2), mid-life commitment to a Christian identity she saw embodied in plant and animal life (Chapter 3), and the 'weak thinking' of her later years in which she related grace to the apocalypse (Chapter 4). Her command is not impulsive or unmindful, but rather the sustained fulfilment of Jesus's summons to love others, and act and make decisions in the world under love's guidance.[7] Following John Keble, she considered poetry the ideal expression of this gentling, compassionate way of being, a lyric mode inherited from Romantic poetry, but that the Tractarians 'disciplined and tamed' into a religious and moral trigger for love and sympathy.[8] She later argued that 'hearing' was the only sense capable of tuning into the 'intangible and invisible', and that believers were ideally prepared for the reception of invisible messages through art forms like poetry that encouraged close attention.[9] For Keble too, poetry obliquely reserved religious truths in a form that allowed for the personal expression of faith and devotion, but that tempered it by directing the imagination, reason, and affections towards God. John Henry Newman described this truth as the poetic reimagining of the world as part of a divinely 'energized' cosmos in which it was a Christian 'duty' to see things 'taken into divine favour, stamped with his seal, and in training for future happiness'.[10] Drawing on Keble's formal discipline, Rossetti wrote poetry and a carefully measured prose that revealed the new creation and its promised 'future happiness' as one available in the material present to those willing to enter grace through kinship with others.[11]

Rossetti believed that kinship was the basis on which early Christianity unfolded, an ecotheological argument she traced back to the Church Fathers. Tractarianism's revival of the Fathers introduced her to a nondualist reading of grace and nature, human and nonhuman, earthly and divine, while their renewal of Anglicanism as part of a universal Catholic Church also closed the divide between Canterbury and Rome. The non-binary structure of this theology was also distinctly Trinitarian, a doctrine that proposed the ontological inseparability of the Father, Son, and Holy Ghost, and, like Paul's divine body, modelled an interconnectedness in which all things are both distinct and one. The incarnational nature of God's being in Jesus was a constant reminder to Rossetti that all of creation is made of the divine and so interdependent with itself. Rossetti's Jesus was not only God made flesh, but God made into all things, a composite of multiple species, beings, and substances. A Jewish human from Nazareth entwined with God and the Holy Spirit, Jesus was also an animal ('Behold the Lamb of God!' John 1. 36), a plant ('I am the vine', John 15. 5), a grain ('I am the bread', John 6. 35), a rock ('the chief corner stone', Ephesians 2. 20), a light ('I am the light of the world', John 8. 12) and water or wine ('If any man thirst, let him come unto me, and drink', John 7. 37). The revelation of his divinity at the point of his baptism (Matthew 3. 17) was also given through the appearance of the nonhuman in the form of a dove. At the same time, Jesus was the embodiment of grace (John 1. 17) and, as the Christ, the giver of grace to all things (Ephesians 4. 7).[12] Rossetti believed in 'prevenient grace', that which sustains life from its inception while ensuring its transition into the 'new heaven' and 'new earth' described by John in Revelation (21. 1).[13] She also believed that nonhuman life forms were always already graced because they lack the capacity for deliberate cruelty and so comprise a perfected nature that serves as an example of how to live. The human, by contrast, who does 'toil' and 'spin' (Matthew 6. 28), enters into and nourishes grace through good works and the sacraments, and also by modelling her behaviour on the nonhuman. There is thus a practicality to Rossetti's divinization (theosis) of animals and plants, one that she based on her reading of the Sermon on the Mount and Revelation. In these texts, she argued, creation appears as an entangled community of things that do not interact as separate things coming together, but that intra-act through communion with the divine.

The ecotheological reading of creation Rossetti developed across her writing offers a challenge to the modern condemnation of Christianity as the naturalizing force behind inequality between species.[14] Her Anglo-Catholic imagining of the cosmos as a fabric of participation and communal experience embodied in Christ might appear to some readers abstract if not naïve. But her faith focused her on the material realities of nonhuman suffering, as it did her peers. Anglo-Catholics were more sympathetic to animal rights than their High and Low Church counterparts, and believed that because God was revealed analogically through nature, it was the Christian's responsibility to engage with the world as an interconnected and social union. The example of Jesus, Rossetti argued, was also a clear antidote to ideologies like capitalism, imperialism, and inequality that had the potential to undermine the peaceful living-together of species. While no creature or thing was inherently or genetically 'bad' in her thinking, the structures and strategies in which they lived—beholden to what she called 'the almighty dollar'—were.[15] In Jesus's outright rejection of money and belongings Rossetti saw a refusal of both the logic of modernity and the commodification of creation as a resource to be mined and sold. She welcomed the apocalypse as that which would finally arrive to destroy, not the earth, but the 'signs of the times'—materialism, consumption, greed, wealth, power, and cruelty—that threatened to destroy it.[16] Revelation thus announced the beginning of a new and shared perspective on reality nourished by the nonhuman in the New Jerusalem. Like William Blake, Rossetti located the New Jerusalem in London, but she also understood its geography as one that would encompass 'all cities' and all natures, a transfigured world newly adorned with plant and animal life.[17]

This book insists that Rossetti was a practical and political, as well as a spiritual and ecological writer whose vision of an interconnected creation was no less real for being joyful and affirmative. Critics have overplayed Rossetti's gloomy side, one enshrined by Michael Field's memorial sonnet in which they hear her 'moan for ease' and retreat from 'joy in earth and in thy kind'.[18] But, as Rossetti playfully noted, she did not suit the role of melancholy martyr, and wrote to Gabriel: 'If only my figure would shrink somewhat! for a fat poetess is incongruous, especially when seated by the grave of buried hope.'[19] While Rossetti's poetry does reveal a writer anxious that she and her fellow humans might be 'shut out' of grace, any ostensible disquiet is faithfully transfigured and redeemed by her carefully reserved references to the Bible and the Fathers. Rossetti no doubt experienced periods

of despair and ill health from her teenage years until her death, but
to ignore the constant of loving faith she expressed in the created
world and its trees, plants, and animals is to miss the ecological
significance of her work and its rootedness in the localities she tra-
versed. Contrary to critics who suggest Rossetti was an 'urbanite
whose love of nature' was 'not rooted in specific places', I suggest
that her reading of the natural world related to particular environments and species.[20] As the frontispiece of this book shows, Rossetti's
suburban neighbourhood in Marylebone and later Bloomsbury comprised Regent's Park and the Zoological Gardens, Christ Church on
Albany Street, and the British Museum. Many of her allusions to the
natural world are focused on the flora and fauna of the trees, parks,
and garden-lined streets of this area, but she also responded to other
destinations to which she travelled—Somerset, South Ayrshire, Lancashire, Staffordshire, Hastings, Brighton, Seaford, Birchington-on-Sea,
as well as France, Switzerland, Germany, and Italy.[21] Rossetti envisioned the Christian as someone who lovingly related to the specificity
of her immediate community in its organic, inorganic, elemental, and
spiritual diversity. As she wrote in *The Face of the Deep: A Devotional
Commentary on the Apocalypse* (1892), 'We know on the highest Authority
that not one sparrow is overlooked' and that, she read in Revelation 5. 13,
every creature 'in heaven, and on the earth, and under the earth, and
such as are in the sea' is blessed and loved.[22]

This introduction provides a context in which to read this narrative
of Rossetti's life and writing. The first section reads Rossetti in relation
to current Victorian ecocriticism, which largely diminishes the role
of nineteenth-century Christianity in the development of the environmental movement. It briefly assesses how her work might contribute
to this field in relation to Pre-Raphaelitism and Tractarianism.
The second section establishes Rossetti as an educated and politicized
Christian fully committed to an inclusive understanding of creation. It
also questions the critical perception of her as a sombre and reclusive
poet by situating her in the intellectually vibrant circle of her family
and their associates. The final section anticipates the broader argument
of this book—that Rossetti's ecological faith confirms the significance of
her life and work for an early twenty-first-century present in which
indifference to the spiritual is complicit with an environmental crisis
in which the weak and vulnerable suffer most. It also makes reference

to the wider field of Rossetti studies and introduces her reading of grace and apocalypse as a unique contribution to the intradiscipline of Christianity and ecology.

Victorian Ecocriticism

The critical reluctance to read Rossetti explicitly as an ecological figure corresponds to the comparative belatedness of Victorian studies to ecocriticism, a problem recent scholarship has started to correct. As Jesse Oak Taylor argues, one of the key 'disjunctures between Victorian studies and ecocriticism' has been the 'issue of presentism, the anachronistic mapping of present concerns or ideas onto the artefacts of the past'.[23] Yet the historical intimacy between now and then in relation to ecology, industrial capitalism, and the fossil fuel economy is striking.[24] The Victorians, Taylor asserts, were the 'first inhabitants' of the Anthropocene, and redefined nature beyond pastoralism and Romanticism to encompass transformations in industry, labour, science, and aesthetics, as well as in Christianity. But Christianity has been largely sidelined from those studies willing to explore nineteenth-century ecocritical questions, and dismissed as another form of fetishized nature 'worship' dependent on an egoic spiritual self.[25] The frequent target for such criticism is William Wordsworth, despite the fact that his later and largely discounted Christian poetry unfolds its own participatory ecological vision. Rossetti registers in ecocriticism only minimally, even though her work reveals God in the specificity of an 'embodied, participatory, and social' nature in a state of continual evolution and flux.[26] She was as fascinated by the bracken and maidenhair ferns she collected in Derbyshire as she was by 'galaxies' of 'distinct luminaries', 'belts and atmospheres', 'interstellar spaces', and the 'force of suns and more than suns'.[27] As Chapter 3 argues, critics who suggest Rossetti was not concerned with the specifics of the environment choose to forget her at once empirical and spiritual prose descriptions of the cosmos. When she wrote about stars, for example, she celebrated their divine being as bodies that sing and rejoice together, even as she wondered at the recently discovered vastness of the multiverse in which they are formed, an 'atmosphere' 'full of currents and commotions' replete with 'meteors' and 'planets'.[28] That the solar system was no longer at the centre of existence and was only one of countless 'island universes' or galaxies meant that creation was infinite, as John guessed: 'And there are also many other things which Jesus did, the which, if they should be written every one, I suppose that even the world itself could not contain the books that should be written' (John 21. 25).[29]

The inaccessibility of spaces too far away to comprehend excited Rossetti, whose references to 'lunar thermal energy, solar physics, eclipses, celestial spectroscopy, planetary discovery, double stars, variable stars, nebulae, external galaxies and theories about the structure of the universe' provided her with a series of expressions for the invisible, heavenly, and cosmic.[30] As Chapter 1 explores, the Tractarians believed that 'material phenomena' are 'types' (symbols or shadows) of 'real things unseen', and that the ecosystem in which all things live was inclusive of spirit as well as matter, grace as well as nature.[31] The intimate connection between the seemingly intangible content of faith and the physical forms through which it is revealed in the world meant that everything was a type and therefore sacred. As Kirstie Blair argues, the category 'form' had a variety of meanings for the Tractarians: liturgical (the practice of ritual, phrasing of the sacraments and daily services), structural (the laws and commandments through which the Church was shaped), and aesthetic (the expression of faith in art, architecture, clothing, and decoration).[32] These forms helped the believer comprehend the multiple forms God created over seven days at the beginning of time, an event that Rossetti understood by equating the 'days of creation not as days of twenty-four hours each, but as lapses of time by us unmeasured and immeasurable'.[33] In her reading, the event of creation was ongoing until the end of time, and so comprised species both discovered and yet to be found in this world and on planets still unknown. She inherited the idea that 'all things work together for good' from Wordsworth, whose insight that humans and nonhumans alike are 'workings of one mind', the 'types and symbols of Eternity' was a cornerstone of the Oxford Movement.[34] Wordsworth's view of nature as a 'living, active, organic whole charged with divine meaning' was championed by Newman and Keble, not least because it was expressed in poetry, where imaginative and 'indirect expression' were ideally suited to the unseen and incomprehensible.[35] Like the Church Fathers and seventeenth-century divines, Wordsworth, S. T. Coleridge, Robert Southey, and

Walter Scott were valued by the Tractarians for their translation of Christian typology into an attentive consciousness of a unified creation.[36] Part of Rossetti's mission was to write a form of poetry that could communicate the charge that held this unified creation together as grace, and so reveal the cosmos as the living and dynamic body of God.

The communion of spirit and matter, grace and nature was also manifest in another movement to which Rossetti was affiliated: the Pre-Raphaelite Brotherhood. As Chapter 2 elucidates, their focus on a vibrant natural world in which everyday details like pebbles and leaves were observed alongside angels and haloes drew on what Gabriel called an 'art-Catholic', an at once medieval and Romantic aesthetic analogous to the theology that founded the Oxford Movement. Just as Newman claimed that Tractarian theology was a reaction against 'the dry and superficial character of the religious teaching and literature and the last generation', so Gabriel and his comrades sought to overcome artistic convention by reimagining the natural world with a hyperreal yet scientific precision.[37] As John Holmes states, the Pre-Raphaelites observed the world like naturalists concerned to meticulously record the botanical, ethological, and ecological in 'pursuit of truth'.[38] The interconnectedness of the infinite and abundant variety of the natural world in Pre-Raphaelite art captured what John Ruskin called 'circles of vitality' in which all things are ordered towards God. In 'The Work of Iron' (1858), Ruskin suggested these circles of vitality could transform a seemingly useless substance like rusted iron through oxygen or God's 'breath of life' (Genesis 2. 7) so that it would fortify blood and colour the landscape red, purple, and saffron. Without rust, Ruskin wrote with a prophetic discernment, the earth's 'green and glowing sphere, rich with forest and flower' would become 'the image of the vast furnace of a ghastly engine—a globe of black, lifeless, excoriated metal'.[39] This affinity between iron, oxygen, the earth, and bodies mapped an ecological system inclusive of the divine, which Ruskin publicly praised in the productions of Gabriel, William Holman Hunt, John Everett Millais, James Collinson, Elizabeth Siddal, and Edward Burne-Jones. Some critics have assumed that Rossetti's perception of this affinity was 'mitigated' by her faith, and that her 'imposition of a theological frame' obscures her reading of the natural world.[40] But the evidence of her writing confirms that her Christian faith engendered in her an environmental consciousness through its appeal to a plural creation: from her praise of God an ecological politics emerged.

One way to understand the connection between religion and ecology in Rossetti's work is through Isobel Armstrong's reading of Victorian poetry as dialogic and multiple, the lyric 'I' replaced by a doubleness through which the text internally struggles with itself to give 'equal weight' to its 'stated project' as well as 'polysemic and possible wayward meanings'.[41] Armstrong also argues that this doubleness had a particular meaning for women's poetry. For Armstrong, the female artist was compelled to adopt an 'affective mode' that was 'often simple, often pious, often conventional', but that, when pressed, revealed a 'more difficult' context, meaning, or emotional register. This is certainly the case with Rossetti, whose writing has been both lauded and berated for its apparent simplicity or 'reserve', a specifically Tractarian theory of symbol discussed in Chapter 1.[42] But modern readers have also elevated the 'possible wayward meanings' in her work to such an extent that the complexity of her 'surface' project—the expression of Christian faith—is sometimes underplayed. Her ecological love command is both wayward and declared, the constant refrain of a body of work faithful to Jesus's instruction that 'ye love one another' (John 13. 34) and that pitched grace against the 'signs of the times'. As she learned from William Dodsworth's notorious 1848 Advent sermons, preached at Rossetti's local church during the Christmas period, contemporary revolution and war had grave implications for the land as well as for those who subsisted on it. The 'symptoms of the upheaving of the earth', Dodsworth wrote, were the same as those 'preparatory to the birth of antichrist'.[43] In the same year, John Stuart Mill warned of a world 'with nothing left . . . every flowery waste or natural pasture ploughed up, all quadrupeds or birds which are not domesticated for man's use exterminated as his rivals for food, every hedgerow or superfluous tree rooted out, and scarcely a place left where a wild shrub or flower could grow without being eradicated as a weed in the name of improved agriculture'.[44] For Rossetti, Dodsworth and Mill's concerns dovetailed into a problem of time—not that its end was imminent, but that its unfolding through grace was being obstructed by human cruelty to other beings. Christ, she thought, would never return and initiate a new creation if the old was embattled and self-interested.

Rossetti explored this dilemma in her 1853 poem, 'To what purpose is this waste?', written a few years after she listened to Dodsworth's fervent 1848 sermons. The poem borrowed its title from Matthew 26, a chapter that comes after Jesus's Olivet prophecy, or his 'little apocalypse', wherein he responds to the disciples' request for a 'sign' of 'the end of the world' with a series of warnings about conflict, 'famines, and pestilences, and earthquakes' (24. 3, 7). Dodsworth's sermons cited these prophecies as a 'call to us to watch against the spirit of the times', a warning against the kind of spiritual vacuity that results in the plot to betray and kill Jesus.[45] This plot begins with his anointment at Bethany, wherein a woman approaches Jesus with 'an alabaster box of very precious ointment' (26. 7), and pours it on his head only to be angrily chastised by the disciples. 'To what purpose is this waste?' they declare, 'For this ointment might have been sold for much, and given to the poor' (26. 7–9). But Jesus admonishes the disciples for their unkindness, and reminds them that the woman's 'good work' prepares him for a death that announces the coming of God's kingdom, a genuine answer to the problem of poverty (10–11). He suggests that the disciples will 'have the poor always with' them because their response to the woman is firmly caught within an exchange economy, one that his last few discourses, beginning with the Sermon on the Mount, actively challenge. As Chapter 4 claims, Rossetti took seriously Jesus's command to prepare for the end of time, and called the old creation an 'age of probation' in which beings were called to receive grace through relationship with each other.[46] The narrator of Rossetti's poem thus attributes the 'waste' the disciples wrongly condemn to the abundance of natural diversity in which she lives: the kinship of shells, bees, mice, roses, squirrels, nightingales, acorns, hedgerows, pearls, fish, fruit, trees, water, sun, and moon is presented as a mirror of the mutual recognition between Jesus and the woman.

Like the disciples, the narrator is initially dismissive of this 'waste', and announces that the things of the poem are worthless without a human observer: 'What waste | Of good, where no man dwells' (ll. 30–1). But it is only the human that stands outside of the interconnection creation embodies in the poem, and, like the lilies and birds in Jesus's Sermon on the Mount, it is the nonhuman that teaches the human how to spiritually evolve into relationship. After the warm air and comfortable embrace of the tree lull her into sleep, she wakes to a

newly heightened sensual experience of the 'force of utter Love' that
binds 'All voices of all things' together (ll. 48–9). Her earlier presump-
tion that the world is a resource for humanity is abruptly 'silenced' by
'all hidden things' and 'all secret whisperings'—voices of creation that
join with 'things inanimate' (angels and spirits) to sing together 'one
loud hymn' (ll. 44–5, 49, 60). As the wind, sea, forests, hedges, crops,
and shells sing with the angels, and the bees store nectar to make
honey for others, nonhuman creation is revealed as graced, but also as
saintly. The nonhuman does not need to prepare for the end of time
here because it is brought into life 'Blood-cleansed' and already
wearing the robes of 'Saints' (ll. 75–7). Even the smallest details of
the nonhuman are presented as part of a participatory creation that
was made not for humans to subjugate, but as an expression of God's
love for all:

> And other eyes than our's
> Were made to look on flowers,
> Eyes of small birds and insects small:
> The deep sun-blushing rose
> Round which the prickles close
> Opens her bosom to them all.
> The tiniest living thing
> That soars on feathered wing,
> Or crawls among the long grass out of sight,
> Has just as good a right
> To its appointed portion of delight
> As any King.   (ll. 78–9)

Rossetti's expression of the rights of creation here is part of an animal
welfare movement popularized in eighteenth-century literature.[47]
It echoes poems like Anna Barbauld's 'The Mouse's Petition, Found
in the Trap where he had been Confined all Night' (1773) and Robert
Burns's 'To a Mouse, on turning her up in her nest with the plough'
(1785), both of which berated the human for looking upon nature
as a picture from which they are excised and so seek to control.
As Barbauld wishes the kindness of angels on the mouse, Burns cries
an apology for breaking 'nature's social union' and destroying the
'wee bit housie' of an 'earth born companion', one more 'blest' than
any human.[48] Rossetti too suggested the nonhuman is blessed in a way

the human is not: only the human has 'fallen' from grace because of a transgression, not simply against God, but against creation.

In her study of the commandments, *Letter and Spirit* (1883), Rossetti presented a nuanced reading of the human 'fall' from grace in relation to Adam and Eve's response to the nonhuman. She compared the 'sins' of Adam and Eve and argued that Eve might be forgiven because her actions were driven by a hospitable relationship to others. Adam's sin, Rossetti wrote, was to 'shelter himself at the expense of Eve', a decision 'diametrically opposed to the Divine law' because it broke his connection with those around him and allowed the 'strong' to inflict 'suffering on the weak'.[49] Eve, however, 'made a mistake' based on her attempt to listen and engage with the snake, an action that reveals a 'tenderness of spirit' in Eve that is only undercut by her inability to understand it in relation to 'God's Will'.[50] Both are ultimately guilty for Rossetti because they split creation, nonhuman and human, from God and fail to recognize that God is not 'like His creature', but that every 'creature is like Him', the 'multitudinous ever-multiplying creation' bound together in a polymorphic oneness.[51] Her poetry and prose alike was directed at spotlighting the consequences of ignoring this likeness, or worse, assuming the human as a model for God. Rossetti argued that humans have 'reversed the process of creation' by making 'gods' after their 'own likeness'— power, money, ownership, all of which bend the flow of grace away from creation. In seeing all things 'changed into the same image' in 'the Spirit of the Lord' (2 Corinthians 3. 18), as Paul wrote, the human is joined with the rest of creation as an equal member within it. The narrator of 'To what purpose is this waste?' includes the reader in this shared world by asking her not to 'grudge' nonhuman resources 'while we have enough', and in doing so, presents the anointing woman's local economy of kindness as an alternative to the disciples' outsourcing logic (ll. 90–1). The narrative of the poem suggests that faith constitutes not blind devotion but prayerful attention to the interconnectedness of the immediate environment. While humans 'have heard | And known' this connection, they 'have not understood' it, the narrator confesses (ll. 123–4). To explicate this understanding, the narrator reasserts creation's multiple unity by concluding with a Trinitarian vision at the end of the poem in the line 'O earth, earth, earth' (l. 125). Without recognition of the shared being between things, she warns, it is not only the earth's fate that is compromised, but also those that destroy it, condemned to be 'Exposed and valued at thy worth' and forced to 'stand ashamed and dumb.— | Ah, when the Son of Man shall come' (ll. 131–2).

As this book argues, Rossetti's writing constantly returned to the urgency of living peacefully with creation so as not to disturb the flow of grace through which things are carried into the new creation. While her vision was universal and 'Catholic', its fulfilment was dependent on the believer attending to the local and specific in relation to scripture and the Fathers, which in turn produces a multiplicity of readings that resists the univocal or literal. She argued for the viability of theology as a resistance to the human desire for power and control, especially in relation to what she called the 'misuse or neglect' of the earth.[52] She also understood the cosmic entanglement of things in God as the basis for a material, rather than simply possible, renewal of the earth. Rossetti's contribution to an emergent environmentalism was to resituate this renewal in a theological and ethical framework in which an 'economy of grace', not money, keeps things moving and in relationship with the love of God.[53] As she wrote in her poem for *The Face of the Deep*, 'Tune me, O Lord', the faithful Christian desires to be tuned into a single 'harmony' comprised of the combined notes of multiple beings that are sounded in 'one full responsive vibrant chord' (ll. 1–2). In her note to the poem, Rossetti argued that the immortal state of the new creation is dependent not on the actions of the few in the future, but on the interdependence of human and nonhuman in the present joined in God's 'heart'. As a free gift that the believer is 'free to accept or decline', God's love is eternally available, and blocked only by its opposite: egoic self-preoccupation in which the human is dominated by its own life and outcomes at the expense of other things.[54] This over-identification with self-centric emotion and behaviour, now perceived as a modern disease, was a symptom of a society that no longer functioned within grace for Rossetti. Her 'weak' response to it, non-egoic, affectionate, and habituated to grace, refused the 'strong' thinking of power, anger, money, and violence for a poetry she hoped would shift the consciousness of her readers from a consumerist anxiety into a graced state of communion.

Education and Politics

Rossetti was an educated, political, and meditative writer, and identified herself as a poet, author, and teacher.[55] She worked innovatively
with scripture, the Church Fathers, and a broad tradition of Christian
poetry to show her readers how to enter into grace and relate lovingly
to the created world. Her experiments with form and genre resulted in
both a devotional prose in which she combined scripture, exegesis,
and verse commentary, and a poetics that played with metrically
melodious if bold rhythms that sometimes gently, sometimes urgently
sought to persuade readers of her vision. As a child, she was influenced
not only by Christian poetry, but by medieval tales and eighteenth-
century horror stories, as well as contemporary science (the family
were close friends with Charles Lyell). Rossetti also contributed to a
weekly family magazine called *Hodge-Podge*, an anthology that included
a short ecological commentary on the 'smoky, smithy' climate of
nineteenth-century London.[56] As one of the 'two storms' of the family
with Gabriel (William and Maria were the 'two calms'), she had
always been encouraged to read and study, and was, her grandfather
declared, '*Avrà più spirit di tutti*'.[57] Her Italian émigré father, Gabriele,
was a Dante scholar and translator, and her mother, Frances Polidori,
was keen to pass on her own education in French, Spanish, Italian,
German, Greek, and Latin.[58] A former governess to John Shelley
(brother of Percy Bysshe) and sister of Byron's physician, John Polidori,
Frances introduced the Rossetti children to a culturally and historically
plural intellectual world, and trained them in languages, maths, science,
literature, and theology.[59] Alongside the Bible, Rossetti was soon reading
Dante, Plato, Augustine, Aquinas, George Herbert, and William Blake,
as well as Oxford Movement writers such as Newman, Keble, Edward
Bouverie Pusey, and Isaac Williams.

   This library incorporates an unusual combination of influences that
resonate across her writing. While her personal library was small (she
spent little on anything except rent and food, owning few clothes or
other possessions), she had access to her grandfather Gaetano Polidori's
collections at Holmer Green, Buckinghamshire and at his villa in Park
Village East as well as her family's shared books. She also lived near the
British Museum and owned her own 'ticket' for its Reading Room from
1860, where she consulted the archives while writing a series of entries

on Italian authors for the *Imperial Dictionary of Universal Biography* and her never-completed book on Ann Radcliffe for the *Eminent Women* series.[60] Given the extent of her theological reach, distinct ecological reading of Anglo-Catholic doctrine, and wide social circle (which included Gabriel's Pre-Raphaelite friends, Ruskin, Collinson, Hunt, and Siddal, as well as those who admired her writing, like Algernon Charles Swinburne, Lewis Carroll, Barbara Leigh Smith Bodichon, Gerard Manley Hopkins, Dora Greenwell, Julia Cameron, and William Bell Scott), it is strange that many readers still regard Rossetti as a solitary mystic disconnected from the world around her. The fault lies in part with her brother, William, who shaped the early reception of her life and writing from the end of the nineteenth century. Eager to protect a fantasy of Rossetti as a sheltered and unread extempore versifier, William portrayed her as an apolitical writer who at 'no point of her life' was 'a great devourer of books', who 'knew nothing' of 'science and philosophy', and who studied theology 'very little indeed'.[61] Her first biographer, Mackenzie Bell, also recorded several of her (male) acquaintances all of whom echoed William's certainty that her 'habits of composition were eminently of a spontaneous kind' wherein she 'rapidly' 'scribbled' poetry 'impelled' by 'her feelings'. One observer claimed that she 'wrote for hours with no mental effort', and another that she 'shut her eyes' before writing to conjure 'all the scene'.[62]

Modern biographers are equally vague in regard to her role as a public intellectual. Jan Marsh appears to concur with William that Rossetti 'developed no interest in scholarship', but her admirable biography makes countless references to Rossetti's engagement with literature, theology, and art. Kathleen Jones too contends that Rossetti was an 'enigmatic figure' whose main writing subject was 'suffering', but her biography is also attentive to Rossetti's involvement with Gabriel's circle of artists and writers, as well as the Italian 'exiles, patriots, politicians, literary men, musicians' invited home by her father.[63] Frances Thomas almost completely evades Rossetti's erudition, and makes the unlikely suggestion that Rossetti avoided Gabriel's acquaintances and confined herself only to close family and the 'Reverend Mr Dodsworth'.[64] Lona Mosk Packer's notorious invention of a love affair between Rossetti and Gabriel's friend, William Bell Scott, is equally implausible; while Georgina Battiscombe, alert to the significance of Anglo-Catholicism in Rossetti's life, portrays a poet frustrated and curbed by Victorian society and religious duty.[65] These biographies have all been invaluable in situating Rossetti in nineteenth-century British culture. But their tendency to attribute the gloominess of some of her narrators to her life has obscured Rossetti's lively and inventive engagement with spirituality and the diversity of creation. Only Bell's biography, which is arguably more balanced than William's records, directly reverses this trend in the assertion that 'none valued really great books more than she'.[66] As this book illustrates, although Rossetti was reluctant to openly perform her knowledge, she was extraordinarily well read, intensely political, and capable of outlining a religious vision of a transformed world in which things shared an equal relationship to resources and God.

Like the writers she most valued—Plato, Augustine, Dante, and Blake—Rossetti welcomed the reign of God as a 'radical and subversive challenge to the world, its powers and authorities'. While her vision is not as fiery as Blake's, she consistently appealed to Jesus and the early Church as 'paradigms' of 'polity and action'.[67] The cause by which she was most energized, as Chapter 3 shows, was the anti-vivisection movement to which she uncompromisingly dedicated herself until the end of her life. She was also painfully aware of the damaging effects of London's smog-filled environment on her health, and suffered from both Graves' disease and breast cancer, and was turned down from volunteering with Florence Nightingale because of severe climate-sensitive symptoms.[68] Her health did not impede her political consciousness, however. She opposed slavery ('for slavery, I loathe and abhor'), was appalled by the British empire ('so much injustice & bloodshed have (I believe) founded & upheld our rule'), and firmly rejected hierarchy based on rank and wealth, especially in the Church.[69] She worked for the poor at Christ Church, Albany Street, and for 'fallen' women at the St Mary Magdalene refuge in Highgate; she donated to the 'workless Lancashire people' affected by the mid-century depression in the cotton industry; and advocated for the 'Protection of Minors' bill against child prostitution.[70] Rossetti was also a determined thinker, who fought to retain copyright over her work and acknowledged her inclusion in what she called 'the strongminded-woman lists' alongside George Eliot and Augusta Webster.[71] Her refusal to sign Emily Davies's petition for a proposed women's college at Cambridge is much cited as evidence of her compromised gender politics, but even Davies recognized that she declined on religious grounds because it 'did not belong to the Catholic Church'.[72] Rossetti in fact welcomed women's education, and attended several courses on Dante at University College, London, as well as establishing her own schools in early life. Her work, instructive as well as devotional, confirms Plato's assertion that women should, equally with men, be guardians or watchdogs of society.[73]

While she allowed for what she perceived as the Bible's 'unalterable distinction between men and women', Rossetti nevertheless argued for 'female rights', the inclusion of 'married women' in suffrage, women members of parliament, and for women as 'national legislators' as long as men continued as the 'exclusive soldier-representatives of the nation, and engross the whole payment in life and limb for national quarrels'.[74] What is striking about this statement is the language Rossetti used to condemn the idea of women occupying military roles. She moved swiftly from the fact of conflict to its consequences as a form of butchering justified by an economy of physical oppression and legitimized slaughter entirely incompatible with the love command. The implicit connection between the 'payment in life and limb' a female solider might make and the gory horror of cutting up a living being haunted Rossetti's observations on gender, and gestures towards Carol J. Adams's observation that women and animals alike are reduced to fragmented parts by a society obsessed with a cannibalistic and bloody power.[75] The connection was alarmingly apparent to Rossetti, who was as troubled by the experiences suffered by the women she volunteered to help at the St Mary Magdalene refuge as she was by the savagery of vivisection. Vivisection, like the mistreatment of any living thing, was abhorrent to Rossetti because it shattered God's covenant made 'between me and you and every living creature that is with you' (Genesis 9. 12). Her private exegesis of Genesis illuminated the discrepancy between the mistreatment of animals and a covenant that is uncomfortable with the human consumption of blood. While Rossetti was not a vegetarian, she tended towards a diet that took 'for meat', every 'herb bearing seed' and 'tree yielding seed' (Genesis 1. 28–9), and perceived plant life as at once symbol and material incarnation of a baptismal network of roots through which holy water was carried to all beings.

Rossetti also recognized in the vegetal a way of being in creation without ego or individual identity. This is evident in her many readings of the Sermon on the Mount as a text that asks the human to attentively 'consider the lilies of the field' (Matthew 6. 28) as types of communal cognition and behaviour. As the philosopher Michael Marder argues, plant thinking constitutes a 'fluid, receptive, dispersed, non-oppositional, non-representational, immanent, and material-practical' approach to the world that actively challenges a dualistic ontology of power and absolutes.[76] Gianni Vattimo and Santiago Zabala equate Marder's plant thinking with weak thinking, a sensitivity to the fragile foundations of nonhuman and human lives and thought that rejects the 'strong structures of metaphysics' for a relational, ethical, and attentive hermeneutics.[77] For the Catholic Vattimo, weak thinking specifically configures faith as tolerance, charity, love, and an openness to a plurality of subjectivities and kinships.[78] To be faithful, he suggests, one must think with the same mind as Christ, one that Paul describes in Philippians: 'Let this mind be in you, which was also in Christ Jesus: Who, being in the form of God, thought it not robbery to be equal with God: But made himself of no reputation, and took upon him the form of a servant, and was made in the likeness of men' (2. 5–7). Philippians 2 was a key text for Rossetti, one that outlines Christ's kenōsis or self-emptying to become human as a renunciation of power, authority, and transcendence. In Vattimo's reading of the kenōtic moment, Christ twists away from the strong claims of God to embrace the weak claims of charity and love, a material kindness and consolation that reveals Christianity itself as a weak religion of brokenness, crucifixion, and unknowing. Rossetti also found in Christianity a politics in which the weak, vulnerable, and poor are valued, and into which its participants are invited to empty themselves before God as members of one divine body. As Chapter 4 discusses, she conceived of kenōsis as a moment of emptying and nothingness that ultimately resulted in theosis, the divinization of things through Christ's Incarnation. God's love and mercy, she wrote in her poem 'Seven vials hold Thy wrath', is an 'empty plenitude', 'Infinitude | Boundlessly overflowing with all good, | All lovingkindness' (ll. 2–4, 6).[79]

An Ecological Love Command

Through kenōsis and weakness, Rossetti suggested that the world can appear Edenic and paradisiacal, and revealed creation as a multi-species kinship in which things receive grace and flourish through intimacy and fellowship with each other and God. She considered it her Christian duty to prepare her readers to undergo transformation through a shift into this weak perspective. But she was also willing to explore the consequences of failing to prepare for change, as her sonnet 'The World' (1854) illustrated. Revising the Petrarchan love sonnet to focus on an excessive erotic desire for consumption and self-gratification, Rossetti separated God's loving creation from its manifestation in the human ego as sensualism and avarice. This voracious world is one in which things are disconnected and commodified, plant life mere bait to 'woo' the narrator with a promise of 'full satiety', and the animal diminished to a beast-like and monstrous 'horror' that threatens to pull her into a hell-like vortex (ll. 1, 6, 10). Baying at the narrator to sell her soul, this world is claustrophobically hedonic and grasping, and intent on setting its inhabitants against one another. But the same world is portrayed as a non-hierarchical and symbiotic entanglement in her sonnet sequence, 'Later Life: A Double Sonnet of Sonnets', which maps the development of faith from its inception at the beginning of time to its fulfilment in the New Jerusalem.[80] In this new creation, things 'feel and see with different hearts and eyes' and are gentled into relationship with each other through love for God (sonnet eight, l. 1). The request of sonnet ten is thus addressed to all things:

> Tread softly! all the earth is holy ground.
>   It may be, could we look with seeing eyes,
>   This spot we stand on is a Paradise
> Where dead have come to life and lost been found,
> Where Faith has triumphed, Martyrdom been crowned,
>   Where fools have foiled the wisdom of the wise;
>   From this same spot the dust of saints may rise   (ll. 1–7)

Here, it is the effort of accepting and 'seeing' the earth as holy that conjures it as a Paradise in the immediate present. The specificity of 'this spot' and 'this same spot' suggests that the particular location in which the reader encounters the poem is itself a site of resurrection and renewal. By presenting the particularity of the narrator and reader's geography as a sacred topophilia, Rossetti suggests that environmental perception creates Paradise. Where 'fools' fail to see the materialization of Paradise around them, the faithful recognize and work to keep their homes and neighbourhoods as places of recovery and new life. It is a devotional perception that goes beyond 'touch or sight', the narrator observes in sonnet twenty-two, one that takes the believer through sensory reality into the 'silent chords' of creation's 'keen magic' (ll. 4, 6, 7).

Apocalypse was not a model of progress towards some distant point in the future for Rossetti, then, but the promise of immediate transformation triggered through the love of things for each other. An interconnected creation in which all things are saved through a mutual love incarnated in the divine body is the defining idea of Rossetti's theology. Yet ecocriticism tends to overlook Christianity, even as it creatively draws on its language and thinking. In *Staying with the Trouble*, for example, Donna Haraway describes an interdependency driven by an 'assembling' vitality in which 'All critters share a common "flesh", laterally, semiotically, and genealogically'.[81] While the idea of 'flesh' invokes the incarnation of the logos through which non-divine things come to know the divine, Haraway elides any reference to the sacred with the exception of a comment that Christians avoid the 'urgency of climate change because it touches too closely on the marrow' of their faith.[82] Dismissing Christian faith and iconography as wholly negative, Haraway turns instead to the spider's web as a metaphor of interdependence, specifically that of the *Pimoa cthulhu*, namesake of her alternative to the Anthropocene, the Chthulucene (a way of becoming-with-each-other). She confesses that she likes the idea of the web because of its proximity to weaving, a '*sensible*' practice that 'performs and manifests the meaningful lived connections for sustaining kinship, behaviour' and 'relational action' for 'humans and nonhumans'.[83] Similarly, Timothy Morton openly disdains what he perceives to be a selfish 'Christian apocalypticism' in *The Ecological Thought*, one so focused on the end of the world it has ceased to care about real life. Morton offers his own image of togetherness in the notion of the 'mesh', a term he claims to have borrowed from the biological sciences, mathematics, and engineering to counter the affectively suspicious warmth and joy embodied in the sentimentality of Christianity.[84] Jane Bennett too equates Christianity with conquest paradigms of human power in her book, *Vibrant Matter*, preferring a vital materialism of matter-energy to conceive of a synchronicity between the seen and unseen. Like Haraway and Morton, Bennett reduces Christianity to a one-dimensional simplification of fundamentalist Evangelicalism, and so leaves no room for the history of radical Christian ecology to which Rossetti's work contributed.[85]

Bennett does, however, conclude her study with a litany, one that rewrites the very creed in which the Trinity is affirmed as the force from which 'all things were made'. She asserts 'a kind of Nicene Creed for would-be vital materialists: "I believe in one matter-energy, the maker of things seen and unseen . . . I believe that encounters with lively matter can chasten my fantasies of human mastery." '[86] Whether derisive mimicry or outright parody, her creed nevertheless invokes an interrelation and entanglement that is material and spiritual. Rossetti's spiritual materialism also rejects human mastery and dominion through its focus on Jesus as a composite of all things, a participatory being whose vitality is not a metaphor like a web or mesh, but rather a body comprising other bodies all of which are loved. The affectively jubilant religious language in which she worked to express her faith embraced creation as more than a conglomerate of parts, and one of her favourite words—'lovely'—allowed her to extend the affection of love into friendship, kindness, attentiveness, and joy. As the source of love, Rossetti's 'altogether lovely' Jesus incarnates love as animating, lived, and co-presencing, the basis of a communion that plants and animals do not need to be taught. Only the antagonistic human needs to be constantly brought back into relation with love through prayer and the sacraments.[87] As Clement of Alexandria argued, the love command is the good life the philosophers have always sought, the basis of a sacred commons that founds the kingdom of God as the mutual self-dedication of things.[88] The lived experience of this commons is membership of the divine body as Paul states: 'And whether one member suffer, all the members suffer with it; or one member be honoured, all the members rejoice with it' (1 Corinthians 12. 26). Or, as Jesus declared, all things should exist in the knowledge that their behaviour impacts directly upon him: 'Verily I say unto you, Inasmuch as ye have done it unto one of the least of these my brethren, ye have done it unto me' (Matthew 25. 40).

As this book argues, Rossetti's ecological love command extended to a wholly inclusive understanding of 'brethren' in which compassion was mutual and reciprocal. Like Francis of Assisi, she perceived all beings and substances as companions, as her poem 'Hurt no living thing' illustrates, published in *Sing-Song: A Nursery Rhyme Book* (1872). Her own illustrations for this poem and its companion piece, 'I caught a little lady bird', revealed both an attention to the smallest and most overlooked elements of creation, and also an unambiguous environmental politics developed by Arthur Hughes in his designs for the published version.[89] He based his own images on her sketches, including one she drew of a tiny constellation of creatures—a worm, grasshopper, cricket, moth, ladybird, gnat, and butterfly—pencilled in above her text:

> Hurt no living thing:
>   Ladybird, nor butterfly,
> Nor moth with dusty wing,
>   Nor cricket chirping cheerily,
> Nor grasshopper so light of leap,
>   Nor dancing gnat, nor beetle fat,
> Nor harmless worms that creep.

The command 'Hurt no living thing' was an unequivocal and inclusive statement Victorian readers might have expected from a poet so publicly committed to the anti-vivisection movement. Hughes's drawing amplified that message by reconfiguring her sketch to place the spider, moth, grasshopper, gnat, and ladybird around a large mole, nose in the air and paws praying to heaven not to be hung by the noose that ominously lingers behind him. As John Clare's poem 'Remembrances' observed, enclosure not only 'levelled every bush & tree & levelled every hill', but it also 'hung the moles for traitors', their executions candid reminders of privatizing creation.[90] Hughes's revisions of Rossetti's illustrations also extended to 'I caught a little ladybird', in which he reframed her drawing of a girl leaping towards a ladybird as an image of a girl with a doll. Rossetti's picture also included the doll, but it lies motionless on a chair at the margins of the page, a 'senseless wooden thing' that stares into nothingness and is unable to age (l. 9). Both captured the poem's comment that the human shares more vitality and love with a nonhuman critter than a human-shaped object forced into enervating social roles. But only Rossetti's animated girl, reaching out towards the bug, revealed the energy behind all her writing about nonhumans, a grace that holds creation buoyant in relationship with itself.

My argument for an ecological love command at the foundation of Rossetti's life and writing is not without precedent in scholarship on the poet. Critics including Diane D'Amico, Mary Arseneau, Karen Dieleman, Linda E. Marshall, Dinah Roe, Elizabeth Ludlow, and Josh King all portray a devotionally sophisticated Christian keen to convey a graced and loving vision of creation and its creator.[91] Ludlow and King in particular read her vision of creation as comprising a spiritual community that 'transcends any national or institutional body' and in which believers are invited into a trans-historical communion of saints.[92] Lynda Palazzo, Lorraine Janzen Kooistra, Heidi Scott, Todd O. Williams, Kelly Sultzbach, Nathan K. Hensley, and Serena Trowbridge also recognize a proto-environmentalism in her writing.[93] The modern poet Peter Larkin even cites 'To what purpose is this waste?' at the beginning of his volume *City-Trappings (Housing Heath or Wood)* (2016) to frame his interest in 'scarcity' as a gift that counters the logic of resource exhaustion.[94] This study is similarly concerned with Rossetti's imagining of a spiritual but also cosmic community that extends to all aspects of creation, the seen—plants, animals, minerals, and fungi—and the unseen—the dead, angels, and spirits. But it is also the first study to identify an ecotheological reading of grace as the foundation for Rossetti's faith and politics. For her call that her readers contemplate 'any creature' as the revelation of Jesus constituted a compelling argument against an Enlightenment individualism that had atomized the world into an existence defined by competition, self-care, and ego. Without Jesus as intermediary, reflection on things would become, she thought, mere pleasure or objectification, and reduce nature to a fetishized pastoral.[95] Rossetti did not romanticize creation, nor endow the human with the role of master caretaker of the earth, but rather envisioned things in relation to each other.[96] In doing so, she refused the now discredited notion that life combatively struggles against itself and eliminates ostensibly weak minorities in an onward march towards evolutionary perfection.[97]

This was not a denial of Darwinism, but rather a reading of evolution as the development of things through shared and common attributes rather than ranked abilities.[98] As Rossetti wrote in *Time Flies: A Reading Diary* (1885), the beginning of time is an 'Origin not of species only but of genera', a plurality of categories in which things are gathered not classified.[99]

Rossetti was committed to a vision of unity and multiplicity in which the act of overlooking or erasing any part of creation was to risk the fragmentation of the divine. In an echo of Colossians 3. 11, 'Christ *is* all, and in all', she wrote in *The Face of the Deep*: 'All who are united to Christ are thereby united to one another', and so joined in God's forgiving communion through theosis and kenōsis.[100] As she learned from the Cappadocian Fathers, God is communion, an idea confirmed in the being of the Trinity as a co-inherence or dance in which three become one in an eternal movement of circular divinity ('perichoresis').[101] This whirling around the other, Gregory of Nyssa observed, signified an endless 'falling in love' in which the believer, human and nonhuman, is held.[102] In Rossetti's version of this falling in love, all things—from gnats to whales, ferns to millipedes, dogs to angels, humans to stones—have 'faith' because they are part of creation, and in loving God they are 'emptied' of the burden of ego and hubris and so 'replenished'.[103] This pneumatology, at once material and mystical, looked back to the Fathers as it gestured towards a fellow feeling and affective kinship in which the ecological and theological become inseparable if not equivalent.[104] Rossetti's insight was to articulate such equivalence in a poetic form that, Keble wrote, 'fill [ed] the soul, even to overflowing', but in an oblique and discerning mode in which nothing, resources or language, is wasted.[105] In doing so, she sought to attune the vision of her reader to what she called the 'parallel revelation' of nature and grace, seen through 'eyes that have been supernaturalized' and so interpret 'not literally', but spiritually and figuratively.[106] From her early poems that vitalize stars and trees to her later reading of apocalypse as renewal, Rossetti's language brings the reader to the experience of dwelling in creation through a relational and loving thinking of it as a radical divine solidarity with an unfolding cosmos.[107]

Notes

1. Christina G. Rossetti, 'Memoranda for my Executor', quoted by kind permission of the Angeli-Dennis Collection, University of British Columbia Special Collections Division, Box 10, 10–12, from facsimile in Bodleian Libraries, Oxford, MS Facs.d.285.

2. Gabriele Rossetti, *Il Mistero dell' Amor Platonico del Medio Evo derivato dai Misteri Antichi* (Londra: Dalla Tipografia di Riccardo e Giovanni E. Taylor, 1840).

3. See Linda E. Marshall, 'What the Dead are Doing Underground: Hades and Heaven in the Writings of Christina Rossetti', *The Victorian Newsletter*, 72 (1987), 55–60.

4. Lynn White, Jr, 'The Historical Roots of Our Ecological Crisis', *Science*, 155.3767 (10 March 1967), 1203–7; see Yi-Fu Tuan's early response to White in 'Our Treatment of the Environment in Ideal and Actuality', *American Scientist*, 58 (May–June 1970), 244–9.

5. Antonio Negri and Michael Hardt, *Empire* (Cambridge, MA: Harvard University Press, 2000); Giorgio Agamben, *The Highest Poverty: Monastic Rules and Form-of-Life*, trans. Adam Kotsko (Stanford: Stanford University Press, 2011).

6. 'Encyclical Letter of Laudato Si' of the Holy Father Francis on Care for our Common Home' (2015), https://laudatosi.com; 'Address of His Holiness Ecumenical Patriarch Bartholomew at the Environmental Symposium, Santa Barbara, CA. November 8, 1997', in Roger S. Gottlieb, *This Sacred Earth: Religion, Nature, Environment* (New York: Routledge, 2004), 229–30.

7. See Victor Paul Furnish, *The Love Command in the New Testament* (Nashville and New York: Abington Press, 1972).

8. G. B. Tennyson, *Victorian Devotional Poetry: The Tractarian Mode* (Cambridge, MA: Harvard University Press, 1981), 26.

9. Christina G. Rossetti, *The Face of the Deep: A Devotional Commentary on the Apocalypse* (London: Society for Promoting Christian Knowledge, 1892), 352.

10. John Henry Newman, Review of *The Theatre of the Greeks; or the History, Literature, and Criticism of the Grecian Drama*, Cambridge 1827, in *The London Review*, 1. 1 (1829), 153–71 (168–70).

11. The Chinese word 'tao' ('way', 'path', 'principle') was sometimes translated into English as 'grace' in the nineteenth century, see, for example, Lao Tzu, E. H. Parker, 'The *Tao-Têh King*, or "Providential Grace" Classic (in Two Divisions)', in *The Dublin Review*, 133.48 (1903), 360–76, and 134.39 (1904), 155–77.

12. Christina G. Rossetti, *Called to Be Saints: The Minor Festivals Devotionally Studied* (London: Society for Promoting Christian Knowledge, 1881), 272–3.

13. Rossetti, *Face of the Deep*, 547.

14. Erica Fudge, *Animal* (London: Reaktion Books, 2002), 15–16.
15. Rossetti, *Face of the Deep*, 272; Rossetti would have encountered the phrase in either Charles Dickens's *American Notes: For General Circulation* (London: Chapman and Hall, 1842); or Edward Bulwer-Lytton's *The Coming Race* (Edinburgh: W. Blackwood and Sons, 1871).
16. Rossetti, *Face of the Deep*, 243.
17. Ibid. 480; on Blake, see Kevin Hutchings, *Imagining Nature: Blake's Environmental Poetics* (Montreal and Kingston: McGill-Queen's University Press, 2002), 60.
18. Michael Field, 'Original Verse. To Christina Rossetti', *The Academy* (1896), 284; 'Michael Field' was the pen name of Katherine Harris Bradley and Edith Emma Cooper; see Josh King, *Imagined Spiritual Communities in Britain's Age of Print* (Columbus: Ohio State University Press, 2015), 243.
19. Christina G. Rossetti to Dante Gabriel Rossetti, 4 August 1881, in Anthony H. Harrison, ed., *The Letters of Christina Rossetti: Volume I 1843–1873; Volume II 1874–1881; Volume III 1882–1886; Volume IV 1887–1894* (Charlottesville and London: The University Press of Virginia, 1997, 1999, 2000, 2004), II, 289; further references are abbreviated to *Letters*.
20. Serena Trowbridge, '"Truth to nature": The Pleasures and Dangers of the Environment in Christina Rossetti's Poetry', in Laurence W. Mazzeno and Ronald D. Morrison, eds., *Victorian Writers and the Environment: Ecocritical Perspectives* (London and New York: Routledge, 2017), 63–78 (65–6).
21. Christina G. Rossetti to Anne Burrows Gilchrist, Autumn 1865, *Letters*, I, 254; Christina G. Rossetti to William Michael Rossetti, 13 August 1878, *Letters*, II, 177–8.
22. Rossetti, *Face of the Deep*, 163.
23. Jesse Oak Taylor, 'Where is Victorian Ecocriticism?' *Victorian Literature and Culture*, 43 (2015), 877–94 (877).
24. Ibid. 878; and see Wendy Parkins, ed., *Victorian Sustainability in Literature and Culture* (London: Routledge, 2018).
25. See, for example, Scott Hess, *William Wordsworth and the Ecology of Authorship* (Charlottesville and London: University of Virginia Press, 2012).
26. Ibid. 2.
27. Christina G. Rossetti, *Seek and Find: A Double Series of Short Studies on the Benedicite* (London: Society for Promoting Christian Knowledge, 1879), 37; Rossetti, *Called to Be Saints*, 446.
28. Rossetti, *Seek and Find*, 17, 24.
29. Anna Henchman, 'Outer Space: Physical Science', in Matthew Bevis, ed., *The Oxford Handbook of Victorian Poetry* (Oxford: Oxford University Press, 2013), 690–708 (691).
30. Linda E. Marshall, 'Astronomy of the Invisible: Contexts for Christina Rossetti's Heavenly Parables', *Women's Writing*, 2.2 (1995), 167–81 (168).
31. John Henry Newman, *Apologia Pro Vita Sua* (1864; London: Penguin, 1994), 37.

32. Kirstie Blair, *Form and Faith in Victorian Poetry and Religion* (Oxford: Oxford University Press, 2012).

33. Rossetti, *Seek and Find*, 87.

34. Ibid. 79; William Wordsworth, *The Prelude* (1850), VI, 636–9, in Jonathan Wordsworth et al., eds., *William Wordsworth: The Prelude 1799, 1805, 1850* (New York and London: W. W. Norton, 1979), 219.

35. Stephen Prickett, *Romanticism and Religion: The Tradition of Coleridge and Wordsworth in the Victorian Church* (Cambridge: Cambridge University Press, 1976), 104; John Keble, 'Memoirs of the Life of Sir Walter Scott by J. G. Lockhart', *British Critic* (1838), in *Occasional Papers and Reviews* (Oxford and London: James Parker and Co., 1877), 1–80 (12).

36. Newman, *Apologia*, 99–100.

37. Ibid. 99.

38. John Holmes, 'Science, Nature, and Knowledge in William Michael Rossetti's "Fancies at Leisure" and "Mrs Holmes Grey"', *Victorian Poetry*, 53.1 (2015), 15–39 (18).

39. John Ruskin, 'The Work of Iron, in Nature, Art, and Policy: A Lecture delivered at Tunbridge Wells, February 16, 1858', in E. T. Cook and Alexander Wedderburn, eds., *The Works of John Ruskin*, 39 vols (London: George Allen, 1905), XVI, 378.

40. Sean C. Grass, 'Nature's Perilous Variety in Rossetti's "Goblin Market"', *Nineteenth-Century Literature*, 51.3 (1996), 356–76 (361); Kathryn Burlinson, '"Frogs and Fat Toads": Christina Rossetti and the Significance of the Nonhuman', in Mary Arseneau, Antony H. Harrison, and Lorraine Janzen Kooistra, eds., *The Culture of Christina Rossetti: Female Poetics and Victorian Contexts* (Athens: Ohio University Press, 1999), 170–93 (88).

41. Isobel Armstrong, *Victorian Poetry: Poetry, Poetics and Politics* (London and New York: Routledge, 1993), 10.

42. Ibid. 324, 341.

43. William Dodsworth, *The Signs of the Times: Sermons Preached in Advent 1848* (London: Joseph Masters, 1849), 89.

44. John Stuart Mill, *Principles of Political Economy with some of their Applications to Social Philosophy*, 2 vols (London: John W. Parker, 1848), II, 316–17.

45. Dodsworth, *Signs of the Times*, 92.

46. Rossetti, *Face of the Deep*, 374.

47. See Kathryn Shevelow, *For the Love of Animals: The Rise of the Animal Protection Movement* (New York: Henry Holt, 2009).

48. See Anna Barbauld, *Poems* (London: Joseph Johnson, 1773); and Robert Burns, *Poems, Chiefly in the Scottish Dialect* (Kilmarnock: John Wilson, 1786).

49. Christina G. Rossetti, *Letter and Spirit: Notes on the Commandments* (London: Society for Promoting Christian Knowledge, 1883), 84.

50. Ibid. 17–18.

51. Ibid. 12–13.

52. Rossetti, *Face of the Deep*, 477.

53. Kathryn Tanner, *Economy of Grace* (Minneapolis: Fortress, 2005).

54. Rossetti, *Face of the Deep*, 489.

55. See her entries in the census records of 1841, 1851, 1871, and 1881, at http://www.nationalarchives.gov.uk.

56. 'Reflections', *Hodge-Podge*, 3 (3 June 1843), in Dinah Roe, *The Rossettis in Wonderland: A Victorian Family History* (London: Haus, 2011), 58.

57. 'She will have more wit (or cleverness) than any of the others', in William Michael Rossetti, *Some Reminiscences of William Michael Rossetti*, 2 vols (New York: Charles Scribner's, 1906), I, 20–1.

58. See Jan Marsh, *Christina Rossetti: A Literary Biography* (London: Pimlico, 1995), 15.

59. Roe, *Wonderland*, 31.

60. The index card recording Rossetti's application for a ticket is dated 17 October 1860: thanks to Lyn Rees at the British Museum's Central Archive for this information; John Francis Waller, ed., *The Imperial Dictionary of Universal Biography*, 3 vols (Glasgow: William Mackenzie, 1857–66).

61. William Michael Rossetti, ed., *The Poetical Works of Christina Georgina Rossetti, with Memoir and Notes* (London: Macmillan, 1904), p. lxix.

62. Mackenzie Bell, *Christina Rossetti: A Biographical and Critical Study* (Boston: Roberts Brothers, 1989), 161.

63. Kathleen Jones, *Learning not to be First: The Life of Christina Rossetti* (Oxford: Oxford University Press, 1992), pp. xi, 56; Rossetti, ed., *Poetical Works*, p. xlviii.

64. Frances Thomas, *Christina Rossetti: A Biography* (London: Virago, 1994), 71–2.

65. Lona Mosk Packer, *Christina Rossetti* (Berkeley and Los Angeles: University of California Press, 1963); Georgina Battiscombe, *Christina Rossetti: A Divided Life* (New York: Holt, Rinehart and Winston, 1981).

66. Bell, *Rossetti*, 160.

67. Andrew Bradstock and Christopher Rowland, *Radical Christian Writings: A Reader* (Oxford: Blackwell, 2002), pp. xvi–xvii.

68. Bell, *Rossetti*, 52.

69. Christina G. Rossetti to Caroline Gemmer, March 1883, *Letters*, III, 102; Christina G. Rossetti to Amelia Barnard Heimann, 29 July 1880, *Letters*, II, 240.

70. Christina G. Rossetti to Amelia Barnard Heimann, 29 September 1862, *Letters*, I, 166.

71. Christina G. Rossetti to Alexander Macmillan, 20 April 1881, *Letters*, II, 269; Christina G. Rossetti to Dante Gabriel Rossetti, 9 August 1881, *Letters*, II, 293.

72. Emily Davies to Anna Richardson, 28 December 1867, in Marsh, *Rossetti*, 365.

73. Plato, *The Republic*, trans. Desmond Lee (Harmondsworth: Penguin, 1955), 229.

74. Christina G. Rossetti to Augusta Webster, 1878, *Letters*, II, 158.

75. Carol J. Adams, *The Sexual Politics of Meat: A Feminist-Vegetarian Critical Theory* (New York and London: Continuum, 1990).

76. Michael Marder, *Plant-Thinking: A Philosophy of Vegetal Life* (New York: Columbia University Press, 2013), 260.

77. Gianni Vattimo and Santiago Zabala, 'Foreword', ibid. 10–17 (11).

78. Gianni Vattimo, *Belief*, trans. Luca D'Isanto and David Webb (Stanford: Stanford University Press, 1999), 44.

79. Published in Rossetti, *Face of the Deep*, 377.

80. 'Later Life' was first published in *A Pageant and Other Poems* (1881); Diane D'Amico, 'Christina Rossetti's *Later Life*: The Neglected Sonnet Sequence', *Victorians Institute Journal*, 9 (1980–1), 21–8.

81. Donna Haraway, *Staying with the Trouble: Making Kin in the Chthulucene* (Durham, NC: Duke University Press, 2016), 103.

82. Christina G. Rossetti, *Time Flies: A Reading Diary* (London: Society for Promoting Christian Knowledge, 1885), 14; Haraway, *Trouble*, 6.

83. Haraway, *Trouble*, 91.

84. Timothy Morton, *The Ecological Thought* (Cambridge, MA: Harvard University Press, 2010), 27–8.

85. Jane Bennett, *Vibrant Matter: A Political Ecology of Things* (Durham, NC: Duke University Press, 2010), 48, 87.

86. Ibid. 122.

87. Rossetti, *Time Flies*, 15.

88. Clement of Alexandria, *Protrepticus*, in Eric Osborn, *The Emergence of Christian Theology* (Cambridge: Cambridge University Press, 1993), 208.

89. Christina G. Rossetti, *Sing Song: A Nursery Rhyme Book* (1868–70), British Library, London, Ashley MS 1371, https://www.bl.uk/collection-items/manuscript-of-sing-song-a-collection-of-nursery-rhymes-by-christina-rossetti; Christina G. Rossetti, *Sing-Song: A Nursery Rhyme Book*, with one hundred and twenty illustrations by Arthur Hughes Engraved by the Brothers Dalziel (London: Macmillan and Co., 1915).

90. John Clare, 'Remembrances' (ll. 68–9), in Eric Robinson, David Powell, and P. M. S. Dawson, eds., *Poems of the Middle Period 1822–1837*, 5 vols (Oxford: Clarendon Press, 1996–2003), IV, 130–4; and see Katey Castellano, *The Ecology of British Romantic Conservatism 1790–1837* (New York: Palgrave Macmillan, 2013), 141–62.

91. Diane D'Amico, *Christina Rossetti: Faith, Gender, and Time* (Baton Rouge: Louisiana State University Press, 1999); Mary Arseneau, *Recovering Christina Rossetti: Female Community and Incarnational Poetics* (New York: Palgrave Macmillan, 2004); Karen Dieleman, *Religious Imaginaries: The Liturgical and Poetic Practices of Elizabeth Barrett Browning, Christina Rossetti, and Adelaide Procter* (Athens: Ohio University Press, 2012); and Marshall, 'Hades and Heaven' and 'Astronomy'.

92. King, *Spiritual Communities*, 237; Elizabeth Ludlow, *Christina Rossetti and the Bible: Waiting with the Saints* (London: Bloomsbury, 2014), 47, 99.

93. Lynda Palazzo, *Christina Rossetti's Feminist Theology* (New York: Palgrave Macmillan, 2002); Lorraine Janzen Kooistra, 'Teaching Victorian Illustrated Poetry: Hands-on Material Culture', *Victorian Review*, 34.2 (2008), 43–61; Heidi Scott, 'Subversive Ecology in Rossetti's *Goblin Market*', *The Explicator*, 65.4 (2010), 219–22; Todd O. Williams, 'Environmental Ethics in Christina Rossetti's *Time Flies*', *Prose Studies*, 33.3 (2011), 217–29; Kelly Sultzbach, 'The Contrary Natures of Christina Rossetti's Goblin Fruits', *Green Letters: Studies in Ecocriticism*, 14.1 (2011), 39–56; Nathan K. Hensley, 'Christina Rossetti's Timescales of Catastrophe', *Nineteenth-Century Contexts*, 38.5 (2016), 399–415; Trowbridge, '"Truth to nature"'.

94. Peter Larkin, *City-Trappings (Housing Heath or Wood)* (London: Veer Books, 2016); on scarcity, see Larkin's *Wordsworth and Coleridge: Promising Losses* (Basingstoke: Palgrave Macmillan, 2012).

95. Rossetti, *Seek and Find*, 326–7.

96. See Chaia Heller, 'For the Love of Nature: Ecology and the Cult of the Romantic', in Greta Gaard, ed., *Ecofeminism: Women, Animals, Nature* (Philadelphia: Temple University Press, 1993), 219–42.

97. For an accessible response to Richard Dawkins's *The Selfish Gene* (Oxford: Oxford University Press, 1976), see Colin Tudge, *Why Genes are Not Selfish and People are Nice: A Challenge to the Dangerous Ideas that Dominate Our Lives* (Edinburgh: Floris Books, 2013).

98. For a different view, see John Holmes, *Darwin's Bards: British and American Poetry in the Age of Evolution* (Edinburgh: Edinburgh University Press, 2009), 23.

99. Rossetti, *Time Flies*, 23.

100. Rossetti, *Face of the Deep*, 209.

101. See Verna Harrison, 'Perichoresis in the Greek Fathers', *St Vladimir's Theological Quarterly*, 35 (1991), 53–65; and Daniel F. Stramara, 'Gregory of Nyssa's Terminology for Trinitarian Perichoresis', *Vigiliae Christianae: A Review of Early Christian Life and Language*, 52.3 (1998), 257–63.

102. Gregory of Nyssa, *De anima et resurrectione*, in Stramara, 'Terminology', 261.

103. Rossetti, *Seek and Find*, 171.

104. The field of religion and ecology is of increasing interest to literary critics and too vast to comprehensively introduce here. The theologies of Pierre Teilhard de Chardin, Sarah Coakley, Catherine Keller, Jürgen Moltmann, and Rosemary Radford Ruether have shaped my own understanding, as well as: Daniel P. Scheid, *The Cosmic Common Good: Religious Grounds for Ecological Ethics* (Oxford: Oxford University Press, 2016); Douglas E. Christie, *The Blue Sapphire of the Mind: Notes for a Contemplative Ecology* (Oxford: Oxford University Press, 2013); Willis Jenkins, *Ecologies of Grace: Environmental Ethics and Christian Theology* (Oxford: Oxford University Press, 2008); John Hart, *Sacramental Commons: Christian Ecological Ethics* (Lanham: Rowman & Littlefield, 2006); and Dieter T. Hessel and Rosemary Radford Ruether, eds., *Christianity*

and Ecology: Seeking the Well-Being of Earth and Humans (Cambridge, MA: Harvard University Press, 2000).

105. Keble, *Life of Scott*, 17.

106. Rossetti, *Face of the Deep*, 116.

107. See Jürgen Moltmann, *God in Creation: A New Theology of Creation and the Spirit of God* (New York: Harper & Row, 1991).

1
What is Catholic is Christian
Tractarian Origins, 1830–1849

One of Rossetti's earliest poems, written at the end of 1844 when she had just turned 14, is 'Earth and Heaven', a nascent vision of a harmonious cosmos. In a series of tightly rhymed couplets, the narrator paints a gently connected world that glows with light while swans glide on flowing water, flowers bloom, and skylarks soar into an ocean 'Sun-rise' (l. 10). Below the ocean waves lie 'jewels' of sea-weed, coral, and amber alongside low-lying plants and climbers that 'nourish' the soil to create an interdependent ecosystem (ll. 11, 16). It is the 'beauty' of these component parts that renders the whole 'Earth' 'full' (l. 18) for the narrator. Heaven promises even 'greater charms', a place where all the elements of creation dwell as they do on earth, but now 'Glowing, indestructible' and free of the 'tainted birth | In the corrupted sons of Earth' (ll. 20–4). While heaven seems out of reach until the end of time, the final lines of the poem reconcile it with material creation:

> Yes; for aye in Heav'n doth dwell
> Glowing, indestructible,
> What here below finds tainted birth
> In the corrupted sons of Earth;
> For, filling there and satisfying
> Man's soul unchanging and undying,
> Earth's fleeting joys and beauties far above,
> In Heaven is Love.   (ll. 21–8)

While the 'aye' of line 21 is a synonym for 'Yes', it also acoustically holds an 'I' figure made more apparent by the double affirmative. Transformed by heaven, the 'aye' joins the other elements of creation in a vision of 'Love' that counters the 'tainted birth' they received at the hands of earth's 'corrupted sons'. The spatial binary between the below of earth and the 'far above' of heaven is overcome by realizing this 'Love' in both realms, an allusion to the life promised when Christ returns. For central to Rossetti's vision was a marriage of earth and heaven where the former is not abandoned or destroyed, but rebuilt. The New Jerusalem, John reports, comes 'down from God out of heaven' (Revelation 21. 2) and is united with earth wherein both are reborn. As Rossetti wrote in her poem 'Sexagesima', first published in *The Face of the Deep: A Devotional Commentary on the Apocalypse* (1892): 'Earth may not pass till heaven shall pass away, | Nor heaven may be renewed | Except with earth' (ll. 13–15). In her earlier poem, this unity is imagined through the dissolution of human-made distinctions between things to confirm a oneness of spirit and matter in love. If there is an 'aye' that 'dwells' in the poem, it is one that senses its meaning as part of a larger material and lived whole that begins on earth and continues, embraced by heaven, in a new creation.

This is an unusually radical vision for a teenage poet, even one born into the prodigious Rossetti family. But Rossetti already had many sources on which to draw, not least the sermons she heard at the Anglo-Catholic Christ Church, Albany Street, which she attended from 1843 to 1876, and Christ Church, Woburn Square, where she worshipped from 1876 to 1894. While the sermons of Albany Street's regular incumbent, William Dodsworth, had a significant influence on Rossetti, as this chapter discusses, those of visiting preacher and leading Tractarian, Edward Bouverie Pusey, also held immense sway.[1] Like Rossetti, Pusey put Jesus Christ at the heart of his sermons, and claimed that the core of his teaching is 'the inculcation of the Great Mystery, expressed in the words to be "in Christ", to be "Members of Christ", "Temples of the Holy Ghost"; that Christ doth dwell really and truly in the hearts of the faithful'.[2] In Christ's actions and grace, Pusey wrote in a sermon for Christmas Eve, there is 'a closer Intercommunion between Heaven and earth, when God the Son came down from Heaven to be Man with men', one that initiates an annual re-visitation, 'born anew in the hearts which watch'.[3] Intercommunion was key to Pusey, both in relation to the spiritual and material, and also between the various branches of the Catholic Church, Roman, Anglican, and Greek.[4] He hoped that the Greek Church might be 'glad to be re-united' with a broader Catholic Church, and referred to Fathers from the Western and Eastern Church in his sermons and devotional writings.[5] Pusey also followed the principle of *lex orandi, lex credenda* (the law of prayer is the law of faith), encouraging in fellow Tractarians as well as his congregations an attentive and meditative relationship to the earliest liturgical texts as well as the Bible. Rossetti found more than just places to worship in the churches she attended, discovering in them vibrant communities, vast libraries, and intimately decorated interiors that sparked her fascination with early Christianity and its reception in the modern Catholic Revival.

This chapter outlines Rossetti's early engagement with Tractarianism through Christ Church, Albany Street, and those she saw preach there. Like many Tractarians, she sought a renewal of Anglicanism as part of a broader Catholicism—an Anglo-Catholicism—that envisioned all believers as part of a communion of saints finally redeemed in the New Jerusalem. But even in her early life, her spirituality was interconnected with the material world in which she walked, conversed, worshipped, and studied. As a movement that saw nature as a codified revelation of the Trinity, Tractarianism directed the believer to the things of the world, human, floral, animal, mineral, as part of a network in which every being was connected with the divine. It also urged Christians to consider it their duty to remain vigilant in ensuring these connections remained unbroken, especially when confronted with what Dodsworth called the 'signs of the times'—natural disasters, war, climate change, and industrialism. As Pusey declared in his sermon 'The Miracles of Prayer': 'Our faith is, that God hears His creatures' prayers, as to every thing which concerns their well-being' and 'specifically' as to 'atmospheric changes, upon which our health and well-being so much depend'.[6] On an ageing planet, Rossetti wrote in 'Advent ("Earth grown old, yet still so green")', these creatures would be myriad, 'Millions' of ancient and evolving beings hidden to human eyes, but seen by God as part of one creation (ll. 1, 6).[7] Many of her earliest poems granted a few of these 'millions' a voice within lyrics in which the 'I' is assumed by a nonhuman thing—a water spirit, a star, the trees, seasons, the sea—all rejoicing in God's love in relationship to other nonhuman things that surround it—the breeze, grass, birds, flowers, the rain, thunder. In doing so, she renewed David's command in the Psalms that 'all the earth' sing 'unto the Lord' and 'bless his name' and turned it into a refusal of the objectification and commodification of the nonhuman. For Rossetti, all things are born into grace and part of a diversely constituted divine body that eternally integrates creation with God.

Before reading these nonhuman songs at the end of the chapter, three sections examine Rossetti's Tractarianism as the basis of her reading of an interconnected creation held together by grace. The first section explores her relationship to the Catholic Revival at Christ Church, Albany Street where she witnessed many of the key Oxford Movement leaders preach. The second focuses on what Rossetti heard in church, especially in regard to Dodsworth's premillennialism and Tractarianism's revival of patristics. The last section looks explicitly at the way her religion required her to thoughtfully engage with theology, that 'dangerous science' Ruskin warned women against pursuing. It focuses on the positive influence of Pusey's mystical and joyful reading of grace on Rossetti, and in doing so complicates the idea of her as an impressionable teenager overwhelmed by his dogmatism. Tractarianism in fact enabled Rossetti's loving ecological faith through its promotion of a universal Catholicism founded on a unity of all things. As she later wrote in *Letter and Spirit: Notes on the Commandments* (1883), the first 'Great' commandment instructs the believer that Catholicism's assertion of the 'inviolable Unity of the Godhead [Athanasian Creed]' is part of a broader Christian 'Mystery of the All-Holy Trinity'. 'What is Catholic underlies what is Christian', she declared, 'on the Catholic basis alone can the Christian structure be raised; even while to raise that superstructure on that foundation is the bounden duty of every soul within reach of the full Divine Revelation'.[8] This revelation was of a world ecosystem in which things depend on each other, nonhuman and human, fleshly and divine, and that would be finally united in the return of Christ at the end of time. Rossetti thought that Christ would not return, however, to an internally atomized creation, and it was in the Tractarian emphasis on communion, presence, and grace that she perceived an incipient environmentalism based on fellowship and companionability.

'The great Catholic Revival'

Rossetti's distinctive reading of Christianity is founded on her commitment to a High Church form of nineteenth-century Anglicanism that sought to reinstate the supernatural within the Church of England. While William, a year older than Christina, claimed that the 'idea of being an "Anglican", and in that sense a Catholic, did not exist in the early years' of their childhood, his sister soon identified with what he called the 'Pusey-ite' Catholic Revival, one with which she was openly 'in sympathy'.[9] Born in 1830, Rossetti was 3 when John Keble delivered his famous Assize Sermon on 'National Apostasy', its title a demand that the Church of England reform and embrace its supernatural authority. Those who agreed with Keble were gathered under several rubrics. As early as 1812, the High Churchman Henry Hadley Norris wrote of a 'Reformed Catholic' movement that by 1865 the established Anglo-Catholic and friend of Rossetti, Richard Frederick Littledale, aligned with 'the great Catholic Revival'.[10] For historians of the Church of England, Norris and Littledale represented two related periods of Catholic reform, the first defined by an intellectual, university-led group called the Oxford Movement; the second by 'Ritualists' who sought to return church worship to a medieval form of Catholicism. The earlier group of reformers were also referred to as Tractarians after the ninety *Tracts for the Times* (1833–41) they composed to outline the nature of their reforms.[11] As Rossetti's friend, William J. E. Bennett, noted, the successes of the earlier movement were all attributable to these Tracts: baptismal regeneration, confirmation, the Eucharist as Real Presence, auricular confession, the restoration of religious communities, and an aesthetic focus on church architecture.[12] While the Tractarians, led by Keble, John Henry Newman, Isaac Williams, and Edward Bouverie Pusey, often differed in their readings of theological law, they shared an academic and antiquarian approach to these issues, appealing to the Church Fathers and early Christianity to justify their belief in an incarnate deity celebrated in the sacramental life of the Church.

   To spotlight Rossetti's association with the Catholic Revival is to affirm both the everyday lived nature of her faith inside and outside of church, and also the breadth of her intellectual engagement with religion as a writer and thinker. She was attracted to the Oxford

Movement in part because of its intellectual and scholarly character, one that introduced her to the mystical and interconnected creation heralded by the early Church. She regularly studied at the British Museum, and secured her own ticket for the newly opened Reading Room in 1860, just three years after it first opened. While she claimed to favour 'Church documents' to other kinds of reading material, she also read deeply in poetry, philosophy, and natural history.[13] Meditating on the history of Christianity, Rossetti agreed with Tractarianism's urgent sense that the Church needed to be rescued from its current state of confused decay—'bad beyond all parallel', William Gladstone wrote, appalled as he was by the 'expulsion of the poor and labouring classes' from churches, the 'baldness of the service', 'the elaborate horrors of the so-called music', and 'indifference' of the 'sleeping congregations'.[14] Echoing Gladstone, she wrote in *The Face of the Deep*: 'Already in England (not to glance at other countries) the signs of the times are ominous: Sunday is being diverted by some to business, by others to pleasure; Church congregations are often meagre, and so services are chilled. Our solemn feasts languish, and our fasts where are they?'[15] Her question was answered very differently by the Tractarians and later Ritualists, and it is between these two groups that her own Anglo-Catholicism emerged. Rossetti's theology was closer to Pusey than Keble or Newman: only the former remained committed to a Catholic Anglicanism willing to engage Ritualism. Keble eventually retreated from what he perceived to be 'Roman' elements of such ritual, while Newman embraced them by converting to Roman Catholicism in 1845. Rossetti also agreed with Pusey's patristic reading of theology, especially in regard to baptism, confession, the Eucharist, and grace, and she remained unperturbed by those who accused him of closet Catholicism.

Much has been made by historians of anti-Catholicism in this period, defined as it was by the Roman Catholic Emancipation Act of 1829, and consequent 'No Popery' protests common around Guy Fawkes Day.[16] But Rossetti felt little anxiety about Rome. Given her inclusive reading of grace, it is not surprising that she welcomed discussion of other religious persuasions. Her attitude is unusual given the particular threat Catholicism was thought to pose to women through the practice of auricular confession, established by the Oxford Movement after its removal from the Anglican Church under Elizabeth I.[17] The notion of male confessors cajoling female penitents to confess their sins and secrets led some to fear confession as a 'source of unspeakable abominations' in which priests might usurp the control husbands and fathers held over their wives and daughters.[18] The fantasy was further aggravated by the 'common view that women predominated' in Tractarian congregations, especially those associated with Ritualism.[19] One curate even bemoaned Ritualism as a conspiring 'female movement' whose clergymen are 'misled' by 'a few' gullible 'ladies' and bored spinsters.[20] Rossetti's friendships with and respect for priests like Littledale, Dodsworth, Bennett, Pusey, Keble, and Newman, however, suggest that these men enabled and encouraged her participation and education within a universal Catholic Church. As William commented, 'she had certainly no strong prejudice against Roman Catholics; she considered them to be living branches of the True Vine, authentic members of the Church of Christ'.[21] Rossetti was content for several of her poems to be reprinted in the *Household Library of Catholic Poets* (1881), and her memorial sonnet, 'Cardinal Newman' (1890), portrayed the convert first and foremost as a 'Champion of the Cross'. Even her broken engagement to James Collinson in 1850, often attributed to his conversion to Rome, had more to do with his rejection of the Pre-Raphaelite Brotherhood and general dreariness.[22]

Rossetti's willingness to accept Catholicism was to some extent inevitable for a young woman brought up in an Italian family surrounded by 'persons entertaining divergent forms of faith or of speculative opinion'.[23] Her grandfather on her mother's side, Gaetano Polidori, raised his sons Roman Catholic after his own faith, and his daughters Anglican, including Rossetti's devout mother, Frances. Frances's marriage to Gabriele Rossetti, an Italian Catholic and political exile who followed the 'gospel utterances of Jesus Christ' rather than Church dogma, had little effect on her own faith, and she, like her daughters, embraced the Catholic Revival.[24] All the Rossetti children were baptized into the Church of England, and as Italian as well as English speakers, their Catholic circle was wide. As Jan Marsh argues, the family regularly received 'members of the Bonaparte entourage, Italian counts and generals and writers', especially after they moved to 50 Charlotte Street in 1835.[25] Gabriele was also the chair of Italian at King's College, London, and a prominent Dante scholar, and his youngest daughter served as his amanuensis from at least the age of 16 during her own studies of Dante.[26] Rossetti, like her mother and sister, remained Anglo-Catholic despite being part of a large extended family open to many religious and mystical persuasions (William and Gabriel later became interested in spiritualism and 'spirit rappings').[27] The Roman Catholicism she associated with her Italian heritage remained a point of fascination for her, as Chapter 3's discussion of her 1865 trip to Italy suggests, but her childhood and teenage involvement with an evolving Anglican Church was the basis of her enduring faith.

Taken to Holy Trinity Church on Marylebone Road, and then St Katharine's Chapel, Regent's Park, as a child, Rossetti finally moved with her mother and sister to Christ Church, Albany Street in 1843, newly built only six years earlier next to Regent's Park and just a short walk from Charlotte Street. Christ Church was commissioned as part of Bishop Charles Blomfield's scheme to construct fifty new churches in London, but it was also partially funded by Pusey, who sought to establish it as a flagship Tractarian parish outside of Oxford.[28] Newman and Pusey selected the Evangelical convert to Tractarianism, William Dodsworth, to oversee Christ Church, and he invited all the major players in the Oxford Movement to lead services there. As its second incumbent, Henry William Burrows, recalled: 'It was a time of fervour and revival of church principles, and it is not too much to say that Christ Church became the leading church in the movement.'[29] Its status as a 'leading' Tractarian church was as much to do with the 'zeal of the congregation' as the influence of prominent Oxford Movement preachers, and both groups raised enough funds to build several large schoolrooms for as many as 871 children by 1839, an open endorsement of religious education.[30] While its members looked back to the Christianity of the early Church, they looked forward in their politics. They established a Young Women's Friendly Society that pre-dated the 1875 Girls' Friendly Society, focused education on girls, Italian-speaking children, and those from poor families, and launched the first Anglican Sisterhood in 1845. Burrows also campaigned to abolish pew rents on the basis that it obscured 'the great principle' that the church is for everyone 'baptized in the parish, as such, and equally'. He reminded his congregation that a system that encourages clergy to favour the wealthy is 'inconsistent with the tracts we have often circulated' and was contrary to the gospels' elevation, not of patrons, but of the poor.[31] The parish were given a free vote, and, like the majority of their fellow worshippers, Christina, Maria, and Frances all voted with Burrows for a democratic restructuring of pews.

Rossetti benefited significantly from an emphasis on communal theological discussion at Christ Church. In his history of the parish, Burrows confirmed that education was central to its mission, and the 'tracts' he referred to in his letter against pew rents comprised the *Tracts for the Times* and numerous sermons and commentaries parishioners were encouraged to study. Religious education was especially important in a period in which Anglicanism was changing so quickly. Burrows required his congregation to fully comprehend the significance of both these tracts and the multiple renovations on the building in which they worshipped. As Karen Dieleman attentively observes, the interior of Christ Church conveyed the way architectural change correlated with theological statute. The chancel and pulpit were both decorated to enhance the significance of Holy Communion, for example, and the font was repositioned opposite the altar to emphasize baptism as the route to grace.[32] Dieleman also elucidates the connection between colour, ornamentation, and the sacrament of baptism at Christ Church, where the red cross in the font that Rossetti so admired was enhanced by a wider architectural commitment to glowing rood screens, painted walls, vibrant hangings, and adorned tiles.[33] Within this environment, Rossetti attended Morning Prayer and Evening Prayer or Holy Communion, both of which were structured by sung psalms, a reading of the Ten Commandments by the priest, a prayer or collect, hymns, a sung Nicene Creed, and a sermon.

During periods of renovation at Christ Church, Rossetti worshipped at St Andrew's on Wells Street, and All Saints, Margaret Street, also ministered by Dodsworth and where Maria became an Associate Sister in 1860.[34] In her 1848 sonnet, 'St Andrew's Church', Rossetti recalled both an aesthetic pleasure in church ritual, as well as feelings of guilt that such prayer was self-indulgent, even decadent. Amidst the 'holy antheming' that rises from the 'white-robed men and boys' through the sanctuary to God, the narrator observes her own 'vanity' in enjoying such ritual, not to censor her pleasure, but to

return herself 'below' to the materiality of the earth and her fellow
beings (ll. 1, 4, 10–11). As Chapter 3 discusses, many church spaces
deliberately used floral and faunal imagery to remind the believer of
her fellowship with creation. This was pronounced in the designs of
the Gothic Revival architect William Butterfield, who renovated both
All Saints and Christ Church, Albany Street in accordance with
Tractarianism's renewed focus on sacramentalism.[35] He also designed
Keble College Chapel in Oxford with a feature mosaic of Francis
of Assisi on the south side of the sanctuary. Rossetti considered
Butterfield's changes a major improvement 'since the old days', his
redecorated Christ Church ornamented with a copy of Raphael's *The
Transfiguration* on the altar, a modernized organ, embellished font,
jewelled communion plate, oak pews, marble floors, and stained-glass
windows.[36] For some observers, these renovations appeared danger-
ously close to a Roman Catholic aesthetic. In a privately compiled
list of London's clergymen and their parishes commissioned by the
editor of *The Times* in 1844, for example, Christ Church is classified
under the label 'Decided Tractarians', only one category below
'As near Romanism as possible'.[37] The document reports that
Christ Church is 'illuminated with the Back Light' with 'everything
arranged to produce "effect"', and compares its ritual to St Paul's,
Knightsbridge, where the service approaches 'v. nearly to that of a
R. C. Cathedral . . . All the responses are chanted—the litany by the
intendent himself:—there are boy choristers in white gowns to assist:—
the Altar is as nearly a "High Altar" as possible [and] there are constant
genuflexions + bowings toward it. The sermon is of course preached
in a surplice.'[38]

Rossetti recognized in this liturgy an echo of the fellowship
and communion inherent to creation. She wrote that it 'is "in the
Churches"' that Christ, the Holy Spirit, 'steadfastness, patience, faith,
hope, love' and the 'Bright and Morning Star' are 'testified', the 'living
branch of that one Holy Catholic Apostolic Church' and the 'house of
God'.[39] For her, the church bears witness to all creation embodied in
the Trinity, and has 'no independent existence' from 'Christ, Whose
mystical body she is' or from the 'Holy Ghost, Whose temple she is'.[40]
But as part of the multiform Christ, the church also incorporates
animal and plant life. Walking by Regent's Park, the Zoological
Society of London, and the Royal Botanic Society on her way to

Christ Church, and past countless small gardens to get to All Saints, the animal and plant life Rossetti observed became part of her everyday religious experience. Many of her fellow congregants remembered when Regent's Park was an 'enclosure enjoyed only by free animals' and the entire parish in which she lived and worshipped belonged to the Department of the Woods and Forests, who regularly assisted the incumbents of Christ Church with the purchase of property for new schools. Burrows even recalled monkeys being brought into these school rooms, 'cheered into patience by the gift of apples or nuts'.[41] The parish exemplifies what Ashton Nichols calls 'urbanature', a space neither solely metropolitan or rural, but within which 'human beings are never cut off from wild nature by human culture'.[42] Exposed to wonders inside and out of the church space, Rossetti was rarely deterred from worship, as her mother's diary attested, and Frances recorded her daughter's trips to church using the phrase 'to litany' or 'Christina to litany'. She wrote in a diary entry from January 1881:

> 18 Tu., 19 W. The hard frost continues to keep us indoors.
> 20 Th. The same weather. William came to see me.
> 21 F. The frost kept all in, except Christina to litany.
> 22 Sat. Frost continues. Mrs Willmer called.
> 23 Sun. Only Christina got to Church. Snow still all about.
> 25 Tu. The frost goes on. Christina went to Church. Mrs Heimann called. (27 Th. William came)
> 26 W. Christina went to litany. A thaw began.[43]

Undeterred by snows, fogs, frosts, and winds, Rossetti intrepidly visited church four times in the same week her mother was 'kept at home by the stormy wind, by which Christina who went to litany was buffeted'.[44] According to Frances, the only other destination Rossetti regularly visited was the British Museum. Tractarianism's appellation 'British Museum religion' constituted at least part of its attraction for a poet who, when the family moved to 56 Euston Square in 1867, often slept 'in the library'.[45] Christ Church and the British Museum provided sources of religious reading material alongside the books she found in family libraries or borrowed from her bibliophile brothers.[46] While her geographical proximity to the leading Tractarian churches of the day, as well as Regent's Park and the Botanic Gardens, brought together grace and nature for Rossetti, it was her willingness to reflect on what she read that animated them. Nowhere is this more apparent in her creative exegesis of both the letter of the Bible and the tradition of the early Church.

Patristics and the Bible

Rossetti's reading of grace as that which allowed all things to synchronously participate in the reality of God and the created world would have been impossible without the influence of Pre-Raphaelite aesthetics, Platonic philosophy, Italian culture, natural history, and the anti-vivisection movement, not to mention her everyday conversations with artists and writers keen to be connected with the Rossetti family. But the foundation of it was in her early apprehension of the relationship between the Bible and early Christianity. As Elizabeth Ludlow argues, Rossetti understood herself to be part of the 'communion of saints' of the Apostles' Creed, one constitutive of the 'Catholic Religion' and 'formative to her conception of the existential dimension of the liturgical practice into which she invites her readers to enter'.[47] Like all Tractarians aware of the sixth Article of the Church of England, she accepted that the Bible was 'sufficient' for 'salvation', but she was also sympathetic with the view that scripture should be read through antiquity, and considered the documents and writings of early councils and the Fathers as 'testimonies' to the original faith.[48] Even after the Apocrypha was removed from the King James Bible in 1885, Rossetti continued to quote from it, especially in her prose. The problem with *sola scriptura* for the Tractarians was that it allowed for private judgement without an authorized guide to interpretation such as that offered by the Fathers, one that was valued because it was historically closest to the time in which Jesus of Nazareth had lived.[49] The early Fathers in particular were considered intimate with the Apostles' view of scriptural truth, whereas later commentaries, such as those by the Caroline Divines, were judged to be too modern. As Newman stated in a review of a study of three early Fathers: 'Whatever then be the true way of interpreting the . . . Apostolical Fathers, if a man begins by summoning before him, instead of betaking himself to them, by seeking to make them evidence for modern dogmas, instead of throwing his mind upon their text, and drawing from them their own doctrines, he will to a certainty miss their sense'.[50] It was for this reason that the Oxford Movement sanctioned Apostolic Succession, which held that the Church's ministry was derived from the original Apostles, to whom all bishops are connected by a chain of consecrated inheritances. This allowed for the lineal transmission of the grace of episcopacy from those twelve figures closest to Jesus through time to establish mystical union with him, and secure the reception of ancient and primitive truths. As part of this succession, the Fathers ensured the validity of those sacraments the Catholic Revival sought to restore, especially baptism, the Eucharist, and confession.

The Church Fathers were celebrated at Christ Church, where their writings were referred to by leading Oxford Movement men including Henry Edward Manning and Walter Hook. But the preachers who had by far the most influence on Rossetti's early faith were Dodsworth and Pusey. Dodsworth was a premillennialist, who believed that an imminent Second Coming would mark the beginning of the Millennium, a thousand-year golden age of peace leading to the Last Judgement. His 1848 sermons on Advent and the Second Coming, published a year later as *The Signs of the Times*, were ardent pleas for his congregants to carefully 'watch' for signs and 'beware' of the 'unbelieving temper' of their own time.[51] For Dodsworth, the 'end of the world' comprised a time of judgement on those who have rejected the Gospel, and only '*after* the LORD has smitten the earth with the rod of His mouth, and with the breath of His lips has slain the wicked' will his 'universal blessedness' hold.[52] He repeated over and over that while God's 'judgment remembers mercy', fear and 'tribulation' are imminent: 'Thus in our LORD's parable, it is said, "Let the tares and the wheat," the emblem of the wicked and the righteous, "both grow together *until the harvest*," and "the harvest is the end of the world"'.[53] Even as Dodsworth insisted he had 'no intention of dogmatizing', he entreated his congregant to 'prepare' for this 'conflict' and 'fearful trial', and was uncompromising in his belief that 'the days in which we live' are worse than any other 'period in the history of Christendom'.[54] This, he declared, was because of the world's 'iniquity', a word he translated as 'lawlessness' to describe his sense of his world's refusal to adhere to political, social, and religious order.[55] In addition to the disorder of unnamed 'political revolutions' and upset social hierarchies, Dodsworth worried, was the problem of ignorance regarding matters of the ancient Church. He combined references to the Old and New Testaments with the writings of Chrysostom, Cyril of Alexandria, and Jerome, and encouraged prayerful meditation on the Fathers alongside Paul and the gospel writers. In doing so, he believed, the Christian would become 'tremblingly alive to our danger' and 'be upon his guard against the insinuating form in which the evil may approach him'.[56]

The force of Dodsworth's Advent sermons affected all three Rossetti women, especially Maria, who feared that the Egyptian mummies in the British Museum would spontaneously resurrect around the corner from where they lived.[57] But Rossetti was spellbound by his reading of Advent as that which marks both the beginning of the liturgical year, and also signals Christ's Second Advent at the end of time.[58] While her later Advent writings rejected Dodsworth's language of fear for one of love, her earlier reflections are less certain. Her narrators often combine a hopeful joy at the absolute love promised by messianic arrival with a sense of disappointment and exhaustion that such a return seems endlessly deferred. 'Heart-sick with hope deferred' for Christ's arrival, these narrators come to see the temporal world as an obstacle to longed-for apocalyptic renewal.[59] Following Rossetti's attendance at Dodsworth's sermons, however, the subject matter of her poems turned away from this youthful swinging between generic despair and hope and towards a concern with preparing readers for apocalypse. These later poems no longer envision the earth as an impediment to Christ's return, but rather as the basis of the new creation prevented from flourishing by egoic, inattentive humans. Two poems written before and after Dodsworth's sermons exemplify this shift. 'The Time of Waiting' (1846), for example, which Rossetti wrote before she heard Dodsworth preach, tracks a transformation from sorrow to hope in neat, three-line rhymed stanzas that end with Christ's 'glorious Resurrection' (l. 57). 'Have Patience' (1848), by contrast, written a month after the Advent sermons, adopts a continuous and relentless poetic form without breaks to communicate a sense of urgent dismay at the earth's degradation. On the surface, 'Have Patience' appears to follow a similar narrative to 'The Time of Waiting', framed as it is by an image of broken goblets and spilled wine that symbolizes the world withering before a new time begins. But the narrator's call for 'patience' in the second poem is one that shifts attention away from a watchful waiting for a 'morrow' (l. 5) that cannot be seen, and towards the things of this world. Her vision redirected, the narrator now sees an environmental imbalance wherein the premature fall of leaves exposes thorns usually hidden by 'green growth' and the sun dries up the dew that feeds the roses, which in turn affects the bees (ll. 16–26). She also shifts the blame for this disturbed symbiotic relationship from 'human kind' in 'The Time of Waiting' (l. 34) to a specifically gendered 'turbulent' 'manhood' in 'Have Patience' (l. 31), the later poem directly indicting those with the power to effect environmental change.

At the end of 'Have Patience', the narrator restores the disorder of the poem, not through an expected reference to the Resurrection, but by using an image of a branch to suggest a renewed time of order: 'The palm-branches, decreed, | And crowns, to be our meed, | Are very near us' (ll. 47–9). This reference had several biblical sources. Palm branches were scattered for Jesus to ride across when he entered Jerusalem on an 'ass's colt' as the 'King of Israel' (John 12. 13–15); and the 'great multitude' of 'all nations, and kindreds, and people, and tongues' in Revelation 7. 9 also carry palms to praise 'God' and 'the Lamb'. Both scenes offer moments of pause between two significant periods: in the gospel narrative, Jesus is welcomed by crowds who quickly revoke their favour and demand his crucifixion; and in Revelation the nations submit to God after the angels hold back the four winds of the earth, but before the opening of the seventh seal. These moments, neither of the present or the future, represent a break in which to see the world differently and initiate change. This is especially apparent in Rossetti's third biblical source, Nehemiah 8. 15, wherein Nehemiah seeks to restore the law of Moses in Jerusalem by rebuilding the walls of the city and reading and explaining the Torah to renew God's covenant. To commemorate deliverance of the Israelites from slavery to wander in the wilderness, those gathered before Nehemiah are commanded to build shelters from olive, pine, myrtle, and palm branches in which to rejoice and pray. The branch in 'Have Patience' thus directs the reader to constantly study and pray on the elements of God's creation in an Advent period where the failure of the season produces what Kate E. Brown calls a 'demand to begin *at every moment*'.[60] This failure is registered not only in Advent's passing each year without the re-arrival of Christ, but also in winter itself, which performs its own apocalypse prior to the new life of spring.[61] For the Tractarians, who believed nature revealed the presence of Christ, the connection between winter and spring illuminated the cyclical nature of creation, one that Dodsworth declared it was the Christian's 'duty' to observe as one of the possible 'premonitory signs of His coming'.[62] As many of Rossetti's 1849 poems attested, 'Symbols', 'Sweet Death', 'Rest', 'Dream Land' and 'Life Hidden' among them, it was the specifics of creation that enabled the believer to reflect on endings, whether present and material or imminent and spiritual.

Both 'Symbols' and 'Sweet Death', written only a few weeks apart, are influenced not only by Dodsworth, but also by the early Fathers to whom Rossetti was introduced at Christ Church. Many of the Fathers explored the mystical oneness of the divine whereby God is embedded in the created order and all things are present in God, allowing human beings to reflect on him through creation.[63] Rossetti had learned from Dodsworth's schema that nature was scarred by elemental changes 'in the sun, and moon, and stars', by the 'distress of nations' (Luke 21. 25), and by 'famines, and pestilences, and earthquakes' (Matthew 24. 7).[64] But from mystical Fathers like Gregory of Nyssa and Basil the Great, she discovered that every detail carried in it the mark or stamp of God, each stone, ant, bee, and mosquito revealing his wisdom and collectively inviting the onlooker into faith.[65] She combined this collective vision with Dodsworth's concern for the world to envision creation as a layered work of art in which its details are syntheses of multiple realities visible and invisible. This also accorded with the Tractarian doctrine of analogy wherein 'material phenomena are both the types and the instruments of real things unseen': concrete elements of the created world are sacraments that reveal spiritual truths like grace and love.[66] The Tractarians privileged poetry as the form most suited to reveal the unseen, one uniquely placed, Keble wrote, to conjure the 'world out of sight' by imitating 'external things' to 'guide' and 'compose' the 'mind to worship and prayer'.[67] While poetry 'lends to Religion her wealth of symbols and similes', he wrote, religion 'restores these again to Poetry', clothing them with 'radiance' so that they appear 'no longer merely symbols' but 'sacraments'.[68] In re-presenting the world in relation to the 'absent and unseen', poetry records God's truths indirectly like a parable, taking 'us by the hand' and leading 'us into the hidden world of Nature affording a wealth of natural analogies'.[69] Newman also argued that religion was 'especially poetical' because its 'disclosures' engage 'the intellect' and so endow the Christian reader with 'a superhuman tendency' for understanding the 'Divine meaning in every event'. Christians have a 'duty' to secure 'a poetical view of things' that at once casts an 'unearthly brightness' across everything they describe, even as it obscures it behind the poet's mask of 'contemplation rather than communication'.[70]

Rossetti's early poetry ideally fulfilled these Tractarian decrees. From her lyrics and sonnets to narrative poems and devotional verses, she was widely admired for her formal rigour and regularity. As George Saintsbury insisted, her 'studied' metre allowed for an 'audacious' content in which she 'skilfully grouped' 'various forms': her poems thus followed a 'continuous flow' while allowing for 'whirls and eddies that form and dissolve again in a rapid'.[71] The confident and meticulous 'infinite variety' of her poetics provided the scope for repeated explorations in which she weighed the question of how to bring together material worlds—her home, church, local parks, the sea—with the immaterial worlds she experienced in prayer, reflection, and grace.[72] In 'Symbols', for example, the narrator approaches the world in relationship by invoking the etymology of symbol as that which rolls together and unifies apparently disparate elements by participating in the meaning of the thing symbolized (as Paul Tillich argued, while signs are distinct from the reality to which they point, symbols co-produce their reality).[73] The narrator begins by intently watching how things are entangled with each other: rosebuds grow in relationship with 'dew and sun and shower' and eggs develop when shaded by a 'green nest' (ll. 2, 8). Despite the promise of these objects, the rosebud opens too early and falls, and the eggs are abandoned by their parents when they fail to hatch on time. The narrator is enraged: nature appears to her to have failed, and she breaks the bough of the tree to force the rosebud to scent the air, and crushes the eggs in an act of 'vengeance' (l. 18). But she also comes to an awareness that 'Their ancient promise had been fair'—that their very being as elements made of God cannot fail regardless of their journey. The epiphany is underlined by the resurrection of the dead in the final verse:

> But the dead branch spoke from the sod,
> And the eggs answered me again:

> Because we failed dost thou complain?
> Is thy wrath just? And what if God,
>   Who waiteth for thy fruits in vain,
>   Should also take the rod?

From the grave, the snapped branch and mutilated eggs remind the narrator that the essential connection between things remains beyond human attempts at desecration. Despite the narrator's ignorance, they remain constant in their 'ancient promise', a line that suggests that the human too might avoid God's 'wrath' if she is faithful to this same vow. This is confirmed by the final allusion to 'the rod', a reference to both faith (God's transformation of Moses's staff into a snake in Exodus 4. 2) and suspicion (God's punishment of Moses for striking a rock a second time with his rod when God has promised to create a spring from it after the first in Numbers 20. 12). While Dodsworth's anxiety at God's ultimate wrath might haunt these lines, the resurrected voices of those things the narrator has destroyed are louder, symbols of a spiritual and material unity under threat only from human naivety or acrimony.

'Sweet Death' also sustains a vision of unified divine reality without end. As Dinah Roe notes, the full stop at the end of the opening line, 'The sweetest blossoms die', turns out to 'be as false and impermanent a conclusion as death itself' as the blossom's demise initiates a poem about 'nature's cycles'.[74] The narrator's commentary on the natural, green world that she passes through on her way to church understands the natural and supernatural together as expressions of one divine reality:

> The sweetest blossoms die.
>   And so it was that, going day by day
>   Unto the Church to praise and pray,
> And crossing the green churchyard thoughtfully,
>   I saw how on the graves the flowers
>   Shed their fresh leaves in showers,
> And how their perfume rose up to the sky
>   Before it passed away.   (ll. 1–8)

Here, the act of prayer within the church space enables a contemplative mode in which the narrator suddenly sees a connection between the flowers, their scent, the rain, and the atmosphere, one that passes away only to then 'nourish the rich earth' in stanza two (l. 10). If life is sweet then death is 'sweeter' because it reveals an affinity between things wherein 'All colours turn to green', a signifier of the divine (ll. 12–16). The permanence and 'truth' of God surpass worldly preoccupations like youth and beauty, as well as spiritual ones like saints and angels (ll. 17–20). But while the concluding lines appear to celebrate an ultimate and heavenly 'full harvest' over the comparatively scarce offerings of an earthly crop, the narrator associates the latter with the Old Testament figure of Ruth to submit a question about how human beings engage with their world. In asking why the Christian might 'shrink' from personal fulfilment to 'glean with Ruth?' (ll. 23–4), the narrator heralds an ethics of welfare and sharing embodied in the practice of gleaning, collecting crops left by landowners for the poor after their commercial reaping is complete (both Deuteronomy and Leviticus ask farmers to leave the corners of their fields unharvested). The open question collapses distinctions, not only between a material and spiritual harvest, gratification and kindness, but also between creator and creation, divine and earthly.

Rossetti's early Advent poems go beyond establishing her as a poet fascinated by analogy, symbolism, and the relationship between the jigsaw-like elements of a created world within a cosmic universe. They also reveal her interest in typology, a doctrine that stressed a continuous and analogous relationship between the Old and New Testaments initiated by the early Church and revived in the nineteenth century. For Tractarians, typology and analogy meant almost the same thing, although the former tended to be used in relation to the recurrence of Old Testament 'characters, events, and prophecies' in the New, while analogy found symbolic precedent for worship in the entire visible world.[75] Both typology and analogy encouraged a creative reimagining of scripture through the connection of ideas, events, and things as a way of mediating the essential incomprehensibility of God. This unknowability was also protected by the doctrine of reserve, a patristic idea the Tractarians revived to defend typology as a method of decoding religious truths necessarily held back from those unwilling to faithfully engage with God. Newman declared that God deliberately fashioned the 'path of thought' toward contemplating his being as a 'rugged and circuitous one' so that the 'very discipline inflicted on our minds in finding Him, may mould them into due devotion to Him when He is found'.[76] By 1849, Dodsworth assumed his Tractarian congregation were familiar with reserve and typology, especially Isaac Williams's 1838 and 1840 tracts 'On Reserve in Communicating Religious Knowledge'.[77] For Williams, biblical forms like songs, prayers, parables, and miracles 'unfolded' divine truth gradually to encourage careful 'study' and 'delight' for the reader willing to be trained over a long period of 'preparation' to receive the 'higher doctrines of our Faith' and obtain God's grace.[78]

As Chapter 4 discusses, Rossetti borrowed Williams's language of 'preparation' to establish her own writing as that which would focus the reader in a probationary period in which to habituate to grace and so welcome the new creation. She also based her 'Harmony on First Corinthians XIII' (1879) on Williams's *Harmony of the Four Evangelists* (1850), and encountered his explicit connection between reserve and poetry in the 'Advertisement' to his own collection of verse, *The Cathedral* (1838).[79] Here, Williams explained that the volume's 'design' represented 'the Doctrine and Discipline of the Church' through 'sacred associations' that shadow forth and symbolize God in a form used by 'our Lord Himself'.[80] He achieved this by following the example of George Herbert in *The Temple* (1633) and organized his poetry like a church filled with material forms of reserve like sepulchral recesses, chapels, and rood screens. Keble too stressed the importance, not only of a reserved poetry, but also of the reserved poet. In 'Sacred Poetry' (1825) Keble wrote that the religious poet must beware of the pitfalls of indulgent 'variety and imagery' in her compositions, and follow the 'grave, simple, sustained melodies' of religious plain chant, 'fervent, yet sober; aweful, but engaging; neither wild and passionate, nor light and airy' but marked with a 'noble simplicity and confidence' in God's truth.[81] The definition might be a description of Rossetti's verse. She consistently masked her profound intellectual grasp of theology and refused to exploit extremes of imagery by using a repentive narrative voice dedicated to an ostensible simplicity. Her early poetry reads like an anthology of poems about shadows, dream states, veils, darkness, and the invisible, all of which invited the reader to unravel their eclipsed meanings.

She also softened Williams's sometimes exclusive-sounding argument to reimagine reserve as a call to all believers to assume a clerical identity in reading and meditating on the Bible, the Fathers, and sermons heard in church. Many critics have assessed her attraction to the doctrine through the association between reticence and female subjectivity, and argued that she reworked reserve as a way to explore female selfhood and community.[82] Adam Mazel also reads her fascination with word play in the context of eighteenth- and nineteenth-century verse cultures of women's 'riddle writing'.[83] For Mazel, Rossetti refused the impulse to conclude and resolve as a way of reminding readers that 'guesses' shape human existence until Revelation, and that before this end time it is faith, and not certainty, that frees the thinking mind.[84] Later in her writing career, Rossetti observed that women tend to be 'the quicker-sighted in matters spiritual' precisely because they cannot be sure of themselves in a world that places them second, a hierarchy that Rossetti suggested will be reversed in the new creation in which those who '"are first shall be last; and the last first"'.[85] Until then, the reserved writer should appear not to 'summon up anything original, or striking, or picturesque, or eloquent, or brilliant' but do so by encoding it through the formal expression of patience and humility.[86] Through reserve, typology, and analogy, women could study their faith and its tradition, and embrace that 'dangerous science' John Ruskin considered off limits for women—'that of theology'.[87]

A 'dangerous science'

Many Tractarians openly disagreed with Ruskin's infamous mandate, and claimed that it was essential for all believers to be religiously educated. Rossetti's friend and later personal confessor, Richard Frederick Littledale, is one example, an Irish clergyman who moved to London in 1857 as curate of St Mary the Virgin in Soho, and who was committed to the issue of women's religious education. His pamphlet, 'The Religious Education of Women' (1872), was published after he had been Rossetti's confessor for several years. While he does not cite Rossetti's writing (perhaps because of her wish to remain reserved), Littledale does refer to Elizabeth Barrett Browning as an exemplary model of the female intellect, and echoed Mary Wollstonecraft and Hannah More's identification of religious study as the pinnacle of women's education.[88] For him, the current state of women's education comprised a superficial system that failed to engage the intellect and so abandoned women in a state of shallow piety suited to the marriage market, not to the Church. Rejecting the idea that religion served only to deepen women's 'tendency to patient self-sacrifice', Littledale described Christian women as 'strong, true, liberal, wise and just, no mere foolish virgins with amiable intentions and expiring lamps' and deserving of 'more exact studies'.[89] If the 'ancient Christian Church' prized 'woman's separate responsibility for her actions', which he believed it did, the existent Church should necessarily hold 'a great career' for women, and affirm that John Stuart Mill's 'phrase "Subjection of Women" is no outgrowth of Christianity'.[90]

Littledale found precedent for his defence of women's education in early Tractarianism, not least the movement's re-establishment of conventual sisterhoods. The Tractarian curate, T. T. Carter, argued as early as 1853 that 'our danger lies' not in the establishment of sisterhoods and female education but 'rather in the opposite direction, in narrowing too much the range of female service, as if domestic duty were women's only calling'. Like Littledale, Carter stated that women required a space for study and contemplation in order that they find 'bonds and sympathies beyond those of home' in 'fellowship of the spirit' and 'consolation in Christ'.[91] Pusey also insisted that women 'ought to understand their own work' and 'education', and stated: 'I think that it is a wrong ambition of men, to wish to have the direction of the work of women. I should fear that it would be for the injury of both.'[92] As Pusey guessed, women joined sisterhoods to be independent, live communally with other women, avoid marriage, and work charitably in social care and education, as well as to live in devotion to God.[93] The religious life offered women a meaningful education, and some of the newly established Anglican convents provided intensely demanding courses involving monthly examinations and papers that were then published in journals or delivered before the community.[94] This was Maria's experience. She was welcomed as an Associate Sister to the flagship Tractarian All Saints Sisterhood on Margaret Street in 1860 only four years after it was established, and became a novice in 1873 and full sister two years later. As a sister, she was tasked with the translation of a Latin Breviary she published privately as *The Day Hours and other Offices as used by the Sisters of All Saints* (1876), and also wrote *Exercises in Idiomatic Italian* (1867), *Aneddoti italiani* (1867), *A Shadow of Dante* (1871), and

Letters to my Bible Class (1872), as a member of All Saints.[95] Rossetti took advantage of the chance to discuss doctrine with Maria, as well as the clergy at Christ Church, and it was through these ecclesiastical institutions that she read the *Tracts for the Times* and listened to Pusey preach.

Pusey played a significant role in reviving sisterhoods in Britain. In 1845 he helped establish the first Anglican sisterhood since Henry VIII's break from Rome in Park Village West, near to Rossetti's maternal family, the Polidoris. The Sisters of the Holy Cross were welcomed by both Pusey and Dodsworth at Christ Church, Albany Street, although Marsh suggests Rossetti may have been intimidated by the darkly clad crew.[96] Admittedly the sisters were initially limited by Pusey's rather too strict 'Rule' for their community, but when the Sisterhood was merged into Priscilla Lydia Sellon's Society of the Sisters of Mercy of the Most Holy Trinity, it became an influential social and charitable body. Sellon worked alongside Pusey to provide education and a soup kitchen for the poor and lodgings for orphaned children. Given this, it is unlikely Rossetti was troubled by the Park Village nuns, and she was already familiar with the idea of sisterhoods from St Katharine's Chapel, which had a long history of granting equal status to its devotional sisters and brothers. While she was not drawn to the conventual life herself, she enjoyed her role as 'Sister Christina' at the St Mary Magdalene Penitentiary for 'fallen women' in Highgate from 1859, and explored sisterhoods in her unpublished novella, *Maude* (1850).[97] But for Rossetti the devotional life was intimately part of a creation that flourished inside and outside of the convent, and she was more inspired by Pusey's affective spirituality and his almost ecstatic openness to the idea of mystical union with the divine body than by the habits of the monastic. Pusey's patristic readings of baptism, confession, the Real Presence, and grace continued to inspire her long after Dodsworth converted to Roman Catholicism, and her spiritual discernment evolved through her engagement with his theology.

Pusey's deeply felt faith was shaped by the German theologian Friedrich Schleiermacher, whose lectures on the New Testament he attended in Berlin in 1825.[98] While Pusey considered Schleiermacher's theology erroneous, he admired 'the direction' in which 'his mind was moving', that is, towards that 'mysterious moment that occurs in every sensory perception, before intuition and feeling have separated'.[99] In a letter to Keble, Pusey distinguished '"feeling" and "feelings": the one the faculty of mind, the other the outward manifestations of that faculty—the emotions', and blamed the 'employment of the latter' in religion as the cause of 'so much mischief and self deception and misery', and the 'neglect of the former' as 'injurious' to the intellect.[100] This distinction is at play throughout Rossetti's early symbolic and reserved poetry, in the taut rhythms of 'Spring Quiet' (1847), for example, or the densely layered sonnets 'Rest' (1849) and 'Remember' (1849), wherein affective expression is measured and restrained. For some readers, such restraint indicates the negative influence of Pusey on her writing as well as her life. Marsh, for example, argues that the 15-year-old Rossetti was especially 'vulnerable' to the teachings of Pusey and Dodsworth and acquired 'an awful sense of unworthiness' from listening to both preach at Christ Church.[101] Accused of *contemptus mundi*, corporal mortification, and extreme fasting, Pusey is even linked by some critics to her alleged breakdown in 1845.[102] But, as with her friend Bennett, Rossetti refused to see Pusey through the lens of anti-Catholic defamation. He was a particular target of the popular press, the word 'Puseyite' adopted to describe an imagined group of secret, predatory, and presumed homosexual agents of Rome sent to corrupt and degrade Protestant Britain.[103] The satirical British weekly, *Punch*, for example, dedicated several articles and images to their 'No Popery' crusade, including a mock advertisement for 'Puseyite Cosmetics' (1850) that offered various fluids 'for blanching the COMPLEXION, and imparting to the FACE that delicate PALLOR which is the recognized indication of severe Thought and Study'.[104] Trollope parodied this anxiety in *Barchester Towers* (1857) by portraying his sycophantic curate Obadiah Slope trembling before 'the iniquities of the Puseyites', whose prayer books 'printed with red letters, and ornamented with a cross on the back' and 'black silk' waistcoats seem to him like symbols 'of Satan'.[105]

But Pusey represented something very different to Rossetti. His rhapsodic presence in Christ Church was described by Sara Coleridge as 'a most earnest and devout spirit, striving to carry out in this world a high religious theory', and he in turn was impressed with the 'exceptional zeal' of a congregation that included the Rossetti women.[106] Pusey was no doubt a serious Christian, and he felt often unworthy before God, 'scarred all over and seamed with sin', as he wrote to Keble.[107] But Rossetti also struggled with the feeling that she was 'unbearable', and claimed to have found 'relief inexpressible' through Pusey, especially in his introduction of 'confession and absolution and spiritual counsel' at Christ Church.[108] His mystical hermeneutics of incarnationalism, theosis, kenōsis, and joy are ever-present in her own theological vision, as is his intuitive, thoughtful, and mystical longing for God in which he connected the love of God to love for others. As Pusey preached in a sermon for Trinity Sunday: 'Holy Scripture hath not said that we should so love God, as to shut out any other love, or any other joy, which does not shut Him out... His love shall make all lovely.'[109] The belief resonates through Rossetti's poem for 'Christmastide', in which Jesus incarnates a 'Love all lovely, love Divine' for and between all things (l. 2).[110]

It was through Pusey too that Rossetti grasped the profound importance of the Church Fathers. His spiritual and mystical pneumatology was founded on a series of patristic references to Clement of Alexandria, Tertullian, Ambrose, and Hippolytus included in his multi-volume *A Library of the Fathers of the Holy Catholic Church Anterior to the Division of the East and West*, published between 1838 and 1881 by John Henry Parker. For Ludlow, Rossetti ideally fulfils Pusey's model reader of these volumes, one he depicts in his edition of Augustine's *Confessions* as an attentive 'student of the Fathers'.[111] Pusey's return to ancient, patristic, and early-modern writings also contributed to his objective of bringing together various communions of the Catholic Church to reinstate it as one whole. He considered the tradition of the Church to have been settled in the first five centuries, and stated that even those who had attempted to reform the Anglican Church 'did not, like Luther, form for us any new system of doctrine' but 'ever appealed to Catholic Antiquity'.[112] His openness to the Churches of the East is represented in the inclusion of Cyril of Alexandria, Athanasius of Alexandria, and Gregory of Nazianzus in his *Library*, as well as a prepared, but unpublished, volume of Gregory of Nyssa's writings. The indwelling and connection modelled in the Trinity also confirmed the importance of intercommunion between Churches and Christians under a broad Catholic tradition for Pusey. He believed that Christ's incarnational declaration, 'I am in the Father, and the Father in me' (John 14. 11), was the basis of the Christian's regeneration through God's presence in all things.[113] By dwelling in the believer, Pusey explained, 'He makes us parts of Himself, so that in the Ancient Church they could boldly say, "He Deifieth Me"; that is, He makes me part of Him of His Body, Who is God'.[114]

Pusey's loving sense of this theotic 'tingling closeness of God!' also underlined his reading of the Real Presence in his multiple, and controversial, writings on the Eucharist as a sacrifice: his university sermon *The Holy Eucharist a Comfort to the Penitent* (1843) provoked his suspension from preaching for two years.[115] For Pusey, Christ was actually but not corporally present in the consecrated bread and wine, his resurrected presence 'truly and really, and yet spiritually and in an ineffable way, His Body and Blood'.[116] This spiritual, rather than physical presence, meant that Christ's being could not be identified by human senses, but rather believed in as something 'Sacramental, supernatural, mystical', a ubiquity both 'without us' as well as 'within us'.[117] The bread and wine become body and blood in Christ's spiritual body, while his resurrected and ascended body waits in heaven until the end of time.[118] Given the controversy surrounding Pusey's reading of the Real Presence, it is significant that Rossetti subscribed to the doctrine, and the implication that inanimate objects like bread and wine had an invisible reality confirmed her sense that all things, material and immaterial, are equal in God. As Pusey argued, the 'Holy Eucharist' suggests the close 'union' of creation with God, a 'foretaste of heavenly sweetness, of blissful calm, of spiritual joy, of transporting love' fully realized in the new creation through Christ.[119] Neither consubstantiation or transubstantiation, Pusey's Real Presence was based on the literal meaning of Jesus's words at the Last Supper, 'this is my body' and 'this is my blood' (Matthew 26. 26–8), statements that for Rossetti confirmed his being as nonhuman as well as human—bread and wine as well as a vine and lamb.

Rossetti quoted these Eucharistic words in her chapter on the Apostle James ('the Great') in her book, *Called to Be Saints: The Minor Festivals Devotionally Studied* (1881), where she aligned Paul's words 'This is My Body, which is broken for you' (1 Corinthians 11. 24) with the Book of Common Prayer version of Psalm 119. 57, 'Thou art my portion, O Lord: I have promised to keep thy law'.[120] The 'law' here comprises an affective theology of God's revealed love in creation and resurrection, and so answers the brokenness of Christ's body, as well as the brokenness of creation itself, with a command to the believer to find her 'portion' or part in God.[121] Rossetti's pairing of the two passages does not simply affirm that the things of creation are 'parts of Himself', as Pusey stated, but that God also belongs to the things of creation: he is their part or share in the cosmos, a vision of Eucharistic harmony Rossetti was drawn to throughout her life. While she later explored this through the doctrine of baptismal grace, to which she was also guided by Pusey, as a young Tractarian poet she turned to song as a way to explore God's real presence in creation, and in doing so extended the space of the church into the world and cosmos. Several critics have noted Rossetti's reading of the world as a sung liturgy.[122] Both Ludlow and Chene Heady identify the 1858 'Earth has clear call of daily bells' as a poem that summons all creation to matins and evensong set amidst the night sky:

> Earth has clear call of daily bells,
> A chancel-vault of gloom and star,
> A rapture where the anthems are,
> A thunder where the organ swells:
> Alas, man's daily life—what else?—
> Is out of tune with daily bells. (ll. 1–6)

For Ludlow, who traces the poem's revision for *Time Flies: A Reading Diary* (1885) and again for *Verses* (1893) under the titles 'Yet a little while' and 'Vanity of Vanities', the poem relates Rossetti's fascination with the 'interface between typology and liturgy'.[123] Like the church interior, creation voices a rhythmic and repeated call to prayer through its own congregation of members. But while the atmosphere 'vibrates' along with the bells, and the thunder plays like an organ, the narrator observes that only 'man' is 'out of tune' with the liturgy: 'what else?' she asks. The human worshipper is invited back into the close union of the Eucharist by the nonhuman here, a model of communion and fellowship.

Rossetti returned repeatedly to the idea that the nonhuman is a paradigm of devotion for the human to 'consider' (Matthew 6. 28). But even in the 1840s, Rossetti wrote several poems in which things sing with other parts of creation to invite the human into a communal chorus directed to God. In 'The Song of the Star' (1847), for example, the star sings to converse with its fellow beings:

> I am a star dwelling on high
> In the azure of the vaulted sky.
> I shine on the land and I shine on the sea,
> And the little breezes talk to me.   (ll. 1–4)

Calm and measured, the star is 'passionless' but loving, interconnected with everything around it—the waves, grass, flowers, fountains, birds, clouds, angels, even planets—and joined with them in a 'cadence musical' that ascends towards heaven (ll. 10, 50). 'Pealing through eternity, | Filling out immensity' (ll. 55–6), the star's song is eternal and unceasing, but also 'Voiceless', its content not auditory but quietly loving:

> Voiceless adoration rise
> To the Heaven above the skies.
> We all chant with a holy harmony,
> No discord marreth our melody;
> Here are no strifes nor envyings,
> But each with love joyously sings,
> For ever and ever floating free
> In the azure light of infinity.   (ll. 63–70)

The communal chant of the nonhuman cannot go out of tune as 'man' does in 'Earth has clear call of daily bells' because it is an expression of shared peacefulness that finds 'extasy' by yielding to a 'flow' that carries it along (l. 38). This flow or energy is grace, that which keeps all things vital and moving towards God, an energy that both creates, manifests, and sustains creation's constituents. In 'The Trees' Counselling' (1847), written a few months after 'The Song of the Star', grace becomes a breeze the narrator perceives waving around the trees of the forest as they talk together in 'leafy' voices. Like the 'voiceless' choir with which the star sings, the trees share their own language of equality and joy: '"Here we all are equal brothers | Here we have nor lord nor peasant"' (ll. 11–12). Sharing a seasonal companionability with 'Little winds', 'Little birds', the sun, moon, stars, and blossoms, the trees hint at a world reminiscent of last-man narratives, in which the nonhuman lives tranquilly and abundantly free of human intervention (ll. 15–16).[124]

But Rossetti did not exclude the human from her many paradisiacal landscapes. The narrator of 'The Trees' Counselling', who strolls 'sorrowfully' alone around the woods, is immediately invited into grace by the trees in order that she '"Learn contentment from this wood"' (l. 29). It is a vision that revises an idealized and bucolic pastoralism as an interdependent 'universe of things' as Shelley wrote in 'Mont Blanc', energized by grace and moved ceaselessly towards an end time of transformation and renewal (ll. 1, 40). While Shelley found only vacancy in his search for the 'secret strength of things', however, Rossetti identified a God in which the human and nonhuman reside in permanent relationship, his Trinitarian being inclusive of a created man, but also a lamb, a vine, a grain, a rock, a light, and water.[125] His silence in the world is not an absence, then, but an invitation to develop a different way of listening, as Rossetti explored in a third poem written in 1847, 'The World's Harmonies'. Here the narrator encourages a synchronic listening to her poem and creation in which things are continually reformed and transformed through their cyclical relationship with each other:

> Oh listen, listen; for the Earth
>   Hath silent melody;
> Green grasses are her lively chords,
>   And blossoms; and each tree,
> Chestnut and oak and sycamore,
>   Makes solemn harmony.
>
> Oh listen, listen; for the Sea
>   Is calling unto us;
> Her notes are the broad liquid waves
>   Mighty and glorious.
> Lo, the first man and the last man
>   Hath heard, shall hearken thus.   (ll. 1–12)

In these first two stanzas Rossetti moves the local into relationship with the cosmic by acoustically translating the geography with which she was familiar—chestnuts, oaks, and sycamores could all be found in Regent's Park—into a cosmic vision of a transformed world in which all things are heard. The harmonies the narrator strives to hear in her repeated call to 'listen' are amplified at the end of time, 'audible', she claims in stanza six, when given 'Before the everlasting

Throne' (ll. 31, 36). This reference to Revelation 7. 9 in which God is revealed to a 'great multitude, which no man could number, of all nations, and kindreds, and people, and tongues' confirms the divine as, the narrator claims, 'the voice of the whole World', one that speaks to the first and to the last (l. 37).

'Sweeter' than even this voice, however, is the 'lowly prayer' of the poor, a sound in which all the angels and spirits 'rejoice' and in which all things are 'undivided' (ll. 40, 42, 47). The song of the weak and vulnerable human that concludes 'The World's Harmonies' rings out only after the reader has listened to the rest of creation sing—its grasses, blossoms, trees, sea, sun, moon, stars, clouds, winds, dews, frost, rain, fishes, beasts, and rainbows. Unlike these things, the human is spiritually, as well as materially 'poor' because she has broken herself from the very things that bring her back into relation with an eternal love finally sounded out at the end of time. But by turning away from this particular 'sin' (l. 48) and embracing the nonhuman, the human can access God as a real and immediate presence in time and learn to hear him speak through the things of his creation. Rossetti invited her readers to engage with and celebrate this diversity as the incarnation of the divine, God a reconciliation of difference, not in sameness, but in an entangled and multiple divine body. Through Tractarianism, she conceived of God as a plural and evolving body into which all things were reconciled, including newly discovered species and organisms. Science and faith are not in conflict for Rossetti, but rather represent different ways of knowing and seeing. She concurred with Pusey's assessment that 'faith *rests* upon the supernatural; science, upon man's natural powers of observation, induction, combination, inference, deduction; faith has to do chiefly with the invisible; science, with this visible order of things'.[126] For Rossetti, the revelation of the invisible through the visible levels creation and reminds the human of the second commandment, 'You shall have no other gods before me' (Exodus 20. 3). She wrote in *Letter and Spirit* that the human exertion of power 'reversed the process of creation' because it caused 'man' to make 'gods after his likeness' and adore 'himself in them'.[127] Such egotism threatened to break the union of all things in God, and so stall the Second Advent and the new creation. As the next chapter argues, Pre-Raphaelitism offered her an aesthetic through which to articulate the urgency of equal fellowship with others, a movement that at once revered the Catholic Revival even as it elevated the vibrancy and specificity of the natural world.

Notes

1. Rossetti's letters show that she was still reading Pusey's work until the very end of her life: see Christina G. Rossetti to William Michael Rossetti, 10 November 1893, in Anthony H. Harrison, ed., *The Letters of Christina Rossetti: Volume 1 1843–1873*; *Volume II 1874–1881*; *Volume III 1882–1886*; *Volume IV 1887–1894* (Charlottesville and London: The University Press of Virginia, 1997, 1999, 2000, 2004), IV, 355; further references are abbreviated to *Letters*.
2. Edward Bouverie Pusey, *Sermons During the Season from Advent to Whitsuntide* (Oxford: John Henry Parker, 1848), pp. v–xxvii (p. v).
3. Ibid. 35–46 (38).
4. Edward Bouverie Pusey, *On the Clause 'And the Son', in Regard to the Eastern Church and the Bonn Conference: A Letter to the Rev. H. P. Liddon* (Oxford: James Parker, 1876), 3.
5. Edward Bouverie Pusey to B. Harrison, 21 February 1840, in Henry Parry Liddon, *Life of Edward Bouverie Pusey*, 4 vols (London: Longmans, 1894), II, 148.
6. Edward Bouverie Pusey, *The Miracles of Prayer: A Sermon Preached Before the University in the Cathedral Church of Christ, in Oxford on Septuagesima Sunday, 1866* (Oxford: John Henry and James Parker, 1866), 31.
7. Undated, first published in Christina G. Rossetti, *Time Flies: A Reading Diary* (London: Society for Promoting Christian Knowledge, 1885), 243.
8. Christina G. Rossetti, *Letter and Spirit: Notes on the Commandments* (London: Society for Promoting Christian Knowledge, 1883), 8–9.
9. William Michael Rossetti, *Some Reminiscences of William Michael Rossetti*, 2 vols (New York: Charles Scribner's, 1906), I, 108, 120–1.
10. Henry Hadley Norris to R. Churton, 30 September 1812, in Peter Benedict Nockles, *The Oxford Movement in Context: Anglican High Churchmanship 1760–1857* (Cambridge: Cambridge University Press, 1994), 154; Richard Frederick Littledale, *The North-Side of the Altar* (London, 1865), 3–4.
11. See Nigel Yates, *Buildings, Faith and Worship: The Liturgical Arrangement of Anglican Churches 1600–1900* (Oxford: Clarendon Press, 1991), 144–5.
12. William J. E. Bennett, 'Some Results of the Tractarian Movement of 1833', in Orby Shipley, ed., *The Church and the World: Essay on Questions of the Day in 1867* (London: Longmans, Green, Reader, and Dyer, 1867), 1–26.
13. Christina G. Rossetti to Miss May, January 1893, in *Letters*, IV, 307.
14. William Gladstone, *The Church of England and Ritualism* (London: Strahan and Co., 1875), 19; reprinted from *The Contemporary Review*, 24 (1874).

15. Christina G. Rossetti, *The Face of the Deep: A Devotional Commentary on the Apocalypse* (London: Society for Promoting Christian Knowledge, 1892), 243.

16. See D. G. Paz, *Popular Anti-Catholicism in Mid-Victorian England* (Stanford: Stanford University Press, 1992), 10.

17. See Edward Bouverie Pusey, *The Entire Absolution of the Penitent* (Oxford: John Henry Parker, 1846).

18. C. J. Blomfield, *A Charge to the Clergy of London* [1842], in James Bentley, *Ritualism and Politics in Victorian Britain: The Attempt to Legislate for Belief* (Oxford: Oxford University Press, 1978), 30.

19. John Shelton Reed, *Glorious Battle: The Cultural Politics of Victorian Anglo-Catholicism* (Nashville and London: Vanderbilt University Press, 1996), 187.

20. Octavius J. Ellis, *Some Time among Ritualists*, 3rd edn (London: Hatchards, 1868), 10–11.

21. Rossetti, *Reminiscences*, I, 72.

22. Eliot Ryder, ed., *The Household Library of Catholic Poets: From Chaucer to the Present Day* (Notre Dame, IN: University of Notre Dame, 1881), 87–8; 'Cardinal Newman' was first published in *The Athenæum*, 3276 (16 August 1890), 225.

23. Rossetti, *Reminiscences*, I, 120.

24. Ibid.

25. Jan Marsh, *Christina Rossetti: A Literary Biography* (London: Pimlico, 1995), 25.

26. Alison Chapman and Joanna Meacock, *A Rossetti Family Chronology* (New York: Palgrave Macmillan, 2007), 35.

27. Rossetti, *Reminiscences*, I, 171.

28. Henry William Burrows, *The Half-Century of Christ Church, Albany Street, St Pancras* (London: Skeffington & Son, 1887), 9.

29. Ibid. 14.

30. Ibid. 12.

31. Henry William Burrows, 'To the Inhabitants of the District and Members of the Congregation of Christ Church, St Pancras' (1 December 1865), in Elizabeth Wordsworth, *Henry William Burrows: Memorials* (London: Kegan Paul, Trench, Trübner, and Co, 1894), 229–32 (229, 230).

32. Karen Dieleman, *Religious Imaginaries: The Liturgical and Poetic Practices of Elizabeth Barrett Browning, Christina Rossetti, and Adelaide Procter* (Athens: Ohio University Press, 2012), 122.

33. Ibid. 124.

34. Marsh, *Rossetti*, 62.

35. Stephen Young, *William Dodsworth 1798–1861: The Origins of Tractarianism in London* (London: Anglo-Catholic History Society, 2002), 1; Paul Thompson, *William Butterfield* (London: Routledge, 1971), 243.

36. Christina G. Rossetti to Caroline Maria Gemmer, 13 February 1873, in *Letters*, I, 419; Burrows, *Half-Century*, 21, 31, 47, 50, 66.

37. 'The Principal Clergy of London: Classified According to their opinions on the Great Church questions of the day', 1844, quoted by kind

permission of the Bodleian Libraries, University of Oxford, MS Add. c.290.

38. Ibid. 7.

39. Rossetti, *Face of the Deep*, 540.

40. Ibid. 541.

41. Burrows, *Half-Century*, 7, 32, 36.

42. Ashton Nichols, *Beyond Romantic Ecocriticism: Toward Urbanatural Roosting* (New York: Palgrave Macmillan, 2011), p. xv.

43. 'Diaries of Frances Mary Lavinia Rossetti', 131 leaves, entries for 18–26 January 1881, quoted by kind permission of the Angeli-Dennis Collection, University of British Columbia Special Collections Division, Box 6–16, 12–17, from facsimile in Bodleian Libraries, Oxford, MS Facs.c.96.

44. Ibid., 14 October 1881.

45. Christina G. Rossetti to William Michael Rossetti, 5 November 1873, *Letters*, I, 437.

46. Diane D'Amico, 'The House of Christina Rossetti: Domestic and Poetic Spaces', *The Journal of Pre-Raphaelite Studies*, 19 (2010), 31–54 (32–3).

47. Elizabeth Ludlow, *Christina Rossetti and the Bible: Waiting with the Saints* (London: Bloomsbury, 2014), 28.

48. Nockles, *Oxford Movement*, 104.

49. Tim Larsen, 'Scripture and Biblical Interpretation', in Stewart J. Brown, Peter B. Nockles, and James Pereiro, eds., *The Oxford Handbook of the Oxford Movement* (Oxford: Oxford University Press, 2017), 231–43.

50. John Henry Newman, Review of William Jacobson, *S. Clementis Romani, S. Ignatii, S. Polycarpi* (Oxonii, 1838), *The British Critic and Theological Review*, 25.49 (January 1839), 49–76 (54).

51. William Dodsworth, *The Signs of the Times: Sermons Preached in Advent 1848* (London: Joseph Masters, 1849), 14–15.

52. Ibid. 40–1.

53. Ibid. 40–3.

54. Ibid. 19–20.

55. Ibid. 22.

56. Ibid. 92.

57. Rossetti, *Time Flies*, 128.

58. See John O. Waller, 'Christ's Second Coming: Christina Rossetti and the Premillennialist William Dodsworth', *Bulletin of the New York Public Library*, 73 (1969), 465–82.

59. See her poem, 'Advent (This Advent moon shines cold and clear)'; Kate E. Brown, 'Futurity and Postponement: Christina Rossetti and the Yearning for Advent', *Intertexts*, 8.1 (2003), 15–21 (18).

60. Brown, 'Futurity', 20.

61. I have written elsewhere on Rossetti's love of winter as the herald of the new life of spring: Emma Mason, 'Christina Rossetti and the Doctrine of Reserve', *Journal of Victorian Culture*, 7.2 (2002), 196–219.

62. Dodsworth, *Signs*, p. vi.
63. See Alister E. McGrath, *The Open Secret: A New Vision for Natural Theology* (Oxford: Wiley-Blackwell, 2008), 191.
64. Dodsworth, *Signs*, 9.
65. Basil the Great, *On Psalm* 32. 3, in John Chryssavgis, 'The Earth as Sacrament: Insights from Orthodox Christian Theology and Spirituality', in Roger S. Gottlieb, ed., *The Oxford Handbook of Religion and Ecology* (Oxford: Oxford University Press, 2006), 92–114 (112).
66. John Henry Newman, *Apologia Pro Vita Sua* (1864; London: Penguin, 1994), 37.
67. John Keble, 'Tract 89: On the Mysticism attributed to the Early Fathers of the Church' [n.d.], *Tracts for the Times by members of the University of Oxford*, 6 vols (London: J. G. F. and J. Rivington, 1841), VI, 143; and *Keble's Lectures on Poetry 1832–1841*, trans. E. K. Francis, 2 vols (Oxford: Clarendon Press, 1912), II, 483.
68. Keble, *Lectures*, II, 481.
69. Keble, 'On the Mysticism', 143.
70. John Henry Newman, 'Poetry: With Reference to Aristotle's Poetics', *The London Review*, 1 (1829), in 'The Newman Reader' (Pittsburgh, PA: The National Institute for Newman Studies, 2007), http://www.newmanreader.org/works/essays/volume1/poetry.html.
71. George Saintsbury, *A History of English Prosody, from the Twelfth Century to the Present Day*, 3 vols (London: Macmillan, 1906–10), III, 353–5.
72. Ibid. 358; see also Michael D. Hurley, *Faith in Poetry: Verse Style as a Mode of Religious Belief* (London: Bloomsbury, 2017).
73. Paul Tillich, *Theology of Culture* (New York: Oxford University Press, 1959), 50.
74. Dinah Roe, *Christina Rossetti's Faithful Imagination: The Devotional Poetry and Prose* (Basingstoke: Palgrave Macmillan, 2006), 46.
75. G. B. Tennyson, *Victorian Devotional Poetry: The Tractarian Mode* (Cambridge, MA: Harvard University Press, 1981), 147.
76. John Henry Newman, *An Essay in Aid of a Grammar of Assent* (1870; New York: Image, 1955), 276.
77. Dodsworth, *Signs*, 12; Isaac Williams, 'Tract 80: On Reserve in Communicating Religious Knowledge (Parts I–III)' (1838), in *Tracts for the Times*, IV; and 'Tract 87: On Reserve in Communicating Religious Knowledge (Conclusion: Parts IV–VI)' (1840), in *Tracts for the Times*, V.
78. Williams, 'Tract 80', Part II, 6.
79. Christina G. Rossetti to the Reverend Charles Gutch, January 1879, *Letters*, II, 191–4; published as 'A Harmony on First Corinthians XIII', *New and Old*, 7 (January 1879), 34–9; republished in Christina G. Rossetti, *Seek and Find: A Double Series of Short Studies on the Benedicite* (London: Society for Promoting Christian Knowledge, 1879), 3.
80. Isaac Williams, *The Cathedral, or, The Catholic and Apostolic Church in England* (Oxford: John Henry Parker, 1838), pp. v–vi.

81. John Keble, 'Sacred Poetry', *The Quarterly Review*, 32 (1825), 211–32 (217, 219–20); reprinted in *Occasional Papers and Reviews by John Keble* (Oxford and London: James Parker and Co., 1877), 81–107.

82. Linda Schofield, 'Being and Understanding: Devotional Poetry of Christina Rossetti and the Tractarians', in David A. Kent, ed., *The Achievement of Christina Rossetti* (Ithaca: Cornell University Press, 1987), 301–21; Isobel Armstrong, *Victorian Poetry: Poetry, Poetics and Politics* (London: Routledge, 1993); Mary Arseneau, *Recovering Christina Rossetti: Female Community and Incarnational Poetics* (New York: Palgrave Macmillan, 2004); Kevin A. Morrison, 'Christina Rossetti's Secrets', *Philological Quarterly*, 90.1 (2011), 97–116; and Mason, 'Doctrine of Reserve'.

83. Adam Mazel, ' "You, Guess": The Enigmas of Christina Rossetti', *Victorian Literature and Culture*, 44 (2016), 511–33 (513).

84. Ibid. 527.

85. Rossetti, *Letter and Spirit*, 57.

86. Rossetti, *Time Flies*, 22.

87. John Ruskin, *Sesame and Lilies* (1865), in E. T. Cook and Alexander Wedderburn, eds., *The Works of John Ruskin*, 39 vols (London: George Allen, 1903–12), XVIII, 127.

88. Mary Wollstonecraft, *Thoughts on the Education of Daughters: with Reflections on Female Conduct, in the more Important Duties of Life* (London: Joseph Johnson, 1787); Hannah More, *Strictures on the Modern System of Female Education: with a View of the Principles and Conduct Prevalent Among Women of Rank and Fortune*, 2 vols (London: T. Cadell Jun. and W. Davies, 1799).

89. Richard Frederick Littledale, 'The Religious Education of Women', *The Contemporary Review*, 20 (June 1872), 1–26 (8–9, 10).

90. Ibid. 14.

91. Thomas Thelluson Carter, *Objections to Sisterhoods Considered in a Letter to a Parent* (London: F. & J. Rivington, 1853), 10, in George Herring, *The Oxford Movement in Practice: The Tractarian Parochial World from the 1830s to the 1870s* (Oxford: Oxford University Press, 2016), 145.

92. Edward Bouverie Pusey to Arthur Stanton, 14 January 1865, in George W. E. Russell, *Arthur Stanton: A Memoir* (London: Longmans, Green and Co, 1917), 57–8.

93. Susan Mumm, *Stolen Daughters, Virgin Mothers: Anglican Sisterhoods in Victorian Britain* (London and New York: Leicester University Press, 1999), 13.

94. Ibid. 72.

95. See Susan Mumm, ed., *All Saints Sisters of the Poor: An Anglican Sisterhood in the Nineteenth Century* (Woodbridge and New York: Boydell, 2001); and Maria Francesca Rossetti, *Exercises in Idiomatic Italian through literal translation from the English*, and *Aneddoti italiani: Italian Anecdotes selected from 'Il Compagno del Passeggio Campestre'*, 2 vols (London: Williams and Norgate, 1867), *A Shadow of Dante: Being an Essay towards Studying Himself, His World and His Pilgrimage* (London, Oxford, and Cambridge: Rivingtons, 1871), *Letters to my Bible Class on Thirty-Nine Sundays* (London and Oxford: SPCK, 1872).

96. Marsh, *Rossetti*, 58.

97. Christina G. Rossetti, *Maude* (1850), in Elaine Showalter, ed., *Christina Rossetti: Maude; Dinah Mulock Craik: On Sisterhoods, a Woman's Thoughts about Women* (London: William Pickering, 1993).

98. George Derrick Westhaver, "The Living Body of the Lord: E. B. Pusey's 'Types and Prophecies of the Old Testament' ", Durham University thesis (2012), http://etheses.dur.ac.uk/6373, 125.

99. Liddon, *Life*, I, 83; Friedrich Schleiermacher, *On Religion: Speeches to its Cultured Despisers* (1799), trans. Richard Crouter (Cambridge: Cambridge University Press, 1996), 31.

100. Edward Bouverie Pusey to John Keble, 18 April 1829, in Westhaver, *Living Body*, 126.

101. Marsh, *Rossetti*, 64, 260.

102. Mumm, *Stolen Daughters*; James A. Kohl, 'A Medical Comment on Christina Rossetti', *Notes and Queries*, 15.213.11 (1968), 423–4.

103. See Reed, *Glorious Battle*, 221 ff.

104. Percival Leigh, 'Puseyite Cosmetics', *Punch*, 10 (9 November 1850), 199, in Dominic Janes, 'Early Victorian Moral Anxiety and the Queer Legacy of the Eighteenth-Century Gothic Revival', in Timothy Willem Jones and Lucinda Matthews-Jones, *Material Religion in Modern Britain: The Spirit of Things* (New York: Palgrave Macmillan, 2015), 125–43 (133).

105. Anthony Trollope, *Barchester Towers* (1857), ed. John Bowen (Oxford: Oxford University Press, 2014), 25.

106. Sara Coleridge to Miss Morris, 7 July 1845, in Edith Coleridge, ed., *Memoirs and Letters of Sara Coleridge*, 2 vols (London: Henry S. King, 1873), I, 333; Burrows, *Half-Century*, 16; Yngve Brilioth, *The Anglican Revival* (London and New York: Longmans Green, 1925), 296; Marsh, *Rossetti*, 64.

107. Edward Bouverie Pusey to John Keble, 26 September 1844, in Liddon, *Life*, III, 96.

108. Christina G. Rossetti to Dante Gabriel Rossetti, 2 December 1881, *Letters*, II, 311.

109. Edward Bouverie Pusey, 'The Rest of Love and Praise', in *Parochial Sermons*, 2 vols (Plymouth: The Devenport Society, 1862), II, 216, in Ian McCormack, 'The History of the History of Pusey', in Rowan Strong and Carol Engelhardt Herringer, eds., *Edward Bouverie Pusey and the Oxford Movement* (London: Anthem Press, 2012), 13–30 (22).

110. Published in Rossetti, *Time Flies*, 251.

111. *The Confessions of S. Augustine Revised from a Former Translation by the Rev. E. B. Pusey*, in *A Library of Fathers of the Holy Catholic Church Anterior to the Division of the East and West*, trans. Members of the English Church, 51 vols (Oxford: John Henry Parker, 1840), I, pp. xxxi–xxxii.

112. Edward Bouverie Pusey, *The Articles treated on in Tract 90 reconsidered and their Interpretation vindicated in a Letter to the Rev. R. W. Jelf, D. D.* (Oxford: John Henry Parker, 1841), 8.

113. Pusey, *On the Clause*, 178–9.

114. Pusey, *Advent to Whitsuntide*, 233.

115. Edward Bouverie Pusey, 'Actualness of the Indwelling of God', *Parochial and Cathedral Sermons* (Oxford: Park and Co., 1882), 472–8 (477); and see Carol Engelhardt Herringer, 'Pusey's Eucharistic Doctrine', in Strong and Herringer, eds., *Pusey*, 91–113.

116. Edward Bouverie Pusey, *The Holy Eucharist a Comfort to the Penitent: A Sermon Preached Before the University in the Cathedral Church of Christ, in Oxford, on the Fourth Sunday after Easter* (New York: D. Appleton, 1843), 3.

117. Edward Bouverie Pusey, *The Presence of Christ in the Holy Eucharist: A Sermon, Preached before the University, in the Cathedral Church of Christ, in Oxford, on the Second Sunday after Epiphany, 1853* (Oxford and London: John Henry Parker, 1853), 21–2.

118. Herringer, 'Pusey's Eucharistic Doctrine', 95.

119. Pusey, *Presence of Christ*, 9, 68–9.

120. Christina G. Rossetti, *Called to Be Saints: The Minor Festivals Devotionally Studied* (London: Society for Promoting Christian Knowledge, 1881), 346.

121. See Columba Breen, 'The Psalms of the Law', *The Furrow*, 15.8 (1964), 516–25.

122. Chene Heady, '"Earth has clear call of daily bells": Nature's Apocalyptic Liturgy in Christina Rossetti's Verses', *Religion and the Arts*, 15 (2011), 148–71 (157).

123. Ludlow, *Rossetti*, 224–5.

124. Timothy Morton, 'Here Comes Everything: The Promise of Object-Oriented Ontology', *Qui Parle: Critical Humanities and Social Sciences*, 19.2 (2011), 163–90 (174).

125. Percy Bysshe Shelley, 'Mont Blanc' (1816), in Donald H. Reiman and Neil Fraistat, eds., *Shelley's Poetry and Prose* (New York and London: W. W. Norton, 2002).

126. Edward Bouverie Pusey, 'The Spirit in which the researches of learning and science should be applied to the study of the Bible', in *Authorized Report of the Church Congress held at Norwich on the 3rd, 4th and 5th October, 1865* (Norwich: Cundall and Miller, 1866), 181–98 (189); see Brian Douglas, *The Eucharistic Theology of Edward Bouverie Pusey: Sources, Context and Doctrine within the Oxford Movement and Beyond* (Leiden and Boston: Brill, 2015), 186–7.

127. Rossetti, *Letter and Spirit*, 77.

2
Kinship and Creation
Amongst the Pre-Raphaelites, 1850–1862

Tractarianism introduced Rossetti to a way of thinking from which she would develop her inclusive reading of grace, but it was her involvement with the Pre-Raphaelites that transformed her perception of the visible and invisible world. At once Christological and ecological, her distinctive and near mystical sense of 'all things' as part of one body is influenced as much by the artistic as by the Christian context in which she was writing, a double lens through which the world revealed itself to her. Critics have always acknowledged the impact of both Christianity and art on Rossetti, but Georgina Battiscombe's proclamation that her poetry was influenced by 'Pre-Raphaelitism' while the 'Oxford Movement had the greater effect upon her life and character' splits two movements that come together in her writing as the foundation of her ecological thinking.[1] The 1850s and 1860s are perhaps the most significant period in Rossetti's spiritual development: instilled by Christ Church, Albany Street, with a work ethic focused on study and reflection, she secured multiple opportunities to read and write—in the context of her brothers' artistic pursuits, Maria's commitment to the conventual life, and various trips taken to escape the London smog. What she learned during this period helped to found an originality of vision minimized in William's histories of the family, which present Rossetti as a fastidious and modest young woman uninterested in reading. Her verse offerings to a Pre-Raphaelite project initiated in 1848 by Gabriel are noticeably more sophisticated than those by other contributors, preoccupied as they are with a visionary fusion of the terrestrial and celestial. She did not attend Brotherhood meetings, not because doing so would have seemed 'like display' as Gabriel suggested, but because she was busy with her own studies and writing projects.[2] Under the name Ellen Alleyn, she contributed seven poems to the group's short-lived periodical, *The Germ: Thoughts towards Nature in Poetry, Literature and Art* (1850), and was drawn to its emphasis on studying 'Nature attentively' and sympathizing 'with what is direct and serious and heartfelt in previous art'.[3] The Brotherhood's focus on a vibrant and luminous natural world spoke to the ideal of a harmonious cosmos Rossetti envisioned through her faith, and she remained committed to a poetics in which natural detail is one with the sacred. Gabriel may well have advised her to write 'from real abundant Nature' and not from 'dreamings', but it is the reciprocal communion of matter and spirit, nature and grace, visible and invisible, that defined her Christology.[4]

One of the challenges of exploring Rossetti's nondual vision of the visible and invisible is tracing the intellectual range of her written responses when she was intent on reserving it. To be or keep something reserved does not mean to obscure it entirely, however. She engaged studiously with Christianity and art in conversation with her family, friends, and those she met during her time as a schoolteacher, governess, and churchgoer. At home with her brothers, as well as during residences at Longleat House in Wiltshire, Frome in Somerset, and at Haigh Hall in Lancashire, Rossetti reflected on her faith through the works of Plato, the Cappadocian Fathers, Francis of Assisi, and William Blake, as well as contemporary novelists and fellow poets. She did not write to showcase what she read, but rather to formulate a space in which to reflect on it as the basis of her vision of grace. As she wrote to the Scottish writer, William Edmonstoune Aytoun, 'poetry is not a mechanism, but an impulse and a reality', a sensuous and considered, affective and intellectual, symbolic and real way of imagining a creation that is both animated by and held in the form of Christ's body. She was thus confident in her vocation, and considered herself part of a community of writers in which 'my love for what is good in the works of others teaches me that there is something above the despicable in mine'.[5] She actively sought positive critical acclaim for her exegetical work on grace and creation and was far from the wallflower William recalled. Most notably she refused the conventual lifestyle. While she was called 'Sister Christina' during her time as a voluntary worker at the Highgate St Mary Magdalene

Penitentiary for 'fallen women', she confessed to her friend and fellow anti-vivisection campaigner, Caroline Gemmer:

> So you think I once trembled on 'the Convent Threshold'—. Not seriously ever, tho' I went thro' a sort of romantic impression on the subject like many young people. No, I feel no drawing in that direction: really, of the two, I might perhaps have less unadaptedness in some ways to the hermit life.[6]

The burst of negatives here betrays her belief that monasticism was incompatible with her commitment to a creation in which all things are connected, even if she would later write to Gabriel that the 'habits of a hermit' held considerable appeal.[7]

This chapter is concerned with how Rossetti evolved her reading of creation as bound by an inherent kinship, or as Cyril of Alexandria put it, a 'kinness'. It suggests that she followed Colossians 1. 15–17 in envisioning Jesus Christ as the 'firstborn' form in which and through which 'every creature' is embraced by grace: 'For by him were all things created, that are in heaven, and that are in earth, visible and invisible' and 'he is before all things, and by him all things consist'. In this radical vision, Christ is incarnated across all things, 'complicating every border between human and animal, human and divine, and divine and other-than-human in all its limitless variety'.[8] Rossetti thus presented different elements of creation as both particular and tangible, as well as unified and symbolic, 'One by one, but all together', as she wrote in her 1845 poem, 'Summer (Hark to the song of greeting!)' (l. 5). Birds, trees, bees, moss, leaves, and rainbows appear to glow in her work because she perceived them under grace as forms of Christ, incarnated into being and renewed by the Church through the sacraments. Pusey even argued that this renewed creation constituted 'a new nature', one that 'is actual, not metaphorical, and by virtue of the Incarnation of our Lord Who took our nature that He might impart His to us'.[9] This 'new nature' speaks directly to the Pre-Raphaelite attention to creation, one conjured through the artist's dramatization of natural phenomena as real presences of God's grace. While Robert Buchanan meant the term 'Fleshly School' as an attack on the Brotherhood in his infamous 1871 review, the phrase nevertheless gestures to the group's embodied vision in which the becoming flesh of word and spirit in Christ holds all things together as one.[10]

Ultimately, it was the Catholicity of the Brotherhood, historically downplayed by the spiritually sceptical William, that allowed Rossetti to draw on and rethink its aesthetics. As the first section suggests, her reading of an early Pre-Raphaelite affinity with what Gabriel called an 'art-Catholic' alongside her ongoing commitment to an evolving Tractarianism helped to found her nondual understanding of creation as that which embraces both the material and the divine. The second section suggests that this vision was also shaped by her encounters with Plato, the Church Fathers, Francis of Assisi, and William Blake, all of whom contributed to her vision of creation as an infinite and eternal network of different species and beings. Her poetry of this period reveals her developing vision of an interdependent creation in which all things—from leaves and sparrows to spirits and angels—dwell harmoniously with each other in a divine body in which earth and heaven are one home. The last section explores how Rossetti envisioned this communal and participatory creation through a 'kinness of nature' modelled in the Sermon on the Mount (Matthew 5–7).[11] Rossetti strove to imagine such kinship between the divine, human, and nonhumans of all kinds, even those goblin critters who appear so unwilling to join with others in her celebrated poem, 'Goblin Market' (1859).

An Art-Catholic

In July 1852, Rossetti modelled for the figure of Jesus in William Holman Hunt's *The Light of the World* (1851–3). Hunt wrote that while she had already sat for Gabriel as the 'pure and docile-hearted damsel' Mary in his *The Girlhood of Mary Virgin* (1848–9) and *Ecce Ancilla Domini!* (1849–50), he considered the combination of 'gravity and sweetness' in her expression better suited to the face of Jesus.[12] The Brotherhood singled out Jesus as the sole recipient of four stars in their 1848 'list of Immortals', a declaration that constituted 'the whole' of their 'Creed'.[13] While Hunt would later become skittish about the document, he remained committed to the idea of Jesus as 'A Poem as well as a poet', a 'Captain of men' whose incarnated being he sought to reveal in his allegorical painting. *The Light of the World* was primarily an Adventist work, a reading of several scriptural passages including Revelation 3. 20 ('Behold, I stand at the door, and knock'), Psalm 119. 105

('Thy word is a lamp unto my feet, and a light unto my path'), and Romans 13. 12 ('The night is far spent, the day is at hand').[14] As John Ruskin wrote, Hunt's risen Christ arrived as 'a living presence among us', and was framed by the specifics of a Surrey orchard—moonlight, ivy, trees, apples, a bat to announce a vividly material world received through the word of God.[15] Symbolic and particular, anticipatory and prophetic, the painting exemplified the aims of the Pre-Raphaelites. Its vibrant colouring and energetic realism summoned the aesthetic, moral, and pious work of early Florentine artists like Giotto, Bellini, and Fra Angelico. In a rejection of the Classicism and 'Academicism' of the Royal Academy, the Brotherhood sought to observe and tell stories about the 'naturalistic facts' of a living world illuminated by sun or moonlight, not spurious objects imprisoned in the dim light of studios.[16] Painting outdoors, at night, in fields, and on walls and ceilings, as well as canvases, the group achieved luminous and hyperreal effects in which empirical observation went beyond the optical into the transcendental.[17] For Ruskin, who advised 'young artists' to 'go to nature in all singleness of heart, and walk with her laboriously and trustingly', Pre-Raphaelite art offered 'space, warmth, and freshness' even when it turned to everyday details: a stone in the foreground, or a blade of grass.[18]

For some, this detail stripped art of its idealism and gestured to an archaic style that many associated with the Oxford Movement, if not Catholicism. When Millais exhibited *Christ in the House of his Parents* (1850) at the Royal Academy, Charles Dickens responded by calling it 'mean, odious, repulsive and revolting' because of its attention to the physiological detail of the Holy Family's bodies amidst a common carpenter's shop.[19] Critics were also appalled by its blunt references to Christ's passion in the injured hand of the child Jesus, which drops blood onto the boy's left foot, the whip-shaped reeds of an unfinished basket, and scattered carpentry nails.[20] Gabriel's *The Passover of the Holy Family: Gathering the Bitter Herbs* (1855–6) also practised a forthright typology in its connection of the sprinkling of blood at Passover (Exodus 12) to Jesus's later sacrifice; and both Millais's *The Return of the Dove to the Ark* (1851) and Charles Allston Collins's *Convent Thoughts* (1851) mesmerized the viewer with radiant typological symbols. Collins's painting extended typology into botany, depicting a young novice (modelled on Maria Rossetti) in a walled garden full of symbolic and empirical details. She holds open an illuminated missal portraying floriated scenes of the Annunciation and crucifixion, is surrounded by roses and lilies (emblems of the Virgin Mary) and water lilies (symbols of purity), and stares thoughtfully at a passionflower. Also known as the 'floral apostle', the *passiflora caerulea* was brought to Europe by Jesuit missionaries who read the white blossom's streaks of purple as a symbol for the Passion of Christ: the corona signified the crown of thorns, the five stamens his wounds, the three styles the nails, and the tendrils the scourges.[21] Collins was no Catholic, but *Punch* was quick to ridicule his emaciated nun as an elevation of the unhealthy body they already associated with Pusey.[22] The vague spirituality of *The Germ* soon led to accusations that it was little more than a 'Puseyite parish magazine' that espoused the Brotherhood's closet Catholicism.[23] Suspicions were further fuelled by the donation of Hunt's *The Light of the World* to Keble College, Oxford by its Anglo-Catholic buyers.[24] Even Ruskin, in an early defence of the Pre-Raphaelites in a letter to *The Times*, could not help but denounce 'their Romanist and Tractarian tendencies'.[25]

William sought to distance the Brotherhood from 'Roman Catholicism, Anglican Tractarianism, or what not', claiming that any association between the two was 'totally' and 'even ludicrously, erroneous'.[26] But the significance of Catholicism and Tractarianism for Pre-Raphaelitism was conspicuous. Even William had to admit to Gabriel's early interest in Roman Catholicism in his 'Art-Catholic', a term that 'embodied conceptions and a point of view related to pictorial art . . . in sentiment though not necessarily in dogma, Catholic—medieval and unmodern'.[27] Sent to Italy to recuperate from ill health in 1843, Gabriel found Catholic 'mass or vespers or whatever they call it' both 'solemn and impressive' and based much of his 1847 manuscript, 'Songs of the Art-Catholic', on the art and architecture he discovered there.[28] William worried that his brother indicated 'definite Christian belief, and of a strangely Roman Catholic kind', and while Gabriel was affected more by what he called the 'emotional influence' of religion than a particular doctrinal system, he was drawn to the Catholic Mass, which he may have attended with his maternal uncle, Henry Polidori.[29] It is not surprising that when the Scottish painter William Bell Scott visited the Rossetti family the following year, he worried that Gabriel, and not Christina, was caught up in 'Oxford Tractarianism'.[30] Pre-Raphaelitism's revival of typological symbolism was founded on

Gabriel's interest in the Bible, Dante, and the *dolce stil novo*, and he valued the 'feeling' of 'worship and service' above all else.[31] Such conviction is embodied in Gabriel's character, Chiaro dell' Erma, in his story 'Hand and Soul', who moves past his anxiety that his faith constitutes little more than love of beauty to a realization that devotion to personal experience through art is itself a form of worship and duty.[32] As George Frederick Stephens wrote in *The Germ*, the 'modern artist does not retire to monasteries, or practise discipline; but he may show his participation in the same high feeling by a firm attachment to truth'.[33] The essay, like Gabriel's story and his 'Sonnets for Pictures', William's poem 'Jesus Wept', and John Orchard's 'On a Whit Sunday Morning', confirmed that religion was central to the group's aesthetic, but that faith constituted not doctrinal adherence but a mystical and reserved depth of feeling.

The only member of the group who did convert to Roman Catholicism was James Collinson. Like Hunt, he chose Rossetti as his model for an image of Jesus designed to accompany his contribution to *The Germ*, 'The Child Jesus: A Record typical of the five Sorrowful Mysteries'. The engraving is deliberately Roman Catholic in its detail: the banner that hangs from Jesus's cross is in the gothic or blackletter script associated with Latin; the child kneels before Jesus to kiss his hand as the laity does after the inaugural mass of a newly ordained priest; and the words presented beneath the engraving in Latin— Psalm 8. 2, 'Out of the mouth of babes and sucklings perfect praise'— are suggestive of an emotional faith associated with Catholicism.[34] Also like Hunt, Collinson overlaid the scriptural location by the Sea of Galilee 'eastward of Nazareth' (l. 30) with a local one, the cliffs, hawthorns, hedgerows, shells, starfish, mossy rocks, honeysuckle, and hawthorn trees resembling the cliffs at Dover to encourage viewers 'to draw a parallel between the Holy Land after the birth of Christ' and Victorian England.[35] Even more striking is the Franciscan element of his Jesus, who bends lovingly towards the created world. A careful observer of natural detail and openly devout, Collinson appeared to Gabriel an ideal match for his youngest sister. While he had been a member of the same Albany Street congregation to which Rossetti belonged, by the time he proposed to her in 1848 he had converted to Roman Catholicism. She initially refused him, accepting a renewed proposal only after he reverted back to Anglicanism. But the two were romantically ill-suited, and theology was their only shared ground. Indeed the impetus behind Collinson's interest in Rome, Cardinal Nicholas Wiseman's 1835–6 lectures on Catholicism in London, were positively reviewed by both Pusey and Newman, both men Rossetti admired, and she was unsurprised when he converted again in 1850.

Rossetti took several trips away during their brief engagement, including one to Longleat House in Somerset, where her aunt, Charlotte Polidori, was governess to Louisa Thynne, daughter of Lord and Lady Bath. Hoping to escape the London fog, she found herself 'literally freezing' in the large house, but enjoyed the park, its lake and the 'rising grounds, and green shady openings, and grand old trees'.[36] Contrary to William's portrait of her at this time as an austere young woman 'trammelled' by her faith and forced to give up chess 'because she thought it made her too eager for a win', Rossetti's letters show her to be in constant, if dry humour, and sharply aware of the natural world around her.[37] As well as dancing at the servants' ball and making her 'first attempt at billiards', she walked around the park's 'gardens and green-houses... one of them entirely devoted to heaths', and noted in her letters the 'noise of the wind' and 'some splendid ivy-overgrown trees'.[38] While she claimed the 'trees, the deer, the scenery' had little impact on her writing, she was especially taken with a 'splendid frog... *sere yellow* spotted with black, and very large', an early indication of her preference for creatures that 'are frequently regarded as odd or uncouth'.[39] Rossetti also spent much of the day reading, and when Lady Bath lent her Montalembert's 1835 *Histoire de Sainte Élisabeth de Hongrie*, she copied out sections for Collinson, who was now at work on his painting, *The Renunciation of Queen Elizabeth of Hungary* (1851).[40] On Collinson's recommendation, she had already read Charles Kingsley's anti-Catholic drama, *The Saint's Tragedy* (1848), which used St Elizabeth as the basis for an attack on Catholicism and Tractarianism, and, familiar with Gabriel and Millais's sketches of the saint, composed her own poem, 'St Elizabeth of Hungary', in 1852. Rossetti remained interested in St Elizabeth long after she ended her relationship with Collinson. Despite William's melodramatic proclamation that his sister's break with Collinson struck a 'staggering blow' at Rossetti's 'peace of mind', there is no discernible shift in tone in either her poetry or letters. She continued to think about St Elizabeth,

but did so in relation to Gabriel and Millais's work as much as
to Collinson's.

While Collinson focused on Elizabeth's martyrdom, Rossetti was
more interested in her role as a visionary. In her poem, she sees
beyond the physical, and gazes out from a soulful holiness in search
of Paradise and Christ:

> Hush, she is a holy thing:
>   Hush, her soul is in her eyes
>   Seeking far in Paradise
> For her Light, her Love, her King.   (ll. 13–16)

Elizabeth's longed-for Paradise is revealed as a Triune space here, one
in which reason (light), passion (love), and divinity (sovereignty) are
brought together through faith.

The harmonizing, perichoretic language of the poem conceived of
Elizabeth as an embodied union of sense and spirit, wisdom and
feeling, her soul and eyes as one in their reaching towards a tangible
and material realm. Removed from a Miltonic realm that can be lost
or regained (William declared that Rossetti 'disliked' *Paradise Lost*),
Elizabeth's Paradise is shaped by a Christianized Platonism in which
sensual and spiritual realities are bound by a divine love in which
material and perfect forms coalesce.[41] But Rossetti also associates her
with the mariological lily and rose to bring out her connection with the
natural world. As she learned from Montalembert, Elizabeth was a
member of the Third Order of St Francis, which, founded after the
orders of Francis and Clare of Assisi, stressed a penitential life in which
'penance' constituted an affective relationship to the created world,
human and nonhuman. Francis is explored further in Chapter 3, but it
is worth noting here his renewed popularity in the period, his tomb and
relics rediscovered in 1818 during an archaeological dig in the basilica
of Assisi.[42] As Collinson and Rossetti worked on their Elizabeth texts,
Francis was being celebrated in publications like *The Edinburgh Review*,
The Gentleman's Magazine, and *The British Quarterly Review*, all of which
emphasized his intimate and sacred relationship with animal and
vegetal life.[43] Montalembert makes much of Elizabeth's Franciscan
heritage, and described her Franciscan convent in Eisenach, the Marburg
hospital to which she dedicated his memory, and their shared canon-
ization in Perugia.[44] Paraphrasing Bonaventure's account of her last

rites, Montalembert also drew on Francis's famous association with birds to relate how 'an immense number of birds, of a species unknown to men before that time' gathered on the roof to speak 'of her in their language' and sing 'with such wondrous sweetness over her tomb'.[45]

The 1840 Italian edition of Montalembert's life also reprinted four of Francis's poems, all of which also appear in an 1816 *Poeti del primo secolo della lingua italiana* owned by Rossetti's father, Gabriele.[46] Francis's Christocentric reading of Trinitarianism wherein the Holy Spirit focuses the believer on her entanglement with the material world animated Rossetti's Jesus, as much as it did his Incarnation in Collinson and Hunt's work. But Hunt went further by fusing Francis with Rossetti in his Jesus to conjure a Saviour that not only subverted Gabriel's domestic depictions of his sister, but also confirmed her role as Francis's ecological heir. Hunt deliberately portrayed Jesus as a harmonizing figure, in which the details of the world, from twilit trees to the weeds that block the door, are illuminated through him as he shines beneath a halo that is also the moon.[47] While his jewelled robes and crown contrast with the simplicity of dress associated with Francis and Rossetti, they invoke the relationship between the entrancing aesthetic of Ritualist liturgy and the domesticated detail of an English orchard, both abundant with living things. The hovering bat, creeping ivy, brambles, nettles, and corn become sacramental symbols of the totality and completeness of God in the painting, and the 'light of the world' (John 8. 14) an ecological mode of interconnection. In his review of the painting, Ruskin heralded a cosmic divinity that represented 'the power of the Spirit' adorned with a 'rayed crown of gold, inwoven with the crown of thorns; not dead thorns, but now bearing soft leaves for the healing of the nations'.[48] Hunt's Jesus permeated the natural world by emitting a glow into which the moon, trees, and plants are absorbed, conjuring his divine body as that into which the onlooker must consciously enter (there is no handle on the side of the door facing Jesus). Symbolic and real, ephemeral and eternal, the Jesus–Rossetti cynosure encompassed a diversity that could only come into being through grace, not simply as that which completes nature, but as that through which the material is entangled irrevocably with the divine.

Rossetti's own refusal of the distinction between creation and divinity was apparent in the first of her contributions to *The Germ*, 'Dream Land' (1849), which elevates the joy of unity with God over anxiety about the transition between the inner and outer self. This joy, revealed in the penultimate line and almost glossed over at the very end of the poem, is preceded by a narrative describing a female figure's journey from a material, vital world into a seemingly eternal period of rest. In rhythms that echo those of Alfred Tennyson's 'The Lady of Shalott' (1833), the figure is led by a star to seek 'Her pleasant lot' amidst a shadowy half-world in which she cannot see or feel (l. 8). The narrator does not track her movement from an outside landscape to an inner 'sunless' space, however (l. 1). Rather she detaches the reader from the expectations of linear time to announce a different kind of joy that lies beyond the dualities of life and death, consciousness and sleep. Like the benumbed figure, the reader also experiences the narrative as if 'through a glass, darkly' (1 Corinthians 13. 12), caught in the poem's anaesthetized atmosphere in which all sensuous elements—the pink morning sun, the cold springs, the singing nightingale—are dulled. But the finality of the 'Rest, rest, for evermore' (l. 25) in which the figure is finally arrested is questioned by its at once topographical and bodily meaning: she is both in a place, on a 'mossy shore' (l. 26), and drawn back into herself, 'at the heart's core' (l. 27). The 'ore' rhyme here also creates a sonic relationship that refutes any clear distinction between place and body, inner and outer, one that signals the distortion of time and space in line 4. Contrary to the poem's drowsy pace, this turn into the heart suggests fulfilment through 'joy' at the end of time:

> Rest, rest, for evermore
> Upon a mossy shore;
> Rest, rest at the heart's core
>   Till time shall cease:
> Sleep that no pain shall wake;
> Night that no morn shall break,
> Till joy shall overtake
>   Her perfect peace.   (ll. 25–32)

This joy signals the New Jerusalem, promised at the end of time to all things who have passed 'Thro' sleep, as thro' a veil' (l. 13). Unlike the Lady of Shalott, and also the narrators of those poems with which 'Dream Land' was printed—Gabriel's 'My Sister's Sleep' and Thomas Woolner's 'Of My Lady in Death'—Rossetti's figure is not condemned to death, nor must she wait suspended until the Last Day.[49] Instead, Rossetti moves her past the waiting time of soul sleep to imagine her in intimate connection with a transformed creation.[50] For her arrival at 'the heart's core' is enabled by her journey through a material landscape: she is pulled into her heart by the fields, singing birds, springs, and mosses.

The narrator's self-emptying into these details of the natural world is also apparent in a series of drawings Rossetti produced for 'Dream Land', described by William as a series of 'three coloured designs' in which a 'sepulchral-looking, white-clad figure, holding a cross' becomes a figure who 'ris[es] and ascend[s] winged; her pinions are golden of butterfly-form'.[51] Celestial and entomological alike, this winged hybrid embodies the joy of a grace-given incorporation with all things as part of God. The drawings may have been produced as a response to Blake's sketch of the Trinity, in which a cruciform body is embraced by a robed figure over which hovers a winged spirit.[52] Included in Gabriel's notebook of Blake's poems and sketches, which he purchased from Samuel Palmer in 1847, Rossetti found in it a model of contemplative pilgrimage congruent with her views on grace as a materially redemptive energy. While Blake's attack on 'Clergymen in the Pulpit Scourging Sin instead of Forgiving it' is sometimes read as a text aimed at Catholicism, it was in fact an indictment of any religion that undermined the sacrament of grace as reconciliation.[53] According to Palmer, Blake thought Catholicism was the least guilty of this, and he claimed in a letter to Rossetti's friend Anne Gilchrist that Blake had 'quite held forth one day to me, on the Roman Catholic Church being the only one which taught the forgiveness of sins; and he repeatedly expressed his belief that there was more *civil* liberty under the Papal government, than any other sovereignty'.[54] This rejection of a secular absolutism to favour a 'divine body of the Saviour' made from the 'Eternal Forms' of 'All Things' anticipated Pusey's 'new nature' as well as Rossetti's redeemed creation in both her poem and illustrations for 'Dream Land'.[55] Whereas Hunt envisioned the artist as a 'priest' in the 'temple of Nature', Rossetti dissolved this priestly model into a poet figure integrated with her surroundings.[56]

As much as Rossetti borrowed from Blake and the Pre-Raphaelites, her vision of a God made manifest through the things of creation is her own, and distinct from such early influences. The divinization or theosis of all things through Christ helped her to revise an Edenic narrative in which only the human develops into the image of God. As her 1853 poem 'Consider the lilies of the field' (1853) attests, flowers, lichen, moss, and weeds all voice God's love and are given the same prophetic and thoughtful status as Jesus confers to them in Matthew 6. 28. It is a vision in which grace is extended to all nonhumans, and one that she could not have developed without reading Blake and the Pre-Raphaelites through her interests in Plato and the early Fathers, as the next section suggests.

From Plato to Nyssa

During the 1850s, Rossetti had a range of available resources through which to further her studies, including Longleat and the public library at nearby Frome (although she bemoaned the absence of a 'good circulating library' there).[57] Frome was also the location of Rossetti's school, established with her mother in 1851 at the suggestion of Lady Bath, who had already secured a position in the area for the Tract-arian clergyman William J. E. Bennett. Bennett had been recently removed from his parish of St Barnabas in Pimlico on the charge of introducing Roman Catholic doctrines and ritual into Protestant worship.[58] He was also widely associated with Ritualism, a liturgical shift that manifested in the use of altar lights, candles and veils, rood screens and grills, the elevation of the Eucharist, prayers for the dead, the burning of incense, the mixing of water and wine in the chalice, and the Three Hours devotion on Good Friday. Many Anglicans were horrified by Ritualism, and Bennett was scapegoated after a series of anti-Ritual riots in London. The first recorded use of the word 'Ritualism' was by the Bishop of London, Charles Blomfield, in his 1850 public letter to *The Times* accepting Bennett's resignation.[59] Writers at *Punch* were particularly savage in their attacks on Bennett, and portrayed him as the lead perpetrator of 'Popery' in the cartoon 'The Puseyite Moth and Roman Candle' (1850) as well as mocking his relocation to a town that sounded so much like 'Rome' (Bennett always spelled his new home 'Froome').[60] Even at Frome, Bennett faced a parliamentary campaign to remove him and it took Pusey to persuade him to stay in post.[61] But Rossetti welcomed Bennett warmly and hired him to offer religious guidance to her new pupils, and wrote that she found him a generous and benevolent presence.[62] She largely approved of Ritualism, especially those changes introduced by Henry William Burrows at Christ Church, such as a sung service, the procession of the clergy and choir from the vestry, the assumption of the Eastward position when celebrating the Eucharist, and the adoption of seasonal coloured coverings for an altar adorned by a back-lit cross.

Rossetti's interest in Ritualism through Bennett and the liturgical dovetailed with her growing interest in the soul and cosmos via Plato and the Church Fathers. As a governess to the Anglo-Catholic family Frances and Colin Lindsay at Haigh Hall in Lancashire in 1855, she had access to their *Bibliotheca Lindesiana*, one of the largest private libraries in the country.[63] Containing thousands of volumes of theology, law, history, archaeology, biography, astronomy, and science, as well as texts on botany, Francis of Assisi, and Floyer Sydenham and Thomas Taylor's five-volume English translation of Plato's works, the library offered Rossetti new ways of thinking about the rationale for Ritualism at a time when it was under attack.[64] She was already interested in Plato, as her poem 'Paradise' (1854) attests, in which the union of the sensual and spiritual echoes that of 'St Elizabeth of Hungary'. 'Paradise' relates a dream in which the narrator sees the perfect forms of a series of elements in creation—flowers, birds, rivers, trees, fruit, and stars—eclipse their earthly counterparts. The blooms of Paradise appear 'More fair' than 'waking eyes | Have seen in all this world of ours' (ll. 3–4); the birds sing 'A tender song so full of grace' (l. 11) it puts the nightingale's song to shame; and a 'fourfold River' flows with 'murmured music' everywhere, refreshing all where earth's draughts fail to reach both 'east' and 'west' (ll. 17, 20, 24). While this fourfold river recalls the 'four heads' of water that stream out of Eden in Genesis 2. 10, the 'healing' leaves of the 'Tree of Life' (ll. 25–9) reference Revelation 22. 2 to remind the reader of the conventional narrative in which Paradise restores a lost Eden at the end of days. But the final stanza offers a different kind of vision. The narrator does not abandon her immediate, waking world for the beautiful forms of an otherworldly realm, but rather reimagines them as part of a telluric Eden present in real time:

> I hope to see these things again,
>> But not as once in dreams by night;

> To see them with my very sight,
> And touch and handle and attain:
> To have all Heaven beneath my feet
>   For narrow way that once they trod;
> To have my part with all the saints,
>   And with my God.   (ll. 41–8)

The narrator's longing to see and feel these ideal forms 'with my very sight, | And touch and handle and attain' refuses the gap between material, protean things, and eternal, changeless abstractions. The stanza is close to Blake's Platonic comparison of the 'World of Imagination' as 'Infinite & Eternal' against the 'finite' and 'Temporal' world of 'Vegetation' in *A Vision of the Last Judgment*: for Blake, 'Every Thing which we see reflected in this Vegetable Glass of Nature' exists in that 'Eternal World' as 'Permanent Realities' comprehended 'in the divine body of the Saviour'.[65] But while Blake's vision can only be seen by those who possess his particular 'Imaginative Eye', Rossetti's poem worked to dispel the illusion of duality and difference for all readers by bringing the earthly and ideal into communion.

The narrator of 'Paradise' not only upturns the transcendent through a terrestrial image of standing firmly on heaven rather than under it, but she also acknowledges that breaking through the limitations of empirical experience is enabled wholly by participation with creation, the saints, and God. Rossetti discovered this participatory faith in the Cappadocian Fathers—Gregory of Nyssa, Basil the Great, Macrina the Younger, and Gregory of Nazianzus—favourites of the early Tractarians and especially significant in the Eastern Church.[66] Nyssa, Basil, and Macrina were siblings, and the latter, one of few recognized female early Christian writers, is often credited with the Cappadocians' relatively positive views on women. They also emphasized the first creation account in Genesis 1. 27 wherein God creates male and female together. As Basil wrote: 'the virtue of man and woman is one, since also the creation is of equal honour for both, and so the reward for both is the same'.[67] Nyssa even claimed that Macrina, a well-read and educated woman, was his 'teacher', as well as active in defining Church teaching across Cappadocia.[68] It is perhaps because of this that Littledale and J. M. Neale cited Nyssa in *A Commentary on the Psalms* as the context for understanding Adam's naming of Eve as 'the mother of all; not mortals, but, of all living', and through which they aligned her with an absolute inclusivity and so with Christ.[69] As Elizabeth Ludlow argues, Nyssa's work was 'repeatedly' recalled in Tractarian literature by writers such as Pusey and Thomas William Allies, as well as Neale and Littledale.[70] While the Cappadocians were absent from Pusey's Latin-focused *Library of the Fathers of the Holy Catholic Church*, many figures not included in the series were frequently cited in Tractarian publications and sermons. Isaac Williams's *Tracts* on reserve, for example, were heavily dependent on the writings of Origen, which are also missing from the series.

Nyssa remained key for the Tractarians because of his role in the historical development of the doctrine of the Trinity, in which he shifted its meaning as the Father and Son as 'one substance' to that of a divine unity of essence or being (*ousia*).[71] At the same time, he famously prioritized the Holy Spirit as the One who comes from the Father through the Son, and established the Spirit as a central connecting point or, as Graham Ward writes, 'the indefinable, ineffable and mysterious heart of God'.[72] All experience is mediated through this relational working together of three particulars in one essence or hypostasis, a harmony that is at once fellowship (*koinōnia*), mingling (*mixis*), and union (*henōsis*).[73] While all things are part of this fellowship, humans must struggle to realize this experience, which involves a creative co-operation with God that is always in process. As Nyssa wrote in his *Life of Moses*, God is located beyond human understanding, but within the faithful experience of divine infinity: 'This truly is the vision of God: never to be satisfied in the desire to see him'.[74] The willingness of the human to see into the darkness of the infinite God without understanding is grace-given. This grace is explicitly Trinitarian in Nyssa's writing, issuing 'from the Father as from a spring', being 'brought into operation by the Son', and then perfected 'by the power of the Spirit'.[75] The dance-like interpenetration of the three in his work also accorded with the later idea of perichoresis, the three whirling about as well as inside each other in what he called a continuous 'falling in love'.[76] Within this incorporative Trinity, each is in itself inclusive, Jesus Christ at once 'Jew, Samaritan, Greek and all humanity', while God and the Holy Spirit constantly rotate like stars that gather everything to them.[77] As creation is divine nature, its component parts are necessarily inclusive and intertwined as part of a communitarian life into which things are ushered by the vitality of the Trinity.

The evidence of God's presence in the cosmos as grace is apparent in the unexpected order and harmony inherent to a universe made up of such vitality, one that prevents opposite motions and forces from annihilating each other. Far from a static mass on which God acts, creation is rather a constantly evolving assemblage 'actively and dynamically combining and recombining', an idea that Nyssa elucidated through the metaphor of music.[78] In his *Inscriptions on the Psalms*, he wrote that the 'order of the universe resembles a musical harmony of varied shapes and colours with a certain order and rhythm which is correct, proper and never dissonant, even if different parts differ greatly'. Just as the musician creates interwoven sounds rather than settling on one note, so the 'blending into a whole from various, separate elements in the universe through an ordered, constant rhythm results'.[79] Rossetti echoed this in her *Time Flies: A Reading Diary* (1885), and insisted that music could only be a metaphor for heaven if 'part of a sequence' rather than a 'single note':

> Therefore, when our Christian heaven is by condescension to man's limited conceptions represented as a heaven of music, that very figure stamps it as a heaven, not of monotony, but of variety. For in music one sound leads unavoidably to a different sound, one harmony paves the way to a diverse harmony.[80]

This harmonious Trinitarianism conceived of God as that which is both immanent and transcendent, moving in all directions at once and cosmically connecting all things through the 'breath of life' of Genesis 2. 7. For Nyssa, this breath sustained a divinized world in which supernatural grace is bound to natural creation, a meeting he explored through an exemplary redeemed being, a hybrid bird–human that is only whole when it holds its bird-like and human elements together. As humans are made in God's image, and God is first seen hovering over the 'face of the waters' (Genesis 1. 2), so 'human nature also was created with wings' and that 'in its wings also it should be like the divine'. If departing from the 'shelter of the wings of God' through sin shed human wings then grace could restore them to '"again grow wings" [cf. Titus 2. 11–12]'.[81]

This image reconnected the human both to God—who holds all things 'under' his wings as a place of 'trust' (Ruth 2. 12) and 'refuge' (Psalm 57. 1)—and to the angels (Exodus 37. 9; Isaiah 6. 2), the wind (2 Samuel 22. 11), the birds (Genesis 1. 21), the winged beasts of Revelation (4. 8), and to time itself (Ecclesiastes 3). The wind and morning are both winged (Psalms 18. 10; 139. 9) and also carry words humans cannot otherwise express: 'for a bird of the air shall carry the voice, and that which hath wings shall tell the matter' (Ecclesiastes 10. 29). Nyssa's analogy also revealed the influence of Plato's dialogue, *Phaedrus*, in which Socrates wrote that 'of all the things that are related to the body, wings have more of the divine in them'. The soul, immortal and self-moving, also has wings, but it is forced to 'shed' them once it loses its 'vision of the truth' by failing to see 'beyond the things we now say "exist"' into the 'true reality' of ideal forms.[82] Only in the 'region beyond heaven' can one witness 'true being' of 'no colour or form; it is intangible, and visible only to intelligence, the soul's guide'. The 'mind of a philosopher', however, can 'grow wings' because of the way 'it uses memory to remain always as close as possible to those things proximity to which gives a god his divine qualities'.[83] Likewise, Nyssa's bird–human is a being that plays on the idea of the image and likeness of God as one that embraces all of creation. Like the perichoretic intercommunion of the Trinity, the divine, human, and animal are assimilated into an ultimate energy, and can be identified in relationship with each other, Nyssa argued, by a shared stamp or 'imprint'.[84] For if the true imprint or 'express image' (Hebrews 1. 3) of God's being is the corporate and communal body of Christ, then all things share this imprint with each other, 'So we, *being* many, are one body in Christ, and every one members one of another' (Romans 12. 5).

By the late 1850s, the idea of the shared imprint became increasingly significant in Rossetti's poetry and prose. 'A Better Resurrection' (1857), for example, staged a newfound embrace of nondualism by setting up a series of oppositions in order to undercut them. The 'better resurrection' of Hebrews 11. 35 sought over the 'resurrection of damnation' in John 5. 29 suggested a hierarchy of rebirths that preface the poem's other dualistic attempts to structure the narrator's experience of faith: she is insensible and quickened, looks left and right, is dead and risen, broken and healed. But Rossetti undoes these tensions by showing how the narrator's identification with stones, leaves, husks, a bowl, is transformed into mutualism through her faith. While a whole ecosystem of failed harvests, freezing weather, droughts, and dusky tedium dwindles, the narrator's willingness to enter into the life of other things sparks an engagement with Jesus that revitalizes everything. For she not only feels connected to these things—her heart is 'like a stone' (l. 2) and her 'life is like a faded leaf' (l. 9)—but she also enters into them. It is only once her life is 'in' a falling leaf that she is able to articulate the request for affective renewal: 'My life is in the falling leaf: | O Jesus, quicken me' (ll. 7–8). As she looks both ways for this quickening, her body imitates the descent of the falling leaf, one that tumbles helix-like to the ground by curving into it even as it acknowledges from where it has been dropped. This sense of balance in the poem allows the narrator to find Jesus both for herself ('O Jesus, quicken me'; 'O Jesus, rise in me', ll. 8, 16), and also for others, her final plea to him a Eucharistic one that symbolizes intercommunion:

> My life is like a broken bowl,
>   A broken bowl that cannot hold
> One drop of water for my soul
>   Or cordial in the searching cold;
> Cast in the fire the perished thing,
>   Melt and remould it, till it be
> A royal cup for Him my King:
>   O Jesus, drink of me.   (ll. 17–24)

Here, Rossetti references the broken bowl in Ecclesiastes 12. 6–7, an image of death that reminds the believer that matter returns to the earth as dust, while the spirit returns to God. She revises this dualistic reading of the body and soul by casting the bowl, and so her life, into a fire where they are both recreated as a cup from which Jesus, the corporate body of all things, can drink and be himself restored. Like Nyssa's bird–human, Rossetti's narrator is 'remoulded' with other living things in order to recognize herself as part of them in Christ. By unveiling a kinship already present in things through acknowledging oneness with them, the narrator ensures a 'better resurrection' that takes her out of the individuality of human ego and into a sacramental life and specific channel of grace.

Rossetti also declared this model of kinship in poems that looked explicitly to the interwoven being of the cyclical natural world. These poems did not take 'nature' as their theme but rather reflected on the relationships between the things of creation as the self-expression and presence of God. Rossetti revealed creation as that in which all things are immanently immersed, including the narrator, in order to wake the reader from the delusion of separateness. She disavowed caretaker environmentalism, in which the human positions itself above the rest of creation as its saviour (or destroyer), to instead invoke a mutual ethics of love worked out in relation with particulars. Her experience of encountering a wounded thrush during her residence in Frome, for example, is one in which her initial impulse to take the bird home and restore it gives way to a realization that its recovery is enabled in connection with creation:

> The other day I found a bird, a thrush I think, which had perhaps fallen out of the nest; it was not fully fledged, and could not fly much; so I took it home with me to bring it up till it could take care of itself, when of course I should have restored it to liberty: but the poor little creature refused to eat or drink; so next day I took it out again, and deposited it in a field near a hedge, in the hope that either it could manage to maintain itself, or that some parent birds would take care of it.[85]

Here Rossetti expresses no regret that she took the thrush into her affectionate protection. Rather she realizes that her care is part of a wider network in which other things—the fields, the hedges, other birds—are included. Her poetry was similarly intimate with the animacy of a world in which unseen energies move things to interact with each other. In 'Winter Rain' (1859), for example, the interdependence of vegetal, aqueous, climatic, and animal presences in the poem gestures towards a connected abundance given through the promise of rainfall. The valleys drink, buds burst, birds nest, flowers bloom, and lambs eat even in the winter. But through a series of repeated hesitations and negations, 'Yet', 'But for', 'Never', 'have no', 'find no', and 'With never', the narrator warns of a time when water might not be so available. The absence of rain threatens both the material and divine, human and nonhuman, as the narrator confirms in the symbol of the lily in the last stanza, both flower and symbol of the divine. The poem suggests not only that the visible and invisible are dependent on each other for the survival of creation, but part of the same body or cosmos united in God.

By locating salvation only inside of material creation, Rossetti went beyond an Enlightenment vision of nature as a mirror of God. Her image of Christ as lily and lily as Christ in 'Winter Rain' presents the two beings as one, both dependent on the 'soaking showers' (l. 16) of winter storms for existence. Rossetti draws on an early Church reading of the Incarnation here as that which is occasioned not by the Fall and original sin, but as the consequence of God's free love for all creatures. Predestined to grace, creation is always already saved and, as the firstborn of all creatures, Jesus is incarnated as an exemplar of this grace. This theology, identified with Irenaeus and later with the Franciscan Duns Scotus, conceived of creation, the Incarnation, and grace as interdependent expressions of God's love and wisdom embodied in Jesus.[86] The barren sterility that 'Winter Rain' cautions against is not a symbol of end times, then, but the consequence of living in isolation from others outside of what Nyssa called the earth's eternal 'conclusive harmony'.[87] Rain becomes a natural baptism in the poem, that which vitalizes physical and spiritual life in Pusey's 'new nature'.[88] While all things eternally belong to Christ's body, they must be continually reawakened to this new nature or life through a baptism of water and spirit. Exemplified by the anointing of Jesus at his own baptism in the Jordan (Luke 4. 18), the reality of baptism was to join the believer to all the elements with which it shared Christ's body. As Chapter 4 confirms, Rossetti later valued baptism as the route to grace for human and nonhuman, both of whom are reborn through it in the old and the new creation.

Even in her earlier baptismal poems, Rossetti envisioned water as a 'quickening' energy that allowed all things in creation to flourish together. In 'The First Day of Spring' (1855), for example, the narrator associates the sap of plants with the waking of birds, flowers, and humans, a baptism that brings with it a 'warmth and bloom' (l. 15) in which she sings and rejoices with the season of spring. But this balmy flourishing of which the narrator is part happens in three locations—the season of spring, the material world, and the kingdom of God—all of which comprise one experience of creation: 'So spring must dawn again with warmth and bloom, | Or in this world, or in the world to come' (ll. 15–16). The conjoining 'or' words in line 16 invite the reader to understand these two lines as an integrated foundation for faith, a trope Rossetti reworked in her 1860 poem, 'Passing away, saith the World, passing away'. As the decaying 'World' is drained of water, 'sapped day by day' by the threat of failure and despair, a reverse baptism attacks the earth, her 'Soul' and God (ll. 1, 2, 10). Through the prayer (l. 17) and love (l. 25) expressed in a series of 'yea' affirmations, however, the narrator is freed to experience the material and metaphysical in tandem. She does not escape a crumbling reality for a paradisiacal otherworld, but confirms creation as the coming together of earth and heaven. As Nyssa argued, all things, worldly and unworldly, share in God's imprint, an idea that looks forward to theories of entanglement and interactive genetic assemblages.[89] For Rossetti this relation is a graced rather than genetic one, an unbreakable connection between the phenomenal and divine that, in Pusey's words, 'engrafts' believers 'into Christ' so that they can 'receive a fuller principle of life, afterwards to be developed and enlarged by the fuller influxes of his grace'.[90] This renewal or moment of kenōtic self-emptying makes room for the indwelling of the divine and so changes the way humans read the world from that of a realm outside into which they step and then retreat, to that of an always unfolding creation of which they are essentially part. Just as the Pre-Raphaelite focus on nature typologically and analogically illuminated creation as a local geography (Hunt's Surrey orchard, Collinson's Dover cliffs), so this revived patristic reading of it sought to focus on what Pusey called 'the most distant and the minutest things and words of Holy Scripture' in 'universal relation' with 'Him, our LORD'.[91]

In response to both Pre-Raphaelitism and the Fathers, Rossetti sought to unite the particular and cosmic in her writing as a way of rejecting anthropological exceptionalism. If Jesus Christ is a hybrid of human (Jesus of Nazareth) and spirit (the Christ), as well as a lamb, vine, bread, stone, light, and water then his Incarnation served as a reminder that all things are at once natural and supernatural. The co-existence of the earthly and spiritual, the divine and creaturely in his person allows the being of God to be materially 'everywhere' as a model for the fellowship of things with each other. Being in all things, God necessitates a community of nature in which the human and nonhuman participate as 'lights' of the world, not because they are all enlightened or rational, but because their nature is light implanted by

God through grace. As Pusey noted in his tract on baptism, the 'workings' of grace are 'as varied as they are unfathomable', a variety that unfolds both in the diversity of living things and the unseen diversity of the Trinity.[92] Both indicate that participation in the whole is dependent on the particularity of existence as a specific if relational thing. The next chapter turns explicitly to the question of particularity in relation to animals and plants. Here Rossetti's eco-logical approach to these questions can be established by acknowledg-ing her understanding of the presence of God made 'real' through kinship. The materiality of God's participative diversity is key to an ecological reading because it requires a responsiveness that radicalizes Christian ethics, each thing in the world becoming a 'Christ to the other'.[93] This is why Pusey insisted on baptismal regeneration as 'actual, not metaphorical', renewing his commitment to the sacra-mental as the only channel of grace. Stripped of grace, creation is reduced to an exploitable resource, a set of objects external to God rather than the lived reality of the human and nonhuman things which comprise it. This was the logic behind vivisection, Rossetti argued. In conceiving of creation as a realm from which the cultured human stands apart, the vivisectionist mutated 'nature' into an object-ive realm of things the human controls, represents, and produces. This has the effect, as Heidegger later noted in a different context, of separating and then alienating humans from creation to the point where they feel superior to it, but homeless within it.[94]

'Kinness of nature'

For Rossetti, to be at home within the world was to participate in grace, that which connects created things to each other through Jesus in what Cyril of Alexandria called a 'kinness of nature'. For some believers, this graced state is accessible only as part of a specific religious community, as Rossetti noted of her sister Maria, who started to work with the All Saints Sisters of the Poor in Marylebone in 1859. By the following year, Maria had enrolled as an Associate Sister at All Saints Sisterhood on Margaret Street and, after several years of training, was initiated as a full Sister in 1875, prompting Rossetti to write to Gabriel: 'I fear we shall soon lose Maria from our hearth in favour of her new "Home"'.[95] But the kind of being at home Rossetti envisioned was a cosmic experience of communality with visible and invisible things unbounded by sisterhoods or brotherhoods. As the dead spirit narrator of 'At Home' (1858) discloses, everyday belonging arises from the experience of familiarity and remembrance, not a constant looking towards tomorrow. This belief had the effect of connecting Rossetti to a created world that included those left behind by promises of a utopian future. She was an 'outer Sister' at Maria's convent, and spent many hours making fifty 'biggish scrapbooks' for hospital patients, and children who were otherwise neglected.[96] Rossetti also volunteered as a 'Sister' at the St Mary Magdalene Penitentiary in Highgate in 1859, and spent so much time there that she missed William Bell Scott's summer visit, writing to Amelia Barnard Heimann that she was 'away almost the whole time at High-gate'.[97] She was not a casual volunteer, and worked for Highgate into the 1870s, eventually being offered the post of Highgate Superintend-ent. While she declined, she remained committed to a position that many considered controversial. As Jan Marsh notes, penitentiary work was deemed inappropriate for unmarried women, and prostitutes were not a group thought especially worthy of charitable care.[98] But Highgate was managed by clergymen including Burrows as a house of mercy rather than a corrective institution and comprised classrooms, a chapel and laundry, as well as dormitories for the women and their guardians. Rossetti also regarded her contribution as a direct imita-tion of Jesus, who not only refuses to dismiss those whom society labels sinners, but chooses to embrace them as those he is specifically sent to assist.

But it was as a writer rather than a philanthropist that Rossetti enabled others to see a world wherein everything is connected through a kinship with God based on the hypostatic unity of the Trinity. This state of being joined to God 'cannot be withdrawn or forfeited' like relationships based on affection or will might be because, for Rossetti, grace comes before all things and moves them into relationship with God as they evolve.[99] Established kinship models between particular things in the world—humans with humans, or plants with the soil—thus map a world of networks ultimately brought together in the divine body. Rossetti explored these ideas further in the 1860s, a period in which she was not only constantly reading, but also writing: she published two major volumes, *Goblin Market and Other Poems* in 1862; and *The Prince's*

Progress and Other Poems in 1866. In her 1863 poem 'Consider', for example, she returned to Matthew 6. 28 to identify humans with the lily and the sparrow in a Trinity held together by 'our Father' (l. 19):

> Consider
> The lilies of the field whose bloom is brief:—
>   We are as they;
>   Like them we fade away,
> As doth a leaf.
>
> Consider
> The sparrows of the air of small account:
>   Our God doth view
> Whether they fall or mount,—
>   He guards us too.
>
> Consider
> The lilies that do neither spin nor toil,
>   Yet are most fair:—
>   What profits all this care
> And all this coil?
>
> Consider
> The birds that have no barn nor harvest-weeks;
>   God gives them food:—
> Much more our Father seeks
>   To do us good.

The emphasis on the word 'Consider' in the opening line of each stanza functions as a repeated command to think like the lily and the bird. As Jesus declares, the human must stop thinking egoically ('Take no thought for your life', Matthew 6. 25) and start thinking like the rest of creation. Similarly, 'Consider' asks the reader to contemplate, reflect on, and attentively estimate the world, not as a series of disparate objects—birds, leaves, blooms—but as particular subjects—lilies, sparrows—that, in God's 'view', the human is 'like'. The melancholy of the reminder that everything dwindles is weakened by the intimacy of a shared fate—'We are as they'—under God's care. The human can only discover the 'good' asserted in the final line of the poem by adopting the same fragility and slightness as the single leaf, the sparrow 'of small account', and the impassive lily (ll. 7, 20). As Jesus claimed, not 'even Solomon in all his glory' was 'arrayed' like the birds and lilies (6. 29), their smallness akin to their scarceness or rarity, both as divine gifts and as threatened species. For the things of the world are 'most fair' when engaged in a form of considering or thinking that reveals life as a sacred entanglement rather than the material gain of 'profits' or of 'coil', a word Rossetti used for its double meaning as endless choice and confusion (ll. 13–15).

The kind of thinking produced in the consideration of others was as much a cognitive as environmental question for Rossetti. Her work implied an ethics of care between things, but she was also interested in what it is like to think like an animal or plant as a way of experiencing grace in communion with other things. The human does not shepherd creation because Jesus already holds all things together, an embrace materially enacted by the congregation of things in the body of the church (Colossians 1. 17–18). As the next chapter argues, the floral and faunal decoration of Anglo-Catholic churches indicated one way of symbolizing this embrace, and Rossetti's later poetry sought to imagine more definitively what it meant to share a likeness with other things. But already in her earlier poem, 'Goblin Market' (1859), the question of finding likeness with things in the world is addressed. The poem was the keynote of her first major publication, *Goblin Market and Other Poems* (1862), a collection that included 'Dream-Land' (now published with a hyphen in the title), 'Winter Rain', 'A Better Resurrection', 'Sweet Death', 'Symbols', and 'Consider the Lilies of the Field', and was lauded by critics for its embodiment of a vibrant and benevolent nature. As a reviewer for *The Athenaeum* declared: 'To read these poems after the laboured and skilful, but not original, verse which has been issued of late, is like passing from a picture gallery, with its well-feigned semblance of nature, to the real nature out-of-doors which greets us with the waving grass and the pleasant shock of the breeze.'[100] These poems offered a way of being in the world through feeling at home in it as a series of interconnections rather than a picture from which some things are excluded.

Part of a volume in which interconnection was valued, 'Goblin Market' might be read as another way of thinking the elements of the divine body, not least through its form. The poem is structured by a series of poetic lists that link things together through either repeated detail (the fruit, the goblins) or similes (used to describe the two sisters at the heart of the narrative). For Erik Gray, these lists are

self-defeating in their excessive sensory detail, which is, as the opening list of fruits exemplifies, indefinite and abstract.[101] But Rossetti's
succession of fruits is slowed deliberately by the elongated amphi-
brach 'together' in line 15 that confirms their communal belonging
to a whole.

> Apples and quinces,
> Lemons and oranges,
> Plump unpecked cherries,
> Melons and raspberries,
> Bloom-down-cheeked peaches,
> Swart-headed mulberries,
> Wild free-born cranberries,
> Crab-apples, dewberries,
> Pine-apples, blackberries,
> Apricots, strawberries;—
> All ripe together　　(ll. 5–15)

The reader is overwhelmed here by fruit varieties and hybrids, which
has the effect of making it difficult to identify specific species: it is much
easier to conceive of them as 'All ripe together'. This list format also
recalls the genealogies of names in the Old Testament, by which
readers are similarly bombarded, but that serve as reminders of the
intricate connections between families and, in Rossetti's poem,
between things. This 'kinness' of creation is even more apparent in
the poem's lists of similes, employed not to distinguish compared
elements through their relationship, but to collapse the difference
between different elements, 'Like a rush-imbedded swan, | Like a
lily from the beck, | Like a moonlit poplar branch, | Like a vessel at
the launch' (ll. 82–5). Analogous to the example of the fruit, the sense
of connection between the swan, lily, moon, tree, and boat suggests a
mode of perception in which all things correspond with each other
without losing the specificity of forms and shapes.

　　These formal elements, however, immediately appear to contradict
the otherwise frighteningly fractured world of 'Goblin Market', one
populated by murderous goblin creatures who have already claimed
the life of the sisters' friend, Jeanie. The poem begins with the
response of these two 'maids', Lizzie and Laura, to the 'Come buy,
come buy' call of the goblins, one to which Laura gives in by bartering
her hair for their fruit, which she devours 'until her lips were sore; |

Then flung the emptied rinds away' (ll. 136–7). As her senses shut down, she yearns for another taste of the fruit, but the goblins have disappeared, leaving her ill and desperate. Only Lizzie, now armed with a silver penny, can find the goblin market, and when she declines to eat their wares, the men force the fruits violently 'Against her mouth to make her eat' (l. 407) and 'claw', 'elbow', 'jostle', 'kick', 'maul', and 'mock' her until they are 'Worn out by her resistance' (ll. 400–1, 428–9, 438). Escaping the attack with her penny jingling, Lizzie kisses the fruit onto her sister's body in a strikingly Eucharistic scene ('Eat me, drink me, love me; | Laura, make much of me', ll. 471–2) in which Laura falls into a dangerous trance only to awaken recovered and revived. For Cynthia Scheinberg, the poem is more sinister still, its Christian symbolism deriving from a 'theological fantasy of Jewish erasure' wherein Hebraic identity and prophecy is revealed to be a 'dangerous temptation for Christian women', both 'honey to the throat | But poison in the blood' (ll. 554–5).[102] The goblins' 'Come buy' indeed echoes Isaiah 55. 1, 'come ye, buy, and eat; yea, come, buy wine and milk without money and without price', wherein Isaiah promises wine and milk to the Jewish people bound in a covenant with God at Sinai. Scheinberg argues that this equates the goblin fruit with Isaiah's text, a disease from which Laura must be redeemed by the Christ-like Lizzie, who redeems them both from predatory merchant men defined by 'distinct anti-Semitic character-istics'. The poem's Christianized and domesticated ending also pro-motes a 'virgin' motherhood or parthenogenesis that seeks to erase the lush and sexual symbolism, not only of the goblin fruit, but also of those Hebrew Scriptures, Isaiah, Jeremiah, Ezekiel, the Song of Songs, the Psalms, to which Rossetti is drawn precisely because of their metaphoric richness.[103]

Rossetti did prioritize a Christocentric nondual experience that contested not only the separation of subject and object, but also distinctions between those of different belief systems. 'Christian and Jew: A Dialogue' (1858), also included in *Goblin Market and Other Poems*, asserted similarly a Christian experience of Paradise from which the Jewish interlocutor is sensorily barred until he asks, 'Can these bones live?' (l. 58) in an echo of God's words to Ezekiel (37. 3). For Scheinberg, the poem feminizes and weakens the Jewish respondent by drawing on prophetic images of Israel as a fallen woman to portray an anguish set up against the 'powerful and morally superior' Christian male voice.[104] Rossetti's insensitivity is explicit in her letter on the poem to her Jewish friend, Amelia Barnard Heimann, to whom she sent her new book as a gift: 'In the volume is one piece of which perhaps you might expect me to make no mention to you: yet this is the very one of which I will ask your permission to speak'. Declaring that she 'cannot bear to be for ever silent on the all-important topic of Christianity', Rossetti wrote that she could not 'love you and yours as I do' without 'longing and praying for faith to be added to your works'.[105] As Marsh writes, while the Heimanns did not take offence, the sentiment of the letter is objectionable.[106] Her poetic dialogue, however, is more nuanced than a straightforward Christian corrective, and is not clearly gendered in the way Scheinberg suggests. For the line 'Can these bones live?', spoken by God in the Old Testament text, is given to the Jewish speaker, who consequently has the agency to animate a valley full of bones, and also to instruct the Christian (now in the role of Ezekiel) to prophesy 'unto the wind' and so participate in the natural world. Rossetti's focus on the wind in the last stanza is also congruous with the poem's depiction of Paradise as a verdant garden in which angels look like rushes and the summer light sustains boughs of vines and leaves (ll. 2, 24, 33–5). These observations about 'Christian and Jew' do not counter Scheinberg's deft critique, but rather suggest that the ecological seeps into Rossetti's work continually. As Ludlow argues in relation to Dodsworth's sermons on Jewish ritual and Rossetti's portrayal of Esther, her model of participatory prayerfulness and theosis sought only inclusiveness.[107] She wrote always in the service of a grace that she believed united rather than divided, albeit one that privileged her own belief system.

Rossetti's reading of God through communion does not erase difference, then, but it does critique the disruption of the co-operative inclusivity of all things. In 'Goblin Market', Rossetti affirmed this inclusivity through similes because they allowed her to ask the question of what it is to be 'like' another thing. She achieved this by comparing the human to the nonhuman and nonhuman to the human: while Lizzie and Laura are described as being like lilies, swans, branches, rocks, eagles, flags, wands, and snowflakes, the nonhuman goblins are like little men, 'Brother with queer brother' (l. 94). As Kelly Sultzbach suggests, the poem spins 'a revolving metaphorical mirror' that creates 'a dizzying array of human-like animals and animal-like humans' that shows 'that humans and non-humans alike inhabit a single world in which all are dynamic players'.[108] For it is precisely the creatureliness of the goblin men that attracts Laura, their tiny bodies tramping like rats, crawling like snails, and furry like wombats, ratels, and cats. Their voices, while shrill, also draw Laura to them with a coo that that sounds 'kind and full of loves' in 'tones as smooth as honey' (ll. 79, 108). As nonhuman critters, the goblins do not appear especially malevolent at the start of the poem, and, as noted, Rossetti preferred the 'odd or uncouth' elements of creation.[109] Lizzie and Laura know to avoid the goblins, not because of how they look, but because of a relentless commercialism indicated by their endless 'Morning and evening' (l. 1) call to sell objects that belong to the body of all things.

The goblins' trade in fruit has a particular scriptural resonance with Genesis, a narrative in which fruit belongs to the trees of life and knowledge as fundamental to the being of everything. God's command that creatures must live off vegetation and find 'meat' in 'every herb bearing seed' and 'every tree' (Genesis 1. 29–30) sanctified plant life, as Rossetti confirmed a few years later in her notes on Genesis, discussed in the next chapter. These 'green things' are given by God for his creatures, and are not on offer as a product to commodify and re-sell. If Rossetti perceived creation as a home in which all things dwell, then to buy and sell within God's 'house of prayer' warranted the same reaction with which Jesus confronted the moneychangers in Matthew 21. 12. Laura infringes on the divine body further by paying for the product with a part of her own body, and Lizzie is only able to protect herself from the exchange by proposing to pay the goblins with a silver penny that Victorian readers would have recognized as without value. By the 1850s, the silver penny was no longer a regular form of currency, and signified only as 'Maundy money', or coins that were minted for and given to the poor by royalty to mark Holy Thursday.[110] The tradition originated in Elizabeth I's distribution of the 'Royal Maundy', one of a series of associations Rossetti makes between Lizzie and the Virgin Queen, and by association, Laura and Elizabeth's sister, Mary, another symbol of the coming together of apparent opposites in the Anglican Catholicism of Tractarianism.[111]

But it is Lizzie's gentle and discerning relationship to the world around her that shields her from the goblins' call and attack. As she observes the flush of the sunset, the sleeping squirrels, rising stars, bending moon, and winking glow-worms, she recognizes herself as one with an environment she must work with rather than against. Unlike Laura, Lizzie sees a world in which she is not poisoned by the fruit, and where the goblins can be addressed as 'good folk' (l. 363) that only morph into 'evil people' (l. 437) in their rapacious compulsion to trade. Even in the horror of their advance, a scene that pervades just over a fifth of the poem, Lizzie stands firm and the goblins eventually give up: she is disoriented but unafraid, and it is with a 'kind heart' and 'inward laughter' that she brings Laura the antidotal 'Goblin pulp and goblin dew' (ll. 461–3, 470). For however horrific their violence, the juice they force on Lizzie becomes a symbol of Christ's remissive body and blood in the sisters' Eucharistic kiss, one that restores Laura both as a sister, and in the poem's domestic and conventual ending, as a mother. While Rossetti probably started 'Goblin Market' before working at Highgate, the female community she envisions at its end is a direct rejection of the masculine logic of atomized labour and competition that was behind the 'fall' of many women in the period. In this reading, the final scene is not so much a vision of serene piety as one of communal and kenōtic love, 'lives bound up in tender lives' in which hands are joined to 'little hands' that 'bid them cling together' (ll. 547, 560–1).[112] Like the 'together' of line 15 that enables the reader to comprehend the diversity of the poem, the togetherness of the final lines is an image of ' "cheer" ':

> 'For there is no friend like a sister
> In calm or stormy weather;
> To cheer one on the tedious way,
> To fetch one if one goes astray,
> To lift one if one totters down,
> To strengthen whilst one stands.' (ll. 562–7)

Rossetti concluded her poem with a picture of a familial and affectionate creation organized by interdependence and defined by a mutualism in which things interact and co-operate with a multiple and reproductive God. As she moved into her late thirties, however, she was increasingly anxious that such co-operation was being obstructed by the human through an egoic exceptionalism that impacted on all species. The next chapter suggests that Rossetti's mature adult life was dominated by a concern for every kind of creature, and her belief that the 'lower' down the natural order of things, the more likely it was to be in communion with the divine, and so to model that connection for its human kin.

Notes

1. Georgina Battiscombe, *Christina Rossetti: A Divided Life* (London: Constable, 1981), 16–17; and see Mary Arseneau, *Recovering Christina Rossetti: Female Community and Incarnational Poetics* (New York: Palgrave Macmillan, 2004), 99–100.

2. Dante Gabriel Rossetti to William Holman Hunt, 23 July 1848, in William E. Fredeman, ed., *The Correspondence of Dante Gabriel Rossetti, The Formative Years: Charlotte Street to Cheyne Walk (1835–1862)*, 2 vols (Cambridge: D. S. Brewer, 2002), I, 66.

3. Rossetti's poems for *The Germ*: 'Dream Land' and 'An End' (issue 1: 1 January); 'A Pause for Thought', 'Song (Oh roses)' and 'A Testimony' (issue 2: 31 January); and 'Repining' and 'Sweet Death' (issue 3: 31 March); she did not contribute to issue 4 (30 April); William Michael Rossetti, 'Introduction', in *The Germ: Thoughts towards Nature in Poetry, Literature and Art: A Facsimile Reprint of the Literary Organ of the Pre-Raphaelite Brotherhood, Published in 1850*, 4 vols (London: Elliot Stock, 1901), I, 5–30 (6).

4. Dante Gabriel Rossetti to Christina G. Rossetti, 8 November 1853, in Fredeman, *Correspondence*, I, 293.

5. Christina G. Rossetti to William Edmonstoune Aytoun, 1 August 1854, in Anthony H. Harrison, ed., *The Letters of Christina Rossetti: Volume 1 1843–1873; Volume II 1874–1881; Volume III 1882–1886; Volume IV 1887–1894* (Charlottesville and London: The University Press of Virginia, 1997, 1999, 2000, 2004), I, 98–9; further references are abbreviated to *Letters*.

6. See Jan Marsh, *Christina Rossetti: A Literary Biography* (London: Pimlico, 1995), 218 ff.; Christina G. Rossetti to Caroline Maria Gemmer, 27 June 1884, *Letters*, III, 196.

7. Christina G. Rossetti to Dante Gabriel Rossetti, 3 March 1865, *Letters*, I, 229.

8. Stephen D. Moore, 'Introduction', in Moore, ed., *Divinanimality: Animal Theory, Creaturely Theology* (New York: Fordham University Press, 2014), 1–16 (13).

9. Edward Bouverie Pusey to John Parker, n.d., in Henry Parry Liddon, *Life of Edward Bouverie Pusey*, 4 vols (London: Longmans, 1894), II, 34; and see Geoffrey Rowell, *The Vision Glorious: Themes and Personalities of the Catholic Revival in Anglicanism* (Oxford: Clarendon Press, 1991), 16–17.

10. 'Thomas Maitland' (Robert Buchanan), 'The Fleshly School of Poetry: Mr. D. G. Rossetti', *Contemporary Review*, 18 (1871), 334–50.

11. Cyril of Alexandria, *Commentary on John*, in Kathryn Tanner, *Christ the Key* (Cambridge: Cambridge University Press, 2010), 73.

12. William Holman Hunt, *Pre-Raphaelitism and the Pre-Raphaelite Brotherhood*, 2 vols (London: Macmillan and Co., 1905), I, 154, 347.

13. 'List of Immortals' (1848), in William E. Fredeman, *The P. R. B. Journal: William Michael Rossetti's Diary of the Pre-Raphaelite Brotherhood 1849–1853* (Oxford: Clarendon Press, 1975), 106–7 (107).

14. Hunt, *Pre-Raphaelitism*, I, 160; Michael Wheeler, *St John and the Victorians* (Cambridge: Cambridge University Press, 2012), 77.

15. John Ruskin, *Modern Painters: Volume III*, in E. T. Cook and Alexander Wedderburn, eds., *The Works of John Ruskin*, 39 vols (London: George Allen, 1903–12), V, 86.

16. William Morris, 'Address on the Collection of Paintings of the Pre-Raphaelite School' (1891), quoted in David Latham, ed., *Haunted Texts: Studies in Pre-Raphaelitism* (Toronto: University of Toronto Press, 2003), 15.

17. Lindsay Smith, *Pre-Raphaelitism: Poetry and Painting* (Tavistock: Northcote House, 1998), 16.

18. John Ruskin, *Pre-Raphaelitism* (London: Smith, Elder, and Co., 1851), in Cook and Wedderburn, eds., *Works*, XII, 337–93 (339).

19. Charles Dickens, 'Old Lamps for New Ones', *Household Words*, 1. 12 (15 June 1850), 265–7.

20. Michaela Giebelhausen, *Painting the Bible: Representation and Belief in Mid-Victorian Britain* (Aldershot: Ashgate, 2005), 66.

21. Debra N. Mancoff, *The Pre-Raphaelite Language of Flowers* (Munich, London, and New York: Prestel, 2012), 12.

22. Dominic James, 'Early Victorian Moral Anxiety and the Queer Legacy of the Eighteenth-Century Gothic Revival', in Timothy Willem Jones and Lucinda Matthews-Jones, eds., *Material Religion in Modern Britain: The Spirit of Things* (New York: Palgrave Macmillan, 2015), 125–46 (133).

23. Humphrey House, *All in Due Time* (London: Hart-Davis, 1955), 152.

24. Andrew M. Stauffer, '*The Germ*', in Elizabeth Prettejohn, ed., *The Cambridge Companion to the Pre-Raphaelites* (Cambridge: Cambridge University Press, 2012) 76–85 (80); Mark Roskill, 'Holman Hunt's Differing Versions of the "Light of the World"', *Victorian Studies*, 6.3 (1963), 228–44 (235).

25. John Ruskin, 'The Pre-Raphaelite Artists', letter to *The Times*, 13 May 1851, in Cook and Wedderburn, eds., *Works*, XII, 320.

26. Rossetti, ed., *Family Letters*, I, 134.

27. William Michael Rossetti, ed., *The Works of Dante Gabriel Rossetti* (London: Ellis, 1911), 661.

28. Dante Gabriel Rossetti to William Michael Rossetti, 1 December 1844, in Fredeman, *Correspondence*, I, 32.

29. Both references are in the note to Gabriel's poem 'Ave', in Rossetti, *Works of Dante Gabriel*, 661; and see Maureen Moran, *Catholic Sensationalism and Victorian Literature* (Liverpool: Liverpool University Press, 2007), 231 ff.

30. William Bell Scott, *Autobiographical Notes of the Life of William Bell Scott*, 2 vols (London: Osgood, McIlvaine, 1892), I, 247; Dinah Roe, *The Rossettis in Wonderland: A Victorian Family History* (London: Haus, 2011), 77.

31. Dante Gabriel Rossetti, 'Hand and Soul', in *The Germ*, I, 23–33; Rossetti, *Works of Dante Gabriel*, 551; and see Sharon Smulders, 'D. G. Rossetti's "Ave", Art-Catholicism, and "Poems" 1870', *Victorian Poetry*, 30.1 (1992), 63–74.

32. Graham Hough, *The Last Romantics* (London: Methuen, 2007), 53.

33. George Frederick Stephens, 'The Purpose and Tendency of Early Italian Art', *The Germ*, II, 58–64.

34. See D. M. R. Bentley, 'The Principal Pre-Raphaelite Pictures of James Collinson', *Victorian Review*, 30.1 (2004), 21–43.

35. Ibid. 25.

36. Christina G. Rossetti to Amelia Barnard Heimann, 14 January 1850, *Letters*, I, 29.

37. William Michael Rossetti, ed., *The Poetical Works of Christina Georgina Rossetti, with Memoir and Notes* (London: Macmillan, 1904), pp. lxvi–lxvii.

38. Christina G. Rossetti to Amelia Barnard Heimann, 14 January 1850, *Letters*, I, 30, and 19 January 1850, *Letters*, I, 33; Christina G. Rossetti to William Michael Rossetti, 25 January 1850, *Letters*, I, 34.

39. Christina G. Rossetti to William Michael Rossetti, 14 January 1850, *Letters*, I, 31; Rossetti, ed., *Poetical Works*, p. ix.

40. Charles Forbes René de Montalembert, *Histoire de Sainte Élisabeth de Hongrie, Duchess de Thuringe* (1835); Christina G. Rossetti to William Michael Rossetti, 25 January 1850, *Letters*, I, 34.

41. Rossetti, ed., *Poetical Works*, p. lxx.

42. Andre Vauchez, *Francis of Assisi: The Life and Afterlife of a Medieval Saint*, trans. Michael F. Cusato (New Haven and London: Yale University Press, 2012), 233.

43. Review, *Histoire de Saint François d'Assise*, Par Emilie Chavin de Malan, in *The Edinburgh Review*, 86.173 (July 1847), 1–42; Review, *Legends of the Monastic Orders*, By Mrs Jameson, *The British Quarterly Review*, 24 (November 1850), 477–500; Francis Harwell, 'Saint Francis and the Franciscans', *The Gentleman's Magazine* (April 1851), 367–75.

44. Charles Forbes René de Montalembert, *The Life of Saint Elizabeth of Hungary, Duchess of Thuringia by the Count de Montalembert*, trans. Mary Hackett (Dublin: James Duffy, 1848), 64, 174, 243.

45. Ibid. 227–8.

46. *Storia di santa Elisabeth d'Ungheria langravia di Turingia del conte di Montalembert*, trans. Nicola Negrelli (Prato: Tipografia di Giuseppe Pontecchi, 1840), 338, 351; Lodovico Valeriani and Urbano Lampredi, *Poeti del primo secolo della lingua italiana in due volumi raccolti* (Florence, 1816).

47. Hunt, *Pre-Raphaelitism*, I, 355.

48. John Ruskin, 'The Light of the World', *The Times*, 5 May 1854, in Cook and Wedderburn, eds., *Works*, XII, 328–32 (329).

49. Smith, *Pre-Raphaelitism*, 119; John Woolford, 'The Advent of Christina Rossetti', *The Review of English Studies*, 62.256 (2011), 618–39.

50. On soul sleep, see Jerome J. McGann, 'The Religious Poetry of Christina Rossetti', *Critical Inquiry*, 10.1 (1983), 127–44.

51. Rossetti, ed., *Poetical Works*, 478.

52. Geoffrey Keynes, *The Note-Book of William Blake called the Rossetti Manuscript* (London: The Nonesuch Press, 1935), facsimile 104.

53. Blake, *A Vision of the Last Judgment* (1810), in Keynes, *Note-Book*, facsimile 69–70; Kathryn R. Barush, *Art and the Sacred Journey in Britain 1790–1850* (London and New York: Routledge, 2016), 101–2.

54. Samuel Palmer to Anne Gilchrist, 2 July 1862, in A. H. Palmer, ed., *The Life and Letters of Samuel Palmer* (London: Seely and Co., 1892), 245.

55. Blake, *A Vision of the Last Judgment*, in Keynes, *Note-Book*, facsimile 69–70.

56. Hunt, *Pre-Raphaelitism*, I, p. xv.

57. Christina G. Rossetti to Amelia Barnard Heimann, 21 June 1853, *Letters*, I, 68–9.

58. John Shelton Reed, *Glorious Battle: The Cultural Politics of Victorian Anglo-Catholicism* (Nashville and London: Vanderbilt University Press, 1996), 57–60.

59. Blomfield's letter was accepted by *The Times* on 9 December 1850, in Dominic Janes, *Victorian Reformation: The Fight over Idolatry in the Church of England 1840–1860* (Oxford: Oxford University Press, 2009), 35.

60. Reed, *Glorious Battle*, 153.

61. Janes, *Reformation*, 72.

62. Christina G. Rossetti to William Michael Rossetti, 22 April 1853, *Letters*, I, 63; Christina G. Rossetti to Amelia Barnard Heimann, 23 May 1853, *Letters*, I, 66.

63. Christina G. Rossetti to Amelia Barnard Heimann, 22 November 1855, *Letters*, I, 104; Jan Marsh, 'Christina Rossetti at Haigh Hall', *The Journal of Pre-Raphaelite Studies*, 17 (Fall 2008), 47–9; Alexander Lindsay, *Sketches of the History of Christian Art*, 3 vols (London: John Murray, 1847).

64. See James Ludovic Lindsay, *Bibliotheca Lindesiana: Catalogue of the Printed Books Preserved at Haigh Hall, Wigan*, 4 vols (Aberdeen: Aberdeen University Press, 1910); the section on Francis is in Volume II, 3603.

65. Keynes, *Note-Book*, 69–70.

66. The history of the Cappadocians has been much revised since the nineteenth century, see Morwenna Ludlow, *Gregory of Nyssa, Ancient and (Post) modern* (Oxford: Oxford University Press, 2007), 13 n. 1.

67. Basil the Great, *Homily on the First Psalm*, in Philip M. Beagon, 'The Cappadocian Fathers, Women and Ecclesiastical Politics', *Vigiliae Christianae: A Review of Early Christian Life and Language*, 49.2 (1995), 165–79 (166).

68. Ibid. 168, 171 ff.; Gregory of Nyssa, *The Life of Saint Macrina*, trans. Kevin Corrigan (Toronto: Peregrina Publishing, 2001), 36.

69. John Mason Neale and Richard Frederick Littledale, *A Commentary on the Psalms, from Primitive and Medieval Writers, and from the Various Office-books and Hymns of the Roman, Mozarabic, Ambrosian, Gallican, Greek, Coptic, Armenian, and Syriac Rites*, 4 vols (London: Joseph Masters, 1868), II, 185; the prayer book version of this text was published 1860–74, and then reissued in a new version 1869–83.

70. Elizabeth Ludlow, *Christina Rossetti and the Bible: Waiting with the Saints* (London: Bloomsbury, 2014), 60; see Thomas William Allies, *Dr Pusey and the Ancient Church* (London: Longmans, Green, Reader, and Dyer, 1866).

71. Ludlow, *Gregory*, 13.

72. Graham Ward, private communication with Sarah Coakley, in *God, Sexuality, and the Self: An Essay on the Trinity* (Cambridge: Cambridge University Press, 2013), 235.

73. Ludlow, *Gregory*, 104.

74. Gregory of Nyssa, *The Life of Moses*, trans. Abraham J. Malherbe and Everett Ferguson (New York: Paulist Press, 1978), 116.

75. Gregory of Nyssa, 'To Ablabius', quoted in Ludlow, *Gregory*, 76 n. 110.

76. Gregory of Nyssa, *De anima et resurrectione*, quoted in Daniel F. Stramara, 'Gregory of Nyssa's Terminology for Trinitarian Perichoresis', *Vigiliae Christianae: A Review of Early Christian Life and Language*, 52.3 (1998), 257–63 (261).

77. Gregory of Nyssa, *In Canticum Canticorum*, quoted ibid. 262.

78. Ludlow, *Gregory*, 142.

79. Gregory of Nyssa, *On the Inscriptions of the Psalms*, trans. Casimir McGambley (Brookline, MA: Holy Cross Orthodox Press, 2008), 18, http://www.lectio-divina.org.

80. Christina G. Rossetti, *Time Flies: A Reading Diary* (London: Society for Promoting Christian Knowledge, 1885), 29.

81. Gregory, *In Canticum Canticorum*, trans. in Anthony Meredith, SJ, *Gregory of Nyssa* (London and New York: Routledge, 1999), 117.

82. Plato, *Phaedrus*, trans. Robin Waterfield (Oxford: Oxford University Press, 2002), 29, 32.

83. Ibid. 30, 32.

84. Gregory of Nyssa, *Homilies on the Beatitudes*, ed. Hubertus R. Drobner and Albert Viciano (Leiden: Brill, 2000), 70.

85. Christina G. Rossetti to Amelia Barnard Heimann, 6 June 1853, *Letters*, 1, 68.

86. Denis Edwards, *Jesus the Wisdom of God: An Ecological Theory* (Eugene, OR: Wipf and Stock, 2005), 71.

87. Gregory of Nyssa, *On the Creation of Man*, quoted in John Chryssavgis, 'The Earth as Sacrament: Insights from Orthodox Christian Theology and Spirituality', in Roger S. Gottlieb, ed., *The Oxford Handbook of Religion and Ecology* (Oxford: Oxford University Press, 2006), 92–114 (95).

88. Edward Bouverie Pusey to John Parker, n.d., in Liddon, *Life of Pusey*, II, 34.

89. See Donna Haraway, *Staying with the Trouble: Making Kin in the Chthulucene* (Durham, NC: Duke University Press, 2016), 60.

90. Edward Bouverie Pusey, 'Tract 67: Scriptural Views of Holy Baptism' (1835), in *Tracts for the Times by Members of the University of Oxford*, 6 vols (London: J. G. F. and J. Rivington; Oxford: J. H. Parker, 1840), II, 24.

91. Ibid. 389–90.

92. Edward Bouverie Pusey, 'Tract 69: Scriptural Views of Holy Baptism continued' (1835), in *Tracts for the Times, Nos. 67, 68, 69* (London: J. G. F. & J. Rivington, 1836), 164.

93. Martin Luther, 'Freedom of a Christian', in Timothy Lull, ed., *Martin Luther's Basic Theological Writings* (Minneapolis: Fortress, 1989), 619–20.

94. See Martin Heidegger, 'The Age of the World Picture' (1938), in *The Question Concerning Technology and Other Essays*, trans. William Lovitt (New York: Harper Perennial, 1977), 115–54; and 'Letter on Humanism' (1947), trans. Frank A. Capuzzi, in David Farrell Krell, ed., *Basic Writings* (New York: HarperSanFrancisco, 1977), 213–65.

95. Christina G. Rossetti to Dante Gabriel Rossetti, 4 May 1874, *Letters*, II, 12–13.

96. Mackenzie Bell, *Christina Rossetti: A Biographical and Critical Study* (Boston: Roberts Brothers, 1989), 60.

97. Christina G. Rossetti to Amelia Barnard Heimann, 3 August 1859, *Letters*, I, 124–5; she was alerted to the charity in an article in *The Morning Chronicle* entitled 'The Bishop of London on "The Social Evil"', 25 March 1858.

98. Marsh, *Rossetti*, 226.

99. Tanner, *Christ the Key*, 76.

100. Review of *Goblin Market, and Other Poems*, in *The Athenæum*, 1800 (26 April 1862), 557–8 (557).

101. Erik Gray, 'Faithful Likenesses: Lists of Similes in Milton, Shelley, and Rossetti', *Texas Studies in Literature and Language*, 48.4 (2006), 291–311.

102. Cynthia Scheinberg, *Women's Poetry and Religion in Victorian England: Jewish Identity and Christian Culture* (Cambridge: Cambridge University Press, 2002), 126 ff.

103. Ibid. 134.

104. Ibid. 123.

105. Christina G. Rossetti to Amelia Barnard Heimann, 4 April 1862, *Letters*, I, 162.

106. Marsh, *Rossetti*, 215.

107. Ludlow, *Rossetti*, 32.

108. Kelly Sultzbach, 'The Contrary Natures of Christina Rossetti's Goblin Fruits', *Green Letters: Studies in Ecocriticism*, 14.1 (2011), 39–56 (48–9).

109. Rossetti, ed., *Poetical Works*, p. ix.

110. Jill Rappoport, *Giving Women: Alliance and Exchange in Victorian Culture* (Oxford: Oxford University Press, 2011), 100.

111. Thanks to Deborah Jackson, University of Maryland, for sharing her reading of Lizzie and Laura as Elizabeth and Mary.

112. Scott Rogers, 'Re-Reading Sisterhood in Christina Rossetti's "Noble Sisters" and "Sister Maude"', *Studies in English Literature 1500–1900*, 43.4 (2003), 859–75; for a different view of the poem, see Heidi Scott, 'Subversive Ecology in Rossetti's *Goblin Market*', *Explicator*, 65.4 (2007), 219–22.

3

Pretty Beasts and Flowers

A Companionable Faith, 1863–1884

In 1870, Rossetti wrote to a potential publisher of *Sing-Song: A Nursery Rhyme Book* (1872) to suggest that she omit 'the ugly human beings' in the volume to make full 'use of the pretty beasts and flowers' on which many of the poems lyricize.[1] Written over one autumn period in 1869, her 'SingSongs', as she musically called them, comprise a long sequence in which a maternal voice affectionately introduces the reader to the moral and ethical landscape of a largely nonhuman world.[2] While many of the poems are riddles, reserving their layered meanings in reticence and understatement, their ecological meaning is manifest in poems like 'Hurt no living thing'.[3] Together, they portray an earthly Eden as present and available, embodied all around in the minutiae and interdependence of creation. *Sing-Song* discloses this creation as a divine body, one comprised of both love and sorrow, innocence and experience, sleeping babies and orphaned infants, frisking lambs and cold dead birds. Rossetti did not, in the end, leave out the ugly or the beautiful, human or nonhuman, and in valuing that which is troubling and bleak as much as that which is joyful and spirited, she made room for all things within the reader's imagination. She ensured that everything had a place in the economy of *Sing-Song* through the maternal being of its speaker, an archetype that she described as 'patient, forgiving, all-outlasting', the 'copy & pledge of Love all-transcending'.[4] As that which gives and houses life, the maternal also represented the Holy Spirit for Rossetti, the part of the Trinity through which creation renews itself through relationship with God. The things on which *Sing-Song* lyricizes—lizards, crows, harebells, pigs, toadstools, frogs, caterpillars—are presented as part of an ongoing, but evolutionary incarnation in the Spirit. In Rossetti's ever-moving and dynamic world, snow falls, nests are built, trees blossom, apples tumble, boats sail, angels fly, and stars spin to manifest the Spirit as both a symbol and presence of God in a material world. No longer caught beyond the human in a far-off limbo, the Spirit is held close in these poems as readers encounter the elements, beasts, and flowers and are positioned with and reconciled to them.

The most striking image of the Holy Spirit in *Sing-Song* is the wind, Rossetti's favourite sound 'after that of the sea'.[5] She imagined an ecological pneumatology through the wind, its restless movement continually evolving and changing the world around it. It blows warmly to 'thaw the flowers and melt the snow'; wanders and whistles 'to and fro'; sweetens the earth by fanning the violets; 'ranges' through March to produce 'changes' in April; withers flowers in Autumn; threatens ships on 'the windy sea'; plays 'cherry bob | With the cherry tree'; and sighs around those who miss their loved ones.[6] Like John's image of the wind, which 'bloweth where it listeth, and thou hearest the sound thereof, but canst not tell whence it cometh, and whither it goeth: so is every one that is born of the Spirit' (3. 8), Rossetti's Spirit-wind is erratic and inexplicable, but always interrelational. Her reworking of John 3. 8 in perhaps the best known of her SingSongs reflects on what it means to perceive a God in relation to the specifics of the natural world:

> Who has seen the wind?
>   Neither I nor you:
> But when the leaves hang trembling
>   The wind is passing thro'.
>
> Who has seen the wind?
>   Neither you nor I:
> But when the trees bow down their heads
>   The wind is passing by.

The force of the wind here imprints onto the leaves and the trees as much as it does the human perceiver, who cannot see it, but senses the wind haptically and affectively as it moves. Unlike Rossetti's other SingSong riddles, 'Who has seen the wind?' begins with the answer, asking readers not to puzzle out a solution, but to assess the wind's dynamism in relation to a world portrayed as animate and in motion.[7] From the lambs in 'On the grassy banks', the waves in 'The horses of the sea', and the fiery flint in 'An emerald is as green as grass', the things of *Sing-Song* have a vitality and agency driven by a God that whirls through creation in both human and nonhuman forms. As Rossetti wrote, 'By analogy of things visible He has shown us things invisible', not only to 'rekindle' hope in an 'end' in which '"Heaven and earth shall pass away"', but as a reminder that the things of both realms will come together as one.[8]

Rossetti realized this vision in her prose study, *Seek and Find: A Double Series of Short Studies on the Benedicite* (1879), wherein she outlined a radically ecological creation gathered by the Holy Spirit and held in grace. The book's objective, like the 'end of all contemplation', she wrote, was to '"see Jesus"' by reflecting on 'any creature' through his body in whom '"dwelleth all"'.[9] Such statements have led some critics to declaim her interest in nature as the abstracted and idealized theology of a city poet removed from the realities of rural life. But Rossetti's London was not an urban metropolis, and the 'urbanatural' environment of Regent's Park, the Zoological Gardens, and the many gardens, terraces, enclosures, and conservatories that she passed on her route to the British Museum brought her close to the creatures she loved. She worked in between the country and the city, and insisted that it was impossible 'for any one to live a happy life' without regular visits to 'the country', even as she claimed that 'my knowledge of what is called nature is that of a town sparrow'.[10] She responded both to the flora and fauna she encountered in London, and to their aesthetic representation in Tractarian churches as part of the turn to a decorated Ritualism associated with William Butterfield and A. W. N. Pugin. Like many middle-class Londoners, she lived in and visited town houses replete with 'indoor gardens', Wardian cases, and terrariums popularized by 'fern-fever', as well as outer plots and terraces.[11] A committed 'fern-hunter', Rossetti also owned several pets, including cats, birds, and a squirrel; she rode horses, and had a particular affection for crocodiles and donkeys, although she favoured dogs and owls above all.[12] In 1868, she wrote to Amelia Barnard Heimann to recount a trip to some 'kind friends' who owned '3 puppies' and a 'pair of owls', the latter 'so tame as to live altogether at large in the grounds'. Her favourite of the pair was the 'happy owl' who flew to her for 'inspection' and then 'freely away', so enjoying the 'advantages of civilization without relinquishing the charms of liberty', part of an ethic of care between human and nonhuman.[13]

Rossetti was one of the first visitors to the 'zoological forest', later called London Zoo, newly open to the public in 1847, and which included an aquarium by 1853.[14] This 'ark in the park' introduced her to elephants, sloths, armadillos, parrots, antelopes, and wild pigs, while Gabriel's personal animal collection brought her into a more intimate relationship with other species. The word 'zoo' also held a double meaning for Rossetti, both a place to visit the things of creation, and a word related to the Greek *zoopoion*, used by the Fathers to signify the vitalizing and life-giving work given by the Holy Spirit through the Eucharist.[15] *Zoopoion* thus incarnates the body in which all things dwell, and so actualized Pusey's 'tingling closeness of God!' in the material and tangible form of what Rossetti called the 'visible Church on earth'.[16] This chapter explores Rossetti's active commitment to protecting the union of creation by countering the fracturing logic of modernity with the inclusive grace of Christianity. During the 1860s and 1870s, Rossetti's interest in geology, biology, and astronomy, the specifics of flora and fauna, and involvement in the antivivisection movement all intensified, causing her to see the world as a congregation of creaturely beings incarnated in God instead of disparate elements of hierarchized scientific catalogues.[17] In doing so, she recognized the commonality of things in grace that also allowed for a valuing of their difference. Her Italian tour in particular renewed her amazement at the relationship between the material and symbolic 'grandeur of nature', and reminded her of Francis of Assisi's companionable grace, in which all things reside together as equals before God.[18] As she wrote in *Time Flies: A Reading Diary* (1885), the 'common type' that all species share may be an 'unconscious' experience, but each is 'the other's looking glass', their 'queer likenesses' only revealed in the new creation.[19] 'Imaging' the world through God was not just a way to repeat the act of creation and then reflect on this in art as Coleridge proposed, then, but to think and perceive as if part of a graced cosmos.[20]

Rossetti also shared her love of the nonhuman with her brothers, both of whom collected and wrote about animals.[21] In the final year of Rossetti's life, William began cataloguing all the species at the Zoological Gardens, guided by his unwell but alert sister, still happily surrounded by her pets.[22] Like Francis, Rossetti elevated the nonhuman as models of being and thought, oblivious to ownership and property, and living interdependently as visible symbols of invisible grace.[23] Francis exhorted 'every creature in heaven, on earth, in the sea and in the depths' to 'give praise, glory, honour, and blessing to Him', and greeted his 'Brother Sun', 'Sister Moon and the stars', 'Brother Wind', 'Sister Water', 'Brother Fire', 'Sister Mother Earth', and 'Sister Bodily Death' as companionable equals.[24] As Bonaventure observed, for Francis nonhumans were like 'syllables' in a 'beautiful song' that God commands humans to hear with undivided attention.[25] This vision of cosmic reconciliation materialized in Rossetti's writing as what John Hart calls a 'sacred commons' in which there is no difference between the human and nonhuman, only between things that live 'in penance' with the 'Body and Blood of our Lord Jesus Christ' and things that do not.[26] She presented vegetal life, for example, as essential aspects of the divine body, especially in its role within the Anglo-Catholic Church. Children's flower services were instituted to teach correspondence to the young; pews were decorated with foliage on Palm Sunday; and the nineteenth-century habit of sending flowers to the sick and poor was implemented on a large scale in the form of Flower Missions, in which boxes of flowers were sent by train to city centres for redistribution to the poor.[27] As Rossetti's friend William J. E. Bennett observed, attention to the 'minuteness of detail' in 'every single atom of creation' impressed on the viewer the 'pencilling of a mere flower, the wing of the smallest insect, the shape and texture of a common leaf' as a template for the church itself. In the altar, for example, Bennett saw 'the shape of a shell', and in the 'voices of the tuneful birds' and 'the beauty of colours in the light and airy wings of the insect tribe' a justification for the wonder of ritual liturgy.[28]

This chapter seeks to illuminate this wonder by revealing Rossetti's perception of the created world as continuous with the divine. While some critics have sought to reduce her fascination with the nonhuman as 'purely devotional', it is apparent in her poetry of this period, as well as in her prose (especially *Seek and Find* and the 1881 *Called to Be Saints: The Minor Festivals Devotionally Studied*), that Rossetti understood grace and nature as co-inherent and mutual.[29] The first section argues that Rossetti perceived the things of creation as companion species all of which share a historical relationship that evolves over time as part of the divine.[30] It also suggests that her understanding of cross-species companionship, in which animals and plants think and have faith, is analogous to a Franciscan model of communion she encountered through Tractarianism, Pre-Raphaelitism, and during her trip to Italy. The second and third sections connect this Franciscan relationship to the creaturely to her loving readings of animals, and then to plants. A fervent anti-vivisectionist, Rossetti was horrified by any practice that threatened to dismember the divine body, and opposed its anthropocentrism with a weakened or kenōtic form of thinking and love she identified with plant being.

Creation as Companion

Like her siblings, Rossetti was 'not brought up to have any foolish prejudices against animals harmless', and admired 'odd or uncouth' creatures like frogs, sea-mice, and insects.[31] But her affection for the nonhuman was more pronounced than it was for her family. William Sharp noted that while Gabriel was interested in collecting animals, he 'never really observed' them 'lovingly and closely' as his sister did, whose 'pictorial eye' Gabriel praised as one that could differentiate mosses, grass weeds, and ivies.[32] The Gilchrists' daughter, Grace, also marvelled at Rossetti's 'nature-loving ken', and admired 'the way in which she would take up, and hold in the hollow of her hand, cold little frogs and clammy toads, or furry many-legged caterpillars, with a fearless love that we country children could never emulate'.[33] Early criticism on Rossetti sentimentalized her 'overflowing' affection for 'animals of every conceivable description, from dormice and hedgehogs' to 'armadillos, sloths, tigers, and elephants', and read her as a poet to whom 'the earth' belonged 'until she died, with all its bloom— and all its animals'.[34] For other critics, however, Rossetti's relationship to 'nature' was obscured by her commitment to a supernatural that was opposed, in Pusey's words, '*not* to what is real, but to what is natural'.[35] Gabriel's friend, Theodore Watts-Dunton, for instance, considered her perception of things 'dimmed' by 'her constant and ever-present apprehension of the *noumenon* underlying the phenomenon'.[36]

But Rossetti's attention to the specificity of local flora and fauna led her to see it in continuity with the noumenal without which the merely material appeared to her lifeless and without spirit. After attending a waxwork exhibition, for example, she noted that she had felt 'shy', not with her fellow visitors, but with the 'waxen crowd' on display. The 'gorgeous assembly' of 'effigies' appeared too perfect to her because they offered no relationship to the things around them. Their 'hollow momentary world' was evident—the dolls were 'things seen'—but as simulacra of 'real people' they could only gesture towards the 'things unseen' of the 'substantial eternal world' comprised of human and nonhuman.[37] Rossetti thus sought a way of conceiving the created visible and invisible world as both vital and immediate, and impervious to abstract or hypothetical systems in which beings are bluntly classified. The nonhuman, she argued, spoke to the human in the same mute manner as the divine itself. This was apparent during her visit to the Scotts at Penkill Castle in South Ayrshire, where she remembered answering a series of 'matutinal taps, supposing myself called: and lo! it was only a tapping of jackdaws or of starlings lodged in the turrets'. While she quickly realized these 'Winged creatures' were 'neither angel visitants nor warning summoners', the birds' song was nevertheless available to the willing listener, for 'any good creature of God may convey a message'.[38] Just as the 'telegraph conveys messages from man to man', she wrote, so birds 'convey messages from the Creator to the human creature'.[39] Rossetti used the analogy to encourage her readers to compare the urgency with which they 'act eagerly, instantly, on telegrams' (as modern readers now respond to electronic communications) with their slower responses to the 'Sender of Providential messages'.[40] By questioning the way her reader decides where to focus her attention, she presented her own case for a common Christian life shared between species embodied in God. The alternative, Rossetti suggested, was to theorize the world as disconnected and disparate, a rationale that leads to the mistreatment and neglect of particularities.

Rossetti condemned the notion of an atomized world made of individuals in a poem for *Time Flies*, in which a frog is mown down by a 'waggoner'.[41] Distracted by his own song about a 'hypothetic frog', the wagon driver is oblivious to his fatal act:

> Unconscious of the carnage done,
> Whistling that waggoner strode on,
> Whistling (it may have happened so)
> 'A Froggy would a-wooing go:'

A hypothetic frog trolled he
Obtuse to a reality.

O rich and poor, O great and small,
Such oversights beset us all:
The mangled frog abides incog,
The uninteresting actual frog;
The hypothetic frog alone
Is the one frog we dwell upon.   (ll. 24–35)

Written in a culture that sentimentalized animals, Rossetti's poem surprises her reader into attending to the specificity of things, however 'uninteresting' or anonymous they might appear. Close observation, the poem intimates, might yield something in addition to taxonomic ranking, and allow the onlooker to see the world in at once discrete and holy terms. For while Rossetti's descriptions of flora and fauna in *Time Flies* always relate back to God, they are also particular—the blossoms of the cudweed, the perfume of the valerian spikenard plant, the venom-less flower of cruciforms, the nesting of birds under wasps' nests for protection, and the 'luminous' and 'non-luminous bodies' of the cosmos.[42] All types and divine analogies of the invisible realm, these things pointed to God's benevolence and revelation in the world in a way that united heaven and earth as one phenomenon. As Rossetti observed in regard to the 'inner bark' of the woodland mezereon shrub, it is 'decked' by God 'with hidden lace' such 'as no needle on earth could embroider', even as this becomes a template for the woven lace worn by human beings.[43]

One of the most striking images in *Time Flies* is of the Christian as 'a chameleon which possesses two independent eyes addicted to looking in opposite directions'. Rossetti contended that onlookers once deemed the creature an 'angelic reptile' because while one eye peered 'frankly downwards fly seeking', the other looked 'skywards' towards heaven. This 'verdict of ignorance', Rossetti proclaimed, has been replaced by a 'verdict of knowledge'—that the chameleon 'simply lives on insects'.[44] Her insight, however, is that by looking both down to earth and up to heaven, the chameleon serves as a connecting point between them, part of a God whose being comprises apparent difference—Father, Son, Holy Ghost—in sameness. She repeated the idea by also describing the Christian as a 'sea anemone', 'sluggish' and 'unbeautiful' on ground, but able to thrive in water through a 'multitude of feelers' that takes in everything around it. A sea creature named for a flower that blooms under water, the anemone consolidates different kinds of being, one that 'gulps all acquisitions into a capacious chasm, and harmonises with the weeds it dwells amongst'.[45] The creature models the Christian as a being able to sense, feel, and become one with the visible and invisible world. In Italy during her tour of Europe in 1865, she wrote that the earth appeared to dissolve into the heavenly, the nation's 'nature treasures' more beautiful than any of its 'art treasures'.[46] At Penkill too, the earth and sky seemed to meet in a 'glory', while its 'leafy' 'pleasures' evoked the 'Garden of Eden'.[47] God's renewal of creation was apparent everywhere the believer chose to look, Rossetti suggested, Italy and Scotland, but also Regent's Park, the grounds at Frome, and by the sea at Brighton and Hastings.

As a keen gardener, amateur botanist, and regular visitor to Gabriel's greenhouse studio and her grandfather's overgrown yard, Rossetti was familiar with the nonhuman world through both its peculiarities and shared complexion. The organisms around her thus appeared both singular and entangled elements connected in the body of God.[48] Catherine Keller argues that this natural complexity equates to a 'physics of quantum nonseparability' in which things exist through interaction, not symbolically, but actually.[49] As modern physics confirms, the particle states of things in the world work with reference to each other even when they are spatially separated. As soon as any attempt is made to measure particles to confirm that they are independent things, they move, and so prevent the objectivism towards which scientism aims. This means that nothing can appear '*outside of its relation* to its observer' and that an understanding of the world divided into 'subject and object, inner world and outer world, body and soul is no longer adequate'.[50] Rather than collapsing into indeterminacy, things emerge through relationships and potential interactions under the observation of something else: things are not 'discovered', but rather disclosed in engagement and participation with other matter. As Rossetti commented, the believer's 'reverent contemplation of the Divine non-exclusiveness' allowed a conception of this observing guardianship as multiple, divine, human, animal, vegetal, mineral.[51] Like Keller, for whom God names the 'infinity enfolding it all psychosomatically together' and provokes 'all its open actualizations', Rossetti saw God both as and in snow, leaf, rose, sparrow, and whale.[52]

While her sense of the world happening through the mindful attention of things for each other is learned from a Tractarian focus on analogy, she also developed it in relation to the 'ecological' saint, Francis of Assisi. As an Anglo-Catholic of Italian descent, Rossetti was familiar with the cultural and religious presence of Francis in the nineteenth century, and had visited several Franciscan churches on her 1865 tour, including San Francesco d'Assisi in Brescia.[53] His tomb recently rediscovered, Francis was now heralded as the salvation of the natural world, the champion of the poor, as well as 'truly the father of painting, as well as of all eloquence, and all Italian poetry'.[54] Dante's elevation of Francis as a 'sun born to light the world', words echoed in the title of Holman Hunt's painting of Jesus, appealed to Maria and Gabriel, as well as to Rossetti. Maria's *A Shadow of Dante* (1871) referred to 'the "seraphic" S. Francis of Assisi' celebrated by Aquinas in the eleventh canto of *Paradiso*, and she also noted his inclusion just below John the Baptist, but above Benedict and Augustine, in Dante's vision of the rose.[55] Gabriel included Francis's poem 'Cristo' in his *The Early Italian Poets* (1861) anthology, and may have intended to include it and others in a revised 'Songs of the Art Catholic'. But no one was more moved than Rossetti when *The Athenæum* announced that the remains of her father were to be interred at the Church of Santa Croce, the principal Franciscan church in Florence and founded by Francis himself.[56]

Rossetti's circle of acquaintances also revered the saint. Hunt identified him as the 'spiritual life' behind Pre-Raphaelitism, and Ruskin, Coventry Patmore, Newman, and Manning all declared themselves members of the Third Order of St Francis (to which St Elizabeth of Hungary also belonged).[57] Many Tractarians elevated Francis as a symbol of reform and devotion, and Newman commented warmly on the Franciscan breviary as a model of Catholic worship.[58] One reviewer attributed Newman's radicalism to Francis, while Littledale claimed that Anglican clergy were in dire need of his 'reforming zeal'.[59] Hundreds of biographies and critical essays on Francis suddenly appeared in the nineteenth century, and proclaimed him a heroic and Romantic Orpheus, and advocate of the exploited, human and nonhuman alike. Of the many hagiographies of Francis published in Rossetti's lifetime, she almost certainly would have known Anna Jameson's chapter on Francis in *Legends of the Monastic Orders* (1850), Frederick W. Faber's translation of Louis François Candide Chalippe's *The Life of S. Francis of Assisi* (1853), and Margaret Oliphant's *Life of St Francis* (1870).[60] The Rossettis' friend Edward Burne-Jones was also obsessed with Francis, and depicted the saint as 'Patience' in a panel for the East Window of Holy Trinity Church, Chelsea that he framed with a border of foliage later reused in his 'Memorial Panels to Christina Rossetti' (1897–9).[61]

Rossetti's relational cosmology under grace was analogous to Francis's sense of the divine, and both rejected the idea of human stewardship over the world for a reading of creation as companion. As Timothy Johnson suggests, Francis perceived the world around him as one into which grace was constantly breaking, and responded by writing what he called 'a new *Praise of the Lord* for his creatures' through whom 'the human race greatly offends the Creator'.[62] This context for his 'Canticle of the Creatures', also called 'The Canticle of Brother Sun', illuminated his commitment to Paul's command that the freedom of human and nonhuman is interdependent: 'For we know that the whole creation groaneth and travaileth in pain together' and 'we know that all things work together for good to them that love God' (Romans 8. 22, 28). Francis's love for the particulars of creation was also an embodiment of the risen Christ's command, 'Go ye into all the world, and preach the gospel to every creature' (Mark 16. 15), one that recognized the agency of the nonhuman to rationally choose to follow God. Jameson, for example, reported that Francis understood 'all living things' as his 'brothers and sisters' because they shared 'a portion of that divine principle by which he himself existed'; and in an echo of William's comment on his sister's preference for the 'odd or uncouth', Oliphant wrote that the saint's 'noble conception of a redeemed world' moved him to embrace even 'the cruellest and least persuasible of animals'.[63] As the many legends and stories of Francis's life record, he prayed in church with a sheep that bleated before the altar of Mary; preached and listened to fields of flowers and birds; rescued and then befriended rabbits caught in traps; secured the civic right of a wolf to be part of and cared for by the community he once terrorized; threw fish back into the water; walked gently on stones; obstructed the cutting down of trees; and talked to lit candles—'brother fire'—as the source of divine light.[64]

Rossetti attributed a similar level of agency to creation in her devotional text, *Annus Domini: A Prayer for Each Day of the Year, Founded on a Text of Holy Scripture* (1874), written during a period in which she was increasingly vocal in her support for animal rights. In her prayer on the 'Counsel of the Lord', for example, she included all creatures in a collective 'our' to refer to a 'will' that is one with God's 'Will'.[65] She also recalled the Book of Common Prayer's reference to sustaining cattle and ravens (Psalms 147. 9) to warn her reader not to 'exceed in meat or drink', and instead give thanks for the 'gifts of fire and water, food and raiment, precious things of the earth and of the sea'.[66] Rossetti compared this recognition that resources are not relative within a finite nature to an abundant 'greenness of hope', a faithful receptivity to God in which grace is granted to 'all the families of the earth' as well as their 'dwelling-place' on it.[67] It was Rossetti's inclusive grace, one that does 'not exclude any', that provoked the author of a review written in 1906 to directly compare *Annus Domini* with A. G. Ferrers Howell's primer of Francis's writings, *Franciscan Days*.[68] But even before this, as early as the 1860s, the Tractarian editor of three hymnals of ancient and medieval poems, Orby Shipley, set Rossetti's 1862 'Good Friday ("Am I a stone")' in 'dialogue' with Francis by including it alongside words from the *Stabat Mater Dolorosa*, thought to have been written by the saint.[69] The poem witnesses the narrator standing insensibly before the crucifixion, measuring the steady drip of Jesus's blood as her fellow mourners weep before the agony of the Passion.[70] Paralysed like 'a stone and not a Sheep', the narrator is separated from the poem's other mourners in the stark and lonely line 12 that formally and affectively isolates her from the other things of creation. But the stanza also echoes Francis's 'Canticle of the Creatures' by presenting the sun and moon both in their natural forms as givers of light and as emotionally intelligent beings:

> Not so the Sun and Moon
>   Which hid their faces in a starless sky,
> A horror of great darkness at broad noon—
>   I, only I.   (ll. 9–12)

Here the sun and moon withdraw their illumination to overshadow the distraught faces of the women disciples, Peter, and the thief, but they also appear to hide their own faces to reveal themselves as mourners before the cross. Their communion with the humans that grieve for Jesus helps to reconcile the stranded narrator with creation. It also sets the scene for the final stanza in which the narrator is gathered into the divine body by a resurrected Christ that gathers all things into the form of sheep:

> Yet give not o'er,
>> But seek Thy sheep, true Shepherd of the flock;
> Greater than Moses, turn and look once more
>> And smite a rock.   (ll. 13–16)

With reference to both Psalm 23, 'The Lord is my Shepherd', and Exodus 17. 6, where Moses strikes a rock to draw water out of Mount Horeb for his people to drink, Rossetti invoked Jesus, not as the bloody body of the first stanza, but as the Shepherd. Only within a vision of fellowship realized in the children of Israel and the interconnectedness of things, does the line 'Yet give not o'er' make sense, a 'give' or gift that is never over or done, an endless grace in which all things are sustained. This grace constituted both a new state of harmony and a coming together of that which was separated, a day of 'union with Thee, and of re-union', from which nothing in creation is excluded, whether human, stellar, lunar, or animal.[71]

'The Covenant of the Rainbow includes animals'

In her notes on Noah, written as part of a commentary on Genesis, Rossetti imagined the ark as a vessel comprising 'nests'.[72] She repeated the observation in *Time Flies*, and remarked that where Genesis 6. 14 has the 'rooms' of the ark, 'the literal Hebrew' records 'not "rooms" but "nests"', the 'homeliest idea of a home'.[73] An 'overhanging presence of love', Rossetti continued, the nest implies 'Warmth and softness', a body of leaves and twigs shaped through the inhabitant's continual presence within it.[74] Like Bachelard, for whom the nest becomes habitable through the suffering of the bird that weaves it together, Rossetti envisioned the nest as a symbol of the love she believed the faithful received following sorrow and adversity.[75] Her notes on Genesis also depict the nest as a secure home in which, she wrote, 'every living creature' is held safe until the dove, sent out to find land, returns with an olive leaf, and God sets a 'bow in the cloud' as a 'token of a covenant between me and the earth' (9. 12–13). Next to her quotation from Genesis 9, she pencilled in the words 'The Covenant of the Rainbow includes animals', indicating her belief that they are part of God's 'time-long promise' to care for the world, but which she considered many humans to have betrayed.[76] For her focus on the detail of animal life broadened into an observance of animal rights, especially her gloss on Genesis 9. 4, 'But flesh with the life thereof, *which* is the blood thereof, shall ye not eat', which she reiterated in her commentary through Leviticus 17. 10, 'I will even set my face against that soul that eateth blood, and will cut him off from among his people'.[77]

While Rossetti was not a vegetarian, she balked at the 'queer dish' of 'preserved kangaroo' Maria and William once tried, and was a lifelong opponent of all forms of animal cruelty, as poems like 'Brother Bruin' attested.[78] 'Brother Bruin' passionately indicts the human for commodifying the nonhuman through its damning narrative of a master who beats his dancing bear to death after the ageing animal refuses to perform. After selling his skin, the man is shunned by society, and dies in the workhouse as 'a grim old sinner', 'unpitied' and unloved (l. 48). The starkness of the parable unequivocally associates animal cruelty with sin, the only barrier to grace. Her whole family were opposed to the 'persecuting, or inconveniencing' of any animal, as William confirmed:

> To stick a pin through a butterfly, or voluntarily to crush a worm on an earthen path, or to give a stamp gratis to a daddy-long-legs, appears to me about as pleasing as to set two cocks fighting, or to plunge a banderilla or a sword into a bull in a bull-fight; and that appears to me not pleasing in the least. Dante Gabriel used to say: 'A black-beetle is a moderately agreeable animal; it is when you squash him that he becomes disagreeable'.[79]

Rossetti also balked at harming even the smallest of critters. On being joined by a 'pill millepede [*sic*]' in her bedroom at Penkill, for example, she recorded feeling a 'sort of good will' towards her 'co-tenant' 'not inconsistent with an impulse to eject it through the window'. Carefully carrying the insect to the window, along with a 'swarm of baby mill-epedes' that suddenly appeared in her hand, she perceived the group as a 'numerous family' happily rehoused in the 'cracks outside'.[80] The incident does not imply a 'conservationist' relationship to fellow creatures.[81] Rather, Rossetti saw the bugs as equals, co-tenants with which she shared God's cosmos and part of a graced as well as ecological chain that, if broken, violated not just an ethical code, but scriptural law.

For Rossetti, the practice of vivisection was an especially abhorrent sin. Through her friend, Caroline Gemmer, she became an eager member of the anti-vivisection movement, and firmly believed that its violence was an offence against God.[82] As Ruskin argued, the question was not whether 'animals had a right to this or that', but rather 'What relation had they to God, what relations mankind had to God, and what was the true sense of feeling as taught to them by Christ the Physician'.[83] Ruskin resigned his appointment as Slade Professor of Art after Oxford University voted to establish a laboratory for animal experimentation in 1885, and joined Frances Power Cobbe's Victoria Street Society for the Protection of Animals Liable to Vivisection (later called the National Anti-Vivisection Society) alongside Rossetti and Manning, as well as figures like Robert Browning and Alfred Tennyson. While many Victorian writers condemned vivisection, there was a pronounced momentum among Tractarians and High Anglicans to condemn the practice in speeches and sermons. As early as 1842, Newman compared the 'Lord's sufferings' to 'the accounts which sometimes meet us of cruelties exercised on brute animals' by both 'barbarous and angry owners who ill-treat their cattle' and the 'cold-blooded and calculating act of men of science, who make experiments on brute animals'.[84] By 1882, Manning determined to put 'an end to that which I believe to be a detestable practice without scientific result, and immoral in itself', and called for vivisection to be prohibited on the basis that 'Nothing can justify, no claim of science, no conjectural result, no hope for discovery, such horrors as these'.[85] The Anglican Archdeacon of Westminster Abbey, Basil Wilberforce, also agreed, and ruled not only that cruelty to animals was 'absolutely scientifically unsound', but that it was in stark contradiction with a belief system in which 'animals other than man, some of whom have been as dear to us as man, will find their place in the Paradise of God'.[86] The prominent Anglo-Catholics, Edward King and Henry Parry Liddon, also stood with Ruskin against the university's decision to perform 'physiological experiments on living animals' because of their commitment to a connected creation.[87] For King, the Christian can only listen 'to the voice of an instructed conscience' when 'in true harmony with himself, with all creation, and with God'; and for Liddon, the very 'work of the Holy Spirit' is to keep creation connected, and 'collect' any 'outlying' and 'less regular creations of the Divine mind' in 'the true self-revelation of God'.[88] Henry William Burrows also preached regularly on the 'intensity of the divine nature' at Rossetti's church, and famously 'taxed' his son for 'shooting rabbits' by burning 'ten shillings' worth of penny stamps' in front of him as a reminder that his actions were not those 'of a gentleman'.[89]

Rossetti expressed her own visceral shock at the practice of vivisection by repeating the word 'horror' when referring to it. One of her early introductions to animal cruelty was a lecture on foreign travel given in 1861 by the rector of Stoke Newington, Thomas Jackson, author of the pro-animal rights *Our Dumb Companions* (1864) and *Our Dumb Neighbours* (1870). She associated Jackson directly with antivivisection, and wrote to William that he had been part of a 'deputation to Napoleon III on the subject of cruelty to poor horses' and had succeeded in ending the 'horror'.[90] She made the connection more obvious in a letter to Gabriel, and, enclosing a petition for him and 'any of your chums' to sign, asked him to take an 'active interest *counter* that horror of horrors Vivisection'.[91] A month later, she wrote to thank her brother for signing the petition:

> I used to believe with you that chloroform was so largely used as to do away with the horror of Vivisection: but a friend has so urged the subject upon me, & has sent me so many printed documents alleging & apparently establishing the contrary, that I have felt impelled to do what little I could to gain help against what . . . is cruelty of revolting magnitude. Mamma is cut to the heart by the details she has read, & has given her dear name also to the cause.[92]

She continued to seek her friends' 'influence against the horrors of Vivisection' and worked until the end of her life to procure signatures for an 'anti-Vivisection Petition to Parliament' that asked the Home Secretary to revoke the medical licences of vivisectionists.[93] This practical approach to the 'anti-V' cause was characteristic of Rossetti's commitment to the campaign. On discovering that the Society for Promoting Christian Knowledge had published a pro-vivisection book by Percy Faraday Franklin, *Our Secret Friends and Foes* (1893), she offered the editor £20 to destroy all remaining copies and then withdrew her subscription from the press.[94] She promoted an 'anti-Vivisection' bazaar in Brighton, attended 'anti-V' meetings in London, and offered several autographed copies of her poem 'A Word for the Dumb', to an anti-vivisection auction at which all were sold.[95] Written in the style of her 'SingSongs', the undated poem eludes puerility by demanding that the reader respect all creatures on the basis of their origin in God:

> Pity the sorrows of a poor old Dog
>   Who wags his tail a-begging in his need:
> Despise not even the sorrows of a Frog,
>   God's creature too, and that's enough to plead:
> Spare Puss who trusts us purring on our hearth:
>   Spare Bunny once so frisky and so free:
> Spare all the harmless tenants of the earth:
>   Spare, and be spared:—or who shall plead for thee?

'A Word for the Dumb' lists many of Rossetti's favourite animals—dogs, rabbits, frogs, and cats—and repeats the idea that all things share with each other a tenancy of creation under God. Through books like William Hayley's *Ballads Founded on Anecdotes Relating to Animals* (1805), she developed a love of domestic animals like rabbits (she announced they should 'live unmolested' in 'rabbit-country') and cats.[96] Even when she lay dying, her thoughts were with her mongrel cat, Muff: as William noted, her last words were not adventual or apocalyptic, but simply 'Don't forget about the kitten'.[97]

It was Rossetti's extraordinary affection for dogs, however, that truly illuminates the way in which she understood the animal world as subjectively alert and evolving consciously alongside other creatures like humans. She estimated the 'expressive countenances and also expressive tails' of dogs with the beauty of Italy as that which passed her 'descriptive faculty', although she enjoyed canine poems such as Gemmer's 'Love Me, Love My Dog', published in the Royal Society for the Prevention of Cruelty to Animals' magazine, *Animal World: An Advocate of Humanity*.[98] During a dull trip to Collinson's family, Rossetti wrote that she was comforted by the presence of a 'very handsome bull-terrier' she named Sol, her only 'sol-ace', she claimed, apart from the postman.[99] At the end of her letters she asked to be remembered to her friends' dogs—Pauline Trevelyan's Skye terrier, Peter ('Hoping Peter is well and waggish'), the Scotts' hound, Olaf (with whom Maria also corresponded)—and was especially enamoured by the several dogs owned by Gabriel's secretary, George Hake.[100] Her 'favourite' of Hake's dogs was a 'black-and-tan terrier' she called 'Delicious Dizzy!'[101] After leaving Hake's to dine in Chelsea one night, Rossetti was elated when Dizzy 'smuggled himself into our cab', and suggested that 'the deep thought of dog' was only 'occasionally revived by the lighter fancy of man'.[102] She soon had no need of Hake as go-between, and wrote to Dizzy directly to ask him to send her love to Gabriel, and to thank him for returning her copy of Swinburne's tragedy, *Erechtheus* (1876), which she urged him to borrow again, suspecting that he had not yet finished it.[103] While her notes about Dizzy are light-hearted, Rossetti was also quite serious when she alluded to Dizzy's 'sociable and intelligent' nature, and she 'happily' anticipated an evolved 'Dog of the future', whose multispecies nature she disclosed by comparing it to a mermaid.[104] Dogs were significant others that offered her a cross-species companionship that modelled, in Donna Haraway's words, a 'kinship claim' she envisioned for all humans and nonhumans.[105]

Rossetti's feelings for dogs went beyond tenderness into friendship, kinship, and an interest in what it means to think and be like another species. She considered every element in creation to be conscious, and all fauna and flora thinking beings capable of faith and compassion for others. This is especially apparent in her affection for the marine worm, *Aphrodita aculeata*, also called the sea-mouse, a creature for whom she searched on various seaside holidays, and had admired in Hake's aquarium collection. When her intimate friend, Charles Bagot Cayley, sent her a pickled sea-mouse as a new year's gift, she responded with 'My Mouse' (1877), a poem that implies that the human is connected to the nonhuman through a Platonic shared memory of the eternal realities of God. The narrator begins by comparing the mouse to Venus. Both are born of the 'foaming seas', she states, both are caught in the gaze of the beholder, and both invoke female sexuality, the mouse through its shape and Venus as a symbol of fertility, beauty, and love. But the mouse also embodies the goddess of sea and sky, Iris, the messenger of the gods and personification of the rainbow: 'Bright bow of that exhausted shower | Which made a world of sweet-herbs flower' (ll. 6–7). Invoking the rainbow through Iris, the sea-mouse recalls God's covenant with the world, and offers a creaturely link between the divine and material. It appears as a hybridic assemblage in Rossetti's poem, god-like and animal, but also 'Part hope', 'Part memory, part anything', gathering all things into its being (ll. 10–11). The narrator reciprocates its inclusivity by recognizing in the mouse multiple mythological and symbolic meanings, as well as its reality as something to which she relates affectively 'in my heart' (l. 15).

The smaller and stranger the creature, the more Rossetti valued it. She read in William's copy of Gilbert White's *The Natural History and Antiquities of Selborne* (1789) that the 'most insignificant insects and reptiles' have the most 'influence in the economy of nature', an idea she heard echoed in Pusey's reverence for 'the most distant and minutest things'.[106] But she also identified with the queer and fiendish. In her double sonnet for *Time Flies*, 'Heaviness may endure', for example, the narrator aligns herself with the owl and dragon to become a companion of monsters. In doing so, she reverses the poem's expression of isolation and grief and moves its darkness into a flash of light:

> Thus I sat mourning like a mournful owl,
>   And like a doleful dragon made ado,
>   Companion of all monsters of the dark:
> When lo! the light cast off its nightly cowl,
>   And up to heaven flashed a carolling lark,
>   And all creation sang its hymn anew.   (ll. 9–14)

Rossetti played on the meaning of 'monster' as a creature that con-joins elements of two or more animal forms (for example, centaurs or wyverns) to reveal creation as a confected body illuminated through companionship. She preferred hybridic creatures because they model creation itself, a composite of multiple things distinct but reconciled in one body. The sea-mouse exemplified such a synthesis: its elliptical and segmented body of overlapping scales is covered with both short hair-like bristles and thorn-like spines made of tiny hexagonal cylinders that allow it to change colour between red, green, and blue. Eventually part of William's collection of aquatic life that Rossetti called his 'bottled monsters', her own sea-mouse signified a loving monstrosity inherent to a gathered creation.[107] As she wrote in the second part of

'Heaviness may endure', 'all creation' sings 'anew' and 'in tune' when it comes together as one choir, a sound that encourages all to join in by granting 'One note for every lovely thing that is' (ll. 1–2, 22, 25).

Rossetti's intimacy with a variety of creatures deepened further in her repeated visits to the Zoological Gardens in Regent's Park, close to her homes in Marylebone and Bloomsbury, and on the way to Christ Church, Albany Street. Rossetti's reports of 'our beloved Zoo' were always animated as she recalled excitedly awaiting the arrival of a new hippopotamus, and feeding barley sugar and carrots to the elephants.[108] She wrote to William:

> We have revisited the z. gardens. Lizards are in strong force, tortoises active, alligators looking up. The weasel-headed armadillo as usual evaded us. A tree-frog came to light, the exact image of a tin toy to follow a magnet in a slop-basin. The blind wombat and neighbouring porcupine broke forth into short-lived hostilities, but apparently without permanent results. The young puma begins to bite. Your glorious sea-anemones:—I well know the strawberry specimen, but do not remember the green and purple. Beware of putting them into *fresh* water, as the result is said to be fatal and nauseating.[109]

The passage illustrates both Rossetti's delight at the diversity of creatures at the zoo, and her new education in the environments of specific species. It is likely that during her stay with Maria at the All Saints branch of Clifton she also visited the newly opened Bristol Zoo, founded in 1835; and she read about ostriches and condors at Surrey Zoo alongside extracts from William Paley's *Natural Theology* (1802) in her mother's commonplace book.[110] Rossetti also shared in Gabriel's personal zoo, one acquired incrementally from Charles Jamrach's animal emporium on Ratcliffe Highway in East London. Jamrach imported, exported, and bred various species from snails to tigers, and Gabriel's collection soon included 'owls, rabbits, dormice, hedgehogs, a woodchuck, a marmot, a kangaroo, wallabies, a deer, armadillos, a raccoon, a raven, a parrot, chameleons, lizards, salamanders, a laughing jackass, a zebu, a succession of wombats' and 'a bull'.[111] Accommodated in Gabriel's garden at Chelsea, and later Birchington-on-Sea in Kent, the animals lived in a state that was far from Edenic, as William reported in 1867:

> The poor little tame barn-owl Jessie has had a horrid end, being found with her head bitten off—it is surmised by the raven ... Two grass-green

parakeets starved to death; a green Jersey lizard killed by a servant because he was regarded as a poisonous eft; a dormouse found with a hole in his throat, conjectured to be done by the other dormice; [the servant's] dog split up the back by a deerhound; a tortoise found dead and shrivelled . . . not to speak of natural but sudden deaths of two robins, a cardinal grosbeak, a salamander, etc. etc. There was also a rabbit eaten up (by cats?) all but his tail [and] a pigeon devoured by a hedgehog—which was afterwards found dead.[112]

Rossetti's prayer in *Annus Domini* that Jesus 'remove violence and cruelty far from our habitations' may have been written with her brother's incompetence (rather than malevolence) in mind.[113] While Gabriel sentimentalized the creaturely, believing his deceased wife's soul to have entered into a chaffinch, Rossetti was more interested in the substance of nature.[114] As a child she was fascinated when a 'black insect' arose from the 'mossy' grave in which she had earlier buried a dead mouse; and her favourite painting in the 1864 Royal Academy exhibition was Edwin Landseer's *Man Proposes, God Disposes*, in which two polar bears chew on the human remains of a shipwreck.[115] While Rossetti would have recognized Landseer's title from Thomas à Kempis's *The Imitation of Christ* (1418–27), her theology rewrites Kempis's understanding of 'creatures' as an 'obstacle' to God's grace and envisions them instead as fellow travellers of whom even the 'least sympathetic' embodied grace.[116]

She argued that is precisely those aspects of creation towards which the human is most likely to bristle that harbour hidden beauty, one that can be glimpsed through the development of close attention and 'reverence'. In *Letter and Spirit: Notes on the Commandments* (1883), she wrote that the human must hone this reverent thinking as a way of approaching 'not only "heaven" and "Jerusalem"', but '"earth" also and our own "head"', and posited that 'In every creature is latent a memorial of its Creator'.[117] By attentively contemplating creation, she sought to see the world as if through 'the mind of Christ', a mode of vision in which the ostensibly 'two worlds' of earth and heaven, seen and unseen, material and immaterial, become one. She wrote 'we should exercise that far higher privilege which appertains to Christians, of having "the mind of Christ"; and then the two worlds, visible and invisible, will become familiar to us even as they were to Him'.[118] The practice of this nondualist perception takes the human beyond the visual and auditory senses into a mode of thinking able to access what Paul calls the 'deep things of God' (1 Corinthians 2. 10). In the same passage, Paul also uses the phrase 'the mind of Christ' (2. 16) to describe a spiritual discernment in which the grace that holds all things together is suddenly apparent to the perceiver, for whom the being of all things is revealed as part of one body. In *Letter and Spirit*, Rossetti argued that by reverentially discerning 'wind, water, fire, the sun, a star, a vine, a door, a lamb', the believer can train her heart to be steady, and her mind to become 'reverential, composed, grave', a state in which she is unbound from the physical into the infinite and eternal.[119] In this graced state, the 'least sympathetic' not only appear part of one reality, but they are revealed as the very aspects that 'set us an example' of how to be with and think about God.[120] Like the modern philosopher of consciousness, Thomas Nagel, Rossetti acknowledged that specific things—whales, seals, ravens, lambs, shells, thistles, bats—have a unique subjective experience that is 'unmeasured, incalculable' by the human observer.[121] But while Nagel famously asserts that the human cannot think like a bat, even if he or she can imagine what it might be like to fly using echolocation or sonar, Rossetti suggested that the nonhuman can think like God, and so models a companionable thinking to the human.

If the created reality of earth and heaven joined is 'an outcome' of God's 'mind' and 'presence', then thinking like God is the same as thinking like creation—in fellowship with other things through which difference is unfolded.[122] The 'mind of Christ' as a 'guide of life' was also ascribed to the anti-vivisectionist in the *Fortnightly Review*, a publication in which Rossetti's own work was often referenced.[123] While the author of the article admitted that some forms of organized religion hold 'that we have no duties to the animal creation', he invites his reader to focus on Jesus's reaction to the idea of vivisection: 'What would our Lord have said, what looks would He have bent, upon a chamber filled with "the unoffending creatures which He loves," dying under torture deliberately and intentionally inflicted?'[124] This what-would-Jesus-do attack on vivisectionism found scriptural validation in the Sermon on the Mount, to which Rossetti turned for evidence of God's indiscriminate and life-giving love for all the things of creation. As Richard Bauckham argues, Jesus's words in his sermon are part of a tradition of wisdom instruction, and ask those present to 'behold' the environment, not simply to reflect on it, but to attend and learn from it.[125] Jesus's creation theology reveals the 'fowls of the air' and 'lilies of the field' as examples of beings that 'teach' through a connection with the world in which they refuse to exploit—sow, reap, toil, or spin—the land that sustains them (Matthew 6. 26–33). In trusting God to provide them with everything they need, the small and transient birds and lilies remind humans that they are one species among many, all of which depend on God for sustenance as foreshadowed in the Psalms (104. 24–8; 145. 15–16). As Bauckham notes, the sermon reveals the way in which humans ignore this reliance on 'the divine provision' of 'the resources of creation' and are preoccupied with their own labour and capabilities to produce food.[126] In contrast, the birds and lilies are more immediately reliant on God, a 'Father of the fatherless' as Rossetti described him, for whom all things are kin.

Rossetti used the phrase 'Father of the fatherless' in her undated poem 'They toil not, neither do they spin', reprinted in *Verses* (1893) after a first appearance in *The Face of the Deep: A Devotional Commentary on the Apocalypse* (1892). In it, the narrator relates the message of the Sermon on the Mount through a ternary God whose form as Father, Son, and Holy Ghost becomes 'Father', 'clother', and 'feeder' (ll. 1–2). But while the nonhuman is commended for its closeness to God, the narrator castigates herself as an example of the human will to assume dominion over the rest of creation. Such egoism, she writes, will be levelled or 'ploughed up' by God in order to be brought back into relationship with grace:

> Clother of the lily, Feeder of the sparrow,
>   Father of the fatherless, dear Lord,
> Tho' Thou set me as a mark against Thine arrow,
>   As a prey unto Thy sword,
> As a ploughed up field beneath Thy harrow,
>   As a captive in Thy cord,
> Let that cord be love   (ll. 1–7)

The narrator demands that God remake her in grace by cutting her down like prey and dragging her until fields until she is bound in his 'cord' of love. Associated with the ploughed field, the narrator becomes part of the earthly alongside the birds and lilies. But the word 'captive' also suggests that she is confined, and waits to be released into a renewed freedom as part of creation. As part of

Rossetti's commentary on Revelation 20. 13 in *The Face of the Deep*, the poem becomes part of a longer gloss on this experience of waiting to feel fully incorporated into creation. Specifically, she describes the purgatorial realm of Hades as a 'pound' not a prison, a place in which stray humans rather than animals are held until earth's restoration at the end of time.[127] Early release is possible, Rossetti argues, but only for the human who can awake to fellowship in the old creation by letting go of her sovereign relationship to it, and tying herself into creation through a cord of love.

One of the most interesting source texts for Rossetti's reading of this interconnection of all things through grace was the Benedicite (also called the 'Song of Creation' or 'Song of the Three Children'), included in the Catholic and Eastern Orthodox versions of the Old Testament Book of Daniel, the Catholic Liturgy of the Hours, and the Anglican Book of Common Prayer. The song, uttered by three men thrown into a furnace for refusing to worship a gold statue of Nebuchadnezzar because of their allegiance to God, provided a way of thinking creation as a chain or 'procession' that Rossetti explored in two revisions of it. The first, *Seek and Find*, opens with a 'Harmony', or collation of passages from scripture that speak to and through each other in the form of a three-column structure or Trinitarian 'intratext-uality'.[128] This in turn is echoed in the three-voiced song of the Benedicite, in which three men praise all elements of God's creation as they burn. Rossetti's catalogue of these elements was based on the 1662 Book of Common Prayer 'Benedicite, omnia opera', in which the men bless 'all ye Works of the Lord', from angels and heavens, ice and snow, seas and floods, beasts and cattle, priests and Christians, to the Father, Son, and Holy Ghost and those who sing the prayer, Ananias, Azaria, and Misael. But while she followed the arrangement and language of the 1662 text, her commentary focuses the reader on the particulars of creation, not simply as 'works', but as companions with which humans share an earth that is also part of a larger cosmos. As Lynda Palazzo argues, in doing so she 'liberates the natural world' from both Tractarian symbolism and exploited commodity 'to full participation in a cosmic order springing to life in Christ the fulfilment of wisdom'.[129]

Seek and Find is divided into two 'series' or parts, 'Creation' and 'Redemption', which granted Rossetti one level on which to detail the physical reality of the created world and a second on which to trace Christ's union with it. This allowed her to reveal nature, not as a symbol of heaven, but as 'the heaven that now is': when loved and attended to, Rossetti suggested, the world becomes at once heaven and earth, an idea underlined by the harmony that opens the text.[130] Here 'God's creatures' are emotional and sentient (they are his 'praise-givers') and have consciousness (they willingly serve Christ). Introduced through their relationship to Christ, each being listed in the Benedicite serves to incarnate the equality of all things, from the sun to the whale to a blade of grass.[131] Through her harmonic contemplation of these intratextual affinities, Rossetti observed a 'Divine non-exclusiveness' in which species are distinct, but incorporated.[132] She offered an interspecies reading of the Athanasian Creed, 'one God in Trinity, and Trinity in Unity', by giving the 'multiform family of living creatures' God embraces two titles: '"the Lamb of God"' and '"the Lion of the tribe of Juda"'.[133] The first, she wrote, is a symbol of God, the second of 'human stock'.[134] In this reading, all things become 'partial expressions' of God, an echo of Plato that revises his reading of perfect forms to rethink his shadows as only what the non-believer sees. As Rossetti wrote in the opening chapter of *Seek and Find*, those who seek 'wisdom' in Christ will discover it in the creaturely.[135] Following a quotation from Job 28, Rossetti suggested that to discern God is to see heaven in creation by looking to 'the ends of the earth' and 'under the whole heaven' (28. 20–8). Like Blake, whose engravings of Job she borrowed from Gabriel, Rossetti understood the book's reading of theodicy as redemptive, and Job as a figure who is restored, not through the regaining of what was lost, but through a new way of seeing in which the same world is revealed anew.[136] Rossetti also aspired to this vision in *Seek and Find*, but with a focus on the environmental that attuned her reader to animals, vegetation, climate, and energy resources and worked to cohere the religious and scientific in a kinship that mirrored her opening harmony.

Rossetti established this connection in her commentary on 'Earth', where she interpreted the 'days of creation not as days of twenty-four hours each, but as lapses of time' that are successive and evolving, 'like the ascending notes of the musical scale'. She conjectured that her own time ('this current period') may still be an ongoing seventh day of creation, in which the human might 'marvel over' both visible creation, as well as those uncharted 'belts and atmospheres' and 'interstellar spaces' in which 'the sun itself may be no more than a sub-centre' of 'attendant worlds'.[137] Amid her star-gazing, she included new planets and universes as part of Christ's incarnated body of created beings, the sun as much 'our fellow-creature' as the fish, and both brought into 'close connexion' with other things through the 'Creator'.[138] She consistently demanded her reader acknowledge the multiplicity of a universe to which the human is most in need of reconnection. Only humans lack the 'faculties to define the limits' of its 'fellow-creatures', she argued, and only humans overlook those that 'exert memory, intelligence, affection'.[139] For Rossetti, Christ was incarnated as a human to illuminate the divinity of all of creation to other humans. She considered the whale an ideal example of a creature the human needed to 'consider' in the way Jesus taught, not as a source of soap, oil, candles, corsets, fishing rods, whips, and shoehorns, but as the '"great fish" of Jonah'.[140] The human is capable of assuming sovereignty over the whale, as all creatures, but never 'for abuse' and always in recognition of their being as 'sentient fellow-creatures'.[141] They are not material from which to make 'pretty fashions in dress' nor the basis of 'scientific problems', Rossetti wrote, and to think of them as such is to damage the human as much as the nonhuman:

> Alas for us, if when the fashion of this world passes away (1 Cor. vii. 31) and partial knowledge is done away (xiii. 9, 10), the groans of a harmless race sacrificed to our vanity or our curiosity should rise up in the judgment with us and condemn us. 'O Lord, Thou preservest man and beast'. (Ps, xxxvi. 6)[142]

Violence against creation, she suggests, not only delays God's transformation of it, but will have severe material and spiritual consequences on both microcosmic and cosmic scales. As she stated in *Time Flies*, perhaps 'the smallest, weakest, most grotesque, *wrong* creature' will 'rise up' in the new creation and 'condemn us' as the human has condemned it in this world.[143]

Her second reimagining of the Benedicite, '"All thy works praise thee, O Lord": A Processional of Creation' (1880), transferred the song from the three burning men to the specific works of God. Each element sings its own three-line lyric about its relationship to God, the poem comprised of choruses sung by distinct groups of beings, from galaxies and nebulae, to medicinal herbs, frost, clouds, mountains, whales, and lambs. In the first and last verse, however, the 'works' join with their fellow beings, not in an ensemble, but in a single voice attuned to one creation: 'I, all-creation, sing my song of praise' (l. 1), the poem begins, and concludes, 'Praise God, praise God, praise God, His creature saith' (l. 191). This nondual embrace of the singular reveals creation as a collective gathered into one grace, even as it comprises a plural diversity of things. For example, Rossetti's revision of the Book of Common Prayer text, 'O ye Stars of Heaven, bless ye the Lord', presents a myriad group of 'Star-hosts numerous, innumerous, | Throng space with energy untumultuous' (ll. 28–9) that are revealed as at once individually luminous spheres of energy as well as a commons of divine workers under God's grace.[144] Her verse on whales too develops the text, 'O ye Whales, and all that move in the Waters', and rethinks it through her beloved word 'monsters' to affectionately elevate both as cheerful and rejoicing creatures in need of shelter and kindness:

> We Whales and Monsters gambol in His sight
> Rejoicing every day and every night,
> Safe in the tender keeping of His Might.   (ll. 124–6)

As the whales and monsters gambol and play, they feel pleasure, joy, and also protection, 'Safe in the tender keeping' of God and redeemed from their portrayal as demonic killers eager to crush ships and their trembling crews. Like this verse, each three-line song serves to disclose a particular element of creation as an animate and conscious being that is also part of a God whom it praises and loves.

'Evergreen love'

In '"All thy works"', Rossetti offered the stage not only to mammals, birds, and the celestial, but also to the vegetal. Like Aquinas, she designated a soul, and so some form of cognition and knowledge, to every aspect of creation, including plant life.[145] The final part of this chapter suggests that Rossetti identified an especially conscious and subjective being in 'all green things'—plants, trees, flowers, fruits, herbs, and gardens—aspects of creation that communally bend towards God in praise. As her verse on green things in '"All thy works"' indicates, the vegetal sings in unison to God:

> We all green things, we blossoms bright or dim,
> Trees, bushes, brushwood, corn and grasses slim,
> We lift our many-favoured lauds to Him.   (ll. 98–100)

Their abundant prayers are celebrated here as 'many-favoured', welcomed by a God that recognized in the vegetal a slow and considered life form whose behaviour modelled the contemplative life. The tree was also life-giving beyond its absorption of carbon dioxide as a model of intricate kinships that branched back to the trees of life and knowledge in Genesis 2. 9 and forward to the renewed tree of life in Revelation 22. 2. As Rossetti noted in *Letter and Spirit*, Jesus's crucifixion 'on the tree' located him as part of a horizontal and continuous network of creation.[146] Her rhizomatic cross was a direct challenge to the scientific and vertical tree of life as a phylogenetic map of embryological development with the conscious human at the top. By contrast, plant life is collective and interdependent with its environment, rooted outside of itself in both the earth and the generative light of the sun and carrying life to other things through its network of roots and leaves.[147] As Rossetti argues in *Seek and Find*, green things reveal a particular kind of divine inclusiveness by mapping the multiple oneness of the divine body:

> Under a form of most sweet beauty the multitudinous unity of a plant sets forth Christ and His members. 'I am the true Vine, and My Father is the Husbandman ... I am the Vine, ye are the branches' (St John xv. 1–8). Everything is held in common and (dare we say so?) for mutual solace and loveliness. Not, indeed, that we bear the Root, but the Root us (see Rom. xi. 18): yet it so bears us that it feeds its branches with its very life, and lives in them as truly as they live by it. Nor does it limit its gift to that of a bare existence; it clothes itself with them as with an added honour; it makes their leaves comely by colour, and their tendrils a very grace by delicacy; it invests them with the fruit which cheereth God and man (see Judges ix. 12, 13).[148]

The plant offered Rossetti not simply an image of the divine body, then, but a living embodiment of its internal workings. As a 'true vine' on which Christians 'are the branches' (John 15. 1–5), the divine body constituted its own plant ecology in which things are receptively oriented towards each other.

As an amateur botanist, Rossetti was familiar with the ecosystem in which the plant carries water through its roots and leaves to the soil and then into the atmosphere. She recognized a direct analogy in Genesis, which relates that plants were created first to enrich the atmosphere with oxygen to allow for the formation of animal life.[149] Their primacy is also a reminder to the human that it comes later and is thus dependent on prior life forms. As Rossetti observed, the root 'bears' the human and 'feeds' its 'branches' with its own vitality.[150] The vegetal divine body is not simply a symbol of diversity, but the realization of the coherence of these things in 'life'. Notably, Rossetti did not turn to the nerves, arteries, or membranes of the human body to conceptualize vitality, and looked instead to the interdependence between plants (which need carbon and expel oxygen) and animals (which require oxygen and expel carbon). As vitalists competed to solve the question of why living matter decomposes while inanimate things decay, Rossetti found evidence of eternity in evergreens like ivy, lavender, camellias, holly, and certain species of fern.[151] These plants were commonly used to decorate Tractarian churches, and signified God's eternal or 'evergreen love', one Rossetti attributed to people and places she perceived to be plant-like. She described Penkill Castle as 'evergreen Penkill', for example, and called Frances her 'evergreen Mother', 'well and blooming' and who sent 'her evergreen love' to others through her daughter.[152] Botany was a respectable subject of study for women in this period, and Rossetti visited the Botanic Gardens as often as she did the Zoological. She also owned a terrarium, collected ferns (which admirers occasionally sent to her as gifts), and signed an 1874 petition against the destruction of part of the New Forest, stating that she was delighted by 'tree-full' landscapes.[153] When she took up gardening in the late 1860s, she wrote that she preferred a 'homely English garden', albeit one that brought the animal into relation with the vegetal, 'not a flower garden only, but strawberries and raspberries and other treats. And several dogs.'[154]

In the 1850s, Rossetti went to stay with the established fern collector, Swynfen Jervis, at Darlaston Hall in Staffordshire, renowned for the famous 'Fernery' he established there amidst mid-century

'Pteridomania'. Located in the 'shady' Trent Valley, Darlaston was rich in woodland and plant life, and geographically near to the leafy public paths around Chester and the river Dee on which she also walked.[155] Her later trips to Newcastle and Wallington Hall were also taken up with close observation of plant life on excursions some of which were led by the botanist, geologist, and owner of Wallington, Walter Calverly Trevelyan. A financial backer of the Pre-Raphaelite project, Trevelyan established a significant natural history collection, one that Rossetti was keen to explore in relation to natural theology.[156] In Ruskin's designs for the new Oxford Natural History Museum, for which Gabriel and Lizzie had been invited to 'design flower and beast borders—crocodiles and various vermin', Rossetti had already perceived a connection between natural history and natural theology.[157] But she also recognized in natural history's observation of evolving organisms and ecosystems a way of understanding the unfolding of grace over time towards its fulfilment in the new creation. Many Christians saw the same parallels between evolution and grace. Pusey, who often pressed dried flowers into the covers of his collection, owned many books on botany, science, and evolution, many of which were written by fellow clergy.[158] Clergy-naturalists including Charles Alexander Johns, George Henslow, Francis Orpen Morris, and William Houghton may have differed in their reactions to Darwin, but they shared a belief in nature as the loving work of God. As Johns argued, the 'trained' eye can find 'being' in the smallest details of 'hedges and by-ways', details classified by scientific terminology, but cared for by God.[159] Henslow also suggested that the theory of evolution strengthened Paley's design argument, and that God had 'adopted Evolution as the method by which He chose to bring about the existence of successive orders of beings until Man appeared upon the scene of Life'.[160]

Rossetti and her family owned several books on botany, including John Gerard's *Herball, or Generall Historie of Plantes* (1537), Richard Phillips's *The Young Botanists* (1810), Peter Parley's *Tales About Plants* (1839), John Lindley's *Elements of Botany* (1849), and a copy of the tenth edition of Carl Linnæus's *Systema Naturae* (1758–9). Rossetti was also familiar with Johns's *Botanical Rambles* (1846), John Hutton Balfour's *Phyto-theology* (1851), Charles Kingsley's *Earth Lore for Children* (1870), and countless essays on botany published in newspapers and periodicals such as Margaret Plues's 'Botanical Rambles' (1867), which appeared next to Rossetti's short story, 'A Safe Investment' in *The Churchman's Shilling Magazine*.[161] This library of ecotheological texts affirmed an evolutionary and green reading of creation compatible with Christianity. Phillips, for example, declared that botany not only inspired 'a partiality for the country, and a desire of investigating the works of nature', but is associated with 'the idea we form of the Deity'. He argued that 'an early attachment to the study of plants' would deter individuals from pursuits like gambling and redirect their attention to 'the lasting beauty of divine nature'.[162] *The Young Botanists* also introduced the reader to Paley, Linnæus's *Systema Naturæ* (1735) and *Dissertation on the Sexes of Plants* (1759), as well as Rousseau's simplified commentary on the classificatory system they outline, *Lettres élémentaires sur la botanique*.[163] The Linnæan system, which orders plants through their sexual reproduction in relation to numbers of stamens and pistils, was widely credited with establishing the first universally accepted conventions for the taxonomic organization of organisms. Linnæus was given centre stage in Oxford's Natural History Museum, where his statue was designed by John Lucas Tupper (whose poems William edited), and the Pre-Raphaelite, Alexander Munro.[164]

Yet Linnæus was unable to account for all organisms. As Theresa Kelley argues, a class of plants he called 'cryptogamia' (ferns, mushrooms, lichens, algae) defied the apparent 'epistemic mastery' of his system. These hidden species confirmed the presence of an 'invisible' world beyond classification that sustained the view that the cosmos comprised unproven and unseen realms.[165] This, together with plants' sensitive and open response to the environment, wherein they take in nutrients, water, and light without appropriating or exploiting these resources, materialized the kindly interdependence Rossetti recognized in all of creation. Several of her contemporaries made the same observation. In *Phyto-theology*, for example, Balfour presented botany as both founded on its relation to other 'departments of science and art'—geology, zoology, medicine, agriculture, horticulture, design—and also the basis of the creation account in Genesis, one entirely in harmony with 'the just ideas which science has given us'.[166] Elizabeth Kent's *Flora Domestica* (1823) also creatively considered botany, not as a banal resistance to what Keats called the impatient 'buzzing' of modernity, but rather as a different way of thinking and

speaking.[167] As Kent writes in a passage Rossetti copied out for
William, flowers 'speak a language, a clear and intelligible language'
of 'affection, benevolence, and piety' that can be traced to the 'earliest
events that history records'.[168] Like the language of reserve, which
veils its meaning while assuming the context of God's love, the
language of flowers was at once an expression of benevolence, and
also an encoded form that challenged social convention.[169] Flowers
were thus used to metaphorically intimate that which could not be
openly articulated, as exemplified in Erasmus Darwin's partially
masked depictions of sexuality in his 1791 *The Botanic Garden*, and in
the affective language in which specific flowers identified emotions
within courtships, friendships, and everyday rituals.[170]

But plant life had an additional significance for Anglo-Catholics,
who reintroduced it into the church as part of a surge of ecclesiastical
refurbishment designed to enable ritual worship. For many Anglo-
Catholics, Anglicanism had all but stripped the church of everything
'that makes worship sensuous'. As the clergyman Henry Christmas
claimed, many worshippers longed for the plant-like 'tracery of roof
and cloister' and 'pillars shooting up in the twilight of the clerestory,
and then expanding into fan-like foliage' once common in Anglican
churches.[171] The consequence of having torn out screens, statues, and
altars, Christmas wrote, had been a 'snapping' of 'the link that bound'
the 'soul and the body in one act of devotion', which in turn abstracted
'earthly objects' from the worshipper and the rest of creation. By
contrast, church decoration, like poetry and art, created a space
'which hallows earthly objects, by regarding them in a symbolical
point of view'.[172]

Architectural and decorative innovations were reintroduced into
the church by the Cambridge Camden Society, inspired by Tractarianism, and which sought to preserve traditional details in the church
like sedilia (decorated seats for clergy) and rood screens (that kept the
chancel distinct from the nave).[173] Pugin's *Treatise on Chancel Screens
and Rood Lofts* (1851) was partly influenced by the Camden group,
as were the sacramental designs of William Butterfield and the
Pre-Raphaelites. But Pugin's designs for screens, as well as altar linens,
stoles, maniples, crests, crosses, rosaries, and church furniture, were
defined by floral forms, and Pugin was soon recognized for what
William Pettit Griffith called his 'architectural botany'.[174] In *Floriated*

Ornament (1849), for example, he argued for a faith derived directly from his experience of nature rather than aesthetics, and recalled his epiphany on seeing plant life as the source of ornamental form at the studio of a fellow designer. Gazing at a plaster cast he assumed to be a 'fine work of the thirteenth century', he realized that it was in fact foliage 'gathered from his garden, and by him cast and adjusted in geometrical form'.[175] On leaving the studio, plant life suddenly appeared to him as the most 'beautiful specimen', a 'Gothic foliage' he sought to recreate inside the church in all its 'irregular and confused effect'.[176] Pugin's irregular Gothic flora and fauna within the church space created a natural or 'ancient Architecture' as Ruskin called it, one 'in sympathy' with 'the vast controlling powers of Nature herself'.[177] By featuring St Francis in his window designs for St Chad's in Birmingham, the first Catholic cathedral to be built in Britain since the Reformation, Pugin reminded churchgoers of the implicit link between worship and nature, one echoed in his floral displays at Christ Church, Albany Street, as well as St Andrew's, Wells Street, and St Mary Magdalene, Munster Square.[178] Butterfield also drew on palm fronds, ivies, spiralling vines, tree knots, and helicoid growths in his designs, and sought to create a forest-like environment especially within churches located in suburban or metropolitan areas.

For some Anglicans, however, floral ornamentation was a dangerous sign of 'Catholicizing'. When the Tractarian Frederick Oakley converted to Catholicism, a priest notorious for his introduction of plants and flowers at Margaret Chapel, and author of a guide to church flowers called *The Catholic Florist* (1851), Bishop Blomfield grew increasingly nervous about the implications of ecclesiastical floral design.[179] In the context of Oakley's desertion, several clergy were indicted for their implementation of vegetal life in the church. William Parks Smith was prosecuted by the Bishop of Exeter, Henry Phillpotts, for 'illegally' placing vases of flowers and a cross covered with flowers on the altar at St John's Chapel, Torquay; Robert Liddell was accused of using evergreens to 'veil' the church at St Paul's Knightsbridge; and the Ecclesiastical Court brought a case against John Purchas of St James, Brighton, author of a handbook of Anglo-Catholic ritual and decoration, for using flowers in worship.[180] When Liddell won his case, he established a precedent for floral decoration that created both an increased demand for flowers (clergy and conventual sisters began to queue as 'early as 4AM' at the Covent Garden flower market) and a market for floral handbooks.[181] William Alexander Barrett's *Flowers and Festivals; or Directions for the Floral Decorations of Churches* (1868), for example, was widely circulated among Tractarian clergy, and is a probable source for *Called to Be Saints*. Addressed to 'the wives and daughters of our parochial clergy', the handbook not only tasked women with responsibility for the sacred space of the church, but encouraged them to read botanical books that also offered lessons in mineralogy, conchology, ornithology, and entomology.[182] At the same time, Barrett introduced his female reader to the relationship between Anglo-Catholicism and the Fathers (who, he claimed, decorated their temples with seasonal floral hangings and garlands), as well as some of the first places of worship in Britain ('built of boughs', he wrote, as imitations of 'the temples of Saturn, which were always under the oak').[183]

Rossetti's own theological botanizing is apparent in both her aesthetic appreciation of the vegetal (she offered a design based on an apple tree to William Morris) and concern for the specifics of plants or her 'floral *intimates*', as she called them.[184] She named her 1876 study of the minor festivals of the Church Calendar *Young Plants and Polished Corners* before retitling it *Called to Be Saints* (1876), the former a reference to Psalm 144's analysis, 'what is man'. Striving to redeem 'man' from his vanity, David offers to 'sing a new song' of humanity in the Psalm, one in which 'sons may be as plants grown up in their youth' and 'our daughters may be as corner stones' (144. 3–12). Both are gathered in the collective phrase 'happy is that people' with sheep and oxen. By extending the concept of humanity to the nonhuman, and associating the feminine with the sturdiness of hewn altar rocks and the masculine with plant life, the psalm constituted its own inclusive ecotheology, one that Rossetti adapted in *Called to Be Saints*. As she wrote in the preface, 'The Key to my Book', her 'nature-portraits' of deliberately local flora (daisies, ivy, holly, mistletoe, groundsel, chickweed, gorse, snowdrops, hepaticas, violets, wood sorrel, cowslips, Veronica, honeysuckle, yellow flag, flowering rush, harebells, pimpernels, ferns, marigolds, blackberries, blackthorn, arbutus, and grass) direct the reader, as Jesus commanded, to 'consider' plants, a task she fulfilled as a writer in her attentive and intimate descriptions.[185] While she assumed the guise of ignorance to emphasize her devotional reading of every aspect of the natural world as a divine archetype, her botanical knowledge is apparent throughout a text so intricately concerned with plant life, and illustrated with careful line drawings of each specimen.[186]

To overlook the conjunction of botanical and theological detail in Rossetti's floral essays in *Called to Be Saints* is to ignore her innovative reading of the participatory convergence of grace and nature. As she argued in her essay on the fern in her entry on 'St Michael and All Angels', the observer requires a way of seeing beyond 'conscious experience' in order to truly see not only 'invisible' things like angels, but also the life of the plant in all its detail and quietude.[187] The unitive and communal relationship Rossetti develops in her discussion of the fern is based on both 'angelic fellowship' and the inter-mutual growth of plant life.[188] While angels encourage a 'love and service of our brethren', she wrote, the 'numberless variations of form and tint' in one fern enable an incorporative perceptual experience, one Rossetti attempted to put into practice in her meticulous account of bracken and maidenhair.[189] She refused to 'describe' ferns 'by generalities', and recognized in them a multiplicity of colours and textures, 'pale, deep, olive-like, glaucous', their foliage 'frosted' with silver and gold and 'glossily smooth, or in a way hairy', between a 'delicacy of thinness, a thick opaque leatheriness, and an absolute rigidity'.[190] She was also fascinated by the haptic semblance of the fern's roots, 'fibrous', 'downy or velvety', and able to spread everywhere without 'structure' or 'habit', as its spores 'congregate' on the leaves 'in dots, stripes, irregular patches, or even as a general coating'. As its looped ends wave like the end of a bishop's staff or 'crozier', Rossetti observed them twist back into the fabric of creation:

> But what an almost infinite variety meets us in the contours of this world of foliage. Leaves ribbon-like, smooth, pendent; stately groups, intricately cut and combined into the form of a crown; airy feathers; young tips curling like a bishop's crozier; dwarf forests of vigorous waving verdure; leaves notched and notched again, twisted, ramified, of a hundred outlines, of a hundred curves, veined in diverse patterns, indefinitely varied.[191]

The attentiveness of this passage is indicative of an observer who is absorbed in the intricate connections, not just between things, but in things. She perceived the elaborately woven fabric of the fern as at once internally entangled and also like the form of the feather, an object related to the fern, she wrote, through its 'learned name Pteris, derived from the Greek "wing" or "feather"'. On cutting the fern's stalk on a slant to reveal its secret inner workings, she reports that the markings inside 'resemble the figure of the imperial spread eagle', sparking 'a thought of wings' that brings her back to 'angels unaware'.[192] Even the 'black and glossy' threads of the fern's stalk 'resemble human hair', a connection that revealed a created likeness and equality between plants and humans.

Rossetti used the forum of *Called to Be Saints* to suggest that the reader can be gathered into the saintliness that awaits all of creation by habitually attending to the specificity of plant life. In her reading of St Thomas, Apostle, for example, she disclosed grace not through hagiographic detail, but through the make-up of 'each individual leaf' of the ivy—curved, peaked, rounded, notched, tapered, rugged, woody, and fringed.[193] Examining holly, she recorded both its 'white and waxy efflorescence' and 'evergreen foliage', and also its connection to the 'holy-tree', its 'leaf the flourishing of hope' and ideal for the 'adornment of churches'.[194] Rossetti was most attentive to weeds, the 'commonest of the common', but often providing food for humans and birds, and marked by an inherent beauty. Chickweed, she wrote, 'flourishes on pink stems', with a 'minute' star-shaped blossom 'formed of five deeply cleft petals set in a five-leafed calyx'.[195] Even when a species is symbolically inscribed, such as 'Our Lady of February', also known as the snowdrop, Rossetti remained precise in her portrait of its bowing stalk, paired leaves, straight-lined veins, and 'bell-shaped flower' in which are 'lodged six fruitful stamens'.[196] Through this detail, she connected the specifics of local flora to Christian typology in order to argue for the embeddedness of all forms and geographies of life in one creation. Writing about mistletoe, for example, Rossetti makes a connection between its English flourishing on apple trees and the Song of Solomon 2. 3, 'As the apple tree among the trees of the wood, so is my Beloved among the sons'.[197] In the interface between the English apple tree and a text that associates the dialogue of lovers with countless beings, from henna blossoms, roses, vines, lilies, brambles, cedars, pomegranates, saffron, myrrh, firs and figs, to roes, foxes, doves, sheep, mountains, fire, and silver, Rossetti affirmed the relational ecology of the created world. God's 'handiwork', she wrote in another essay on the yellow iris, does not demote botanical detail below a theocentric understanding of the world. Rather the nature of creation as a process, or 'procession' as she called it in ' "All thy works" ', reveals an ongoing ethics of interdependence moved by both the physical universe and its metaphysical maker.[198]

While the labyrinthine phytotomy of the plant mapped the integrative structure of the divine body for Rossetti, it also embodied a devotional way of being that was non-cognitive, non-ideational, and non-instrumental. Like angels, the phenomenology of plants was hidden to the human observer, but, with Aquinas, she considered the nutritive, vegetal soul to be capable of instinctual and rational love.[199] Rossetti even compared the process of writing devotionally to the surfacing and unearthing of a 'sensitive plant', and in doing so echoed Pusey's observation that the reception of grace was an 'engrafting' of the Christian 'into Christ'.[200] But she also took seriously the scriptural plant language used to envision Jesus as a 'true vine' and God as his vine-grower: 'Every branch in me that beareth not fruit he taketh away: and every *branch* that beareth fruit, he purgeth it, that it may bring forth more fruit' (John 15. 1–2). Co-constitutional with its environment, the plant is both emptied of ego but also interdependent on everything around it, a kenōtic and Christ-like model of living consonant with Rossetti's sea-anemone. As Plato argued, the 'constitution' of 'trees, plants, and seeds' was 'akin' to the human, even if all are different in 'appearance and awareness'.[201] Chapter 1's reading of 'The Trees' Counselling' confirms Rossetti's love of the vegetal as a pastoral being that evolves with the human as a guide or watcher. She developed the same idea in 'A Dumb Friend' (1863), wherein the narrator recalls a childhood memory of planting a 'green and living tree' that transforms into an evergreen. As the tree grows, it engages affectionately with its environment, secure in a 'stately grace' in which it peacefully ages:

> Wagging its round green head with stately grace
>   In tender winds that kiss it and go by:
>   It shows a green full age; and what show I?
>   A faded wrinkled face.   (ll. 13–16)

A 'faithful pleasant friend' to the narrator, the tree connects her with the world (l. 21). Through it, she hears the robin tune 'his silver tongue' in its branches, witnesses the flowers grow around it, and, from her window, shares with it 'all my secrets wise' (ll. 4, 20). This reciprocal relationship between narrator and tree extends into the final stanza's funereal allusion to the evergreen shade of the cypress. As a classical symbol of mourning and also the material from which many thought the ark had been built, the cypress invokes both life and death for the narrator, and so embodies a self-abandoning or kenōtic experience of both visible and invisible reality.

The 'growing green' of the world, Rossetti wrote in a later poem called 'Easter Monday' (1864), is dependent on such weakness, the life of plants hidden and dependent, even as they disclose vitality in their flowers and buds (l. 1). This efflorescent movement that accompanies the appearance of fruits and flowers, and their temporal self-transfiguration as they evolve from stem to leaf to bud, suggested to Rossetti the same gradual and patient being Jesus argues for in the Sermon on the Mount. She explored this beingness in 'Herself a rose, who bore the Rose', in which the relationship between Mary and Jesus is used to reflect on the distinctions between plant species, gender, and the human and nonhuman. The poem draws on the idea of the *Rosa Mystica*, a title for Mary in Catholic Marian devotion in which Mary is blessed as a mediator between her son and creation and the route through which grace passes into the world. But Rossetti also portrays Mary and Jesus as plants entangled with the elements of creation: she is a 'star' and 'rill' to his 'sun' and 'Fountain' (ll. 9–12). As his mother, Mary creates Jesus, but as a reflection of him, she is made over in his likeness, the two figures eternally mirroring each other to produce a sense of mutualism and interrelation:

> Christ's mirror she of grace and love,
>> Of beauty and of life and death:
>> By hope and love and faith
> Transfigured to His Likeness, 'Dove,
>>> Spouse, Sister, Mother,' Jesus saith.   (ll. 16–20)

Through Jesus, Mary incorporates all things within her, blurring distinctions between nonhuman and human all of whom are graced through her. Her transfiguration in Jesus reveals that she looks like her son not only because all things bear the imprint of God, but because she, like him, contains multiple identities and beings—a bird, a woman, a sister, the mother of God. As a rose that bears a rose, she also shares her vegetal being with him, both able to empty their human egos into the connective and networking interdependence of plant communities.

Plants, like animals, offered Rossetti a kenōtic way of being in which things are animated not by ego, but by an interconnective spirit that places grace and nature forever in communion. But her poetry registered the challenge as much as the joy of emptying the self of ego to enter into the multiple unity of creation. The narrator of 'An Old-World Thicket', for example, also included in the 1881 *Pageant* volume, is bewildered by the 'ingathering' of creation, one she perceives to be shaped by 'wrath and gloom' (ll. 79–80). For while the poem bears the hallmarks of many of her ecotheological poems—birds speak 'more wisdom' than the narrator, the trees shiver with 'compassion'—it is also an apocalyptic poem in which hell threatens the transformation of the created world (ll. 18, 135). The poem is introduced with an epigraph from Dante's *Inferno*, 'Una selva oscura', situating her reader in Dante's disorienting and darkly wooded maze in which creation appears bound together, but mechanistically so in the misery of grace-less solidarity. The wall of trees the narrator of 'An Old-World Thicket' first encounters, for example, aspens, sycamores, elms, ivy, and pines, is haunted by preternatural birds that glow like 'spots of azure' and 'actual coals on fire' (ll. 12–14). While they move in a chimerical and surreal collective, the birds have no specificity, 'Like anything they seemed, and everything', the narrator declares, as she watches them dance in an eerily silent landscape (l. 15). As the hallucinations of a narrator 'overdone with utter weariness', the opening scenes collapse into a world that feels too abundant and full: 'Sweetness of beauty moved me to despair, | Stung me to anger by its mere content' (ll. 37, 46–7). This abundance postpones fulfilment because it is driven by a logic of desire that in fact creates scarcity: this human rapacity for resources creates their shortage, wounding an environment that is supposed to be shared.[202] As Rossetti's narrator declares, her vision resonates with weeping and sobbing, a 'universal sound of lamentation' (l. 71) that echoes the cries of Paul's creation that 'groaneth and travaileth in pain' (Romans 8. 22).

Only when the narrator looks up and sees the sun 'stooped to earth, in slow | Warm dying loveliness brought near and low' does her vision turn from one of despair into anticipation of apocalyptic

transformation (ll. 149–50). Rossetti depends on her reader's familiarity with Revelation as a book that plays on the number seven (seven
years of judgement, seven attributes of the Lamb, seven churches,
seven angels, seven lamps, and so on) to unfold an apocalyptic narrative in the last seven stanzas of her poem. As the sun and moon set,
creation is overcast by 'purple shadows' (l. 153) that conjure Revelation's Babylon, the 'Mother of Harlots and Abominations of the
Earth' (17. 5). It is as if Babylon pours her golden cup into the
landscape of Rossetti's poem, as the birds, trees, and nests become
suddenly aureated (l. 161). This moment of paralysis in the poem,
wherein birds are 'unfledged' and 'gilded' with gold, is suddenly
transformed into joy and kinship in the final three stanzas (ll. 163,
165). Here creation is gathered in a peaceful journey 'homeward', led
by a 'patriarchal ram' that leads 'all his kin' from this old thicket into
the New Jerusalem (ll. 169, 171–2). Those that follow the ram are
lambs, symbols of this renewal that 'frolic' (l. 174) cheerfully and as one:

> Journeying together toward the sunlit west;
> Mild face by face, and woolly breast by breast,
>   Patient, sun-brightened too,
> Still journeying toward the sunset and their rest.   (ll. 177–80)

This warm, sunny, and peaceful pilgrimage towards the 'sunset'
redeems the bleak mirage of the earlier narrative through forgiveness
and participatory grace. As Elizabeth Ludlow notes, the poem is one
of several prodigal poems Rossetti wrote to explore the 'painful
process of repentance', one that always leads to renewal in relationship with God in her work.[203] For the hellish inferno through which
Rossetti's narrator struggles is a creation destroyed, not by God, but
by anthropocentric offences only corrected through the practice of
repentance and work of grace.

'An Old-World Thicket' can be read as a poem about the fragility of
life, not least in an age of climatic ruination, one that leaves the reader
'stunned and horrified by her or his own mortality'.[204] But such an
interpretation is dependent on a dispirited understanding of the quest
Rossetti maps in her poem as bound by a linear reading of time
incompatible with an Anglo-Catholic conception of the afterlife.
Rossetti was forced to confront death in a series of distressing and
quite frightening departures in her later life, starting in November

1876 with her sister Maria, who suffered what a fellow sister at All Saints called a 'very suffering death'.[205] She retreated from social engagements, and was forced to care for both her mother, who was profoundly affected by the bereavement, and also Gabriel, by this point gravely ill, and who also died six years later in April 1882. When her mother died in 1886, Rossetti wrote, 'I have been grieved before but never so desolate as now', and the last years of her life are marked by a slight shift in her theological focus on a created world held together in grace that anticipates the new creation to the transformation of this world by grace at the end of time.[206] Yet, as the final chapter suggests, Rossetti never looked beyond her immediate environment to another idealized future time, but rather invested in an apocalypse in which this world would be radically renewed as the new creation born again through grace. Like the woolly lambs that are 'Still journeying' in 'An Old-World Thicket', creation needed to prepare itself for a crossing from the old world into the New Jerusalem, and have faith that what it found there would be 'sun-brightened' and joyful.

Notes

1. Christina G. Rossetti to Frederick Startridge Ellis, 6 July 1870, in Anthony H. Harrison, ed., *The Letters of Christina Rossetti: Volume 1 1843–1873*; *Volume II 1874–1881*; *Volume III 1882–1886*; *Volume IV 1887–1894* (Charlottesville and London: The University Press of Virginia, 1997, 1999, 2000, 2004), I, 358; further references are abbreviated to *Letters*. Ellis eventually withdrew his support, and *Sing-Song* was published by Routledge in 1872.
2. Christina G. Rossetti to Dante Gabriel Rossetti, 17 September 1878, *Letters*, II, 186.
3. Constance Hassett, *Christina Rossetti: The Patience of Style* (Charlottesville and London: University of Virginia Press, 2005), 124.
4. Christina G. Rossetti to Caroline Gemmer, 26 January 1875, *Letters*, II, 40; and see Elizabeth A. Johnson, *She Who Is: The Mystery of God in Feminist Theological Discourse* (New York: Crossroad Publishing, 1992).
5. Christina G. Rossetti to William Michael Rossetti, 25 January 1850, *Letters*, I, 34.
6. 'I dug and dug amongst the snow', ll. 5–6; 'O wind, why do you never rest', l. 2; 'O wind, where have you been'; 'January cold desolate', ll. 3–4; 'If hope grew on a bush'; 'The wind has such a rainy sound', l. 8; 'Playing at bob cherry', ll. 11–12; 'I have a little husband'.

7. Hassett, *Rossetti*, 121.

8. Christina G. Rossetti, *Seek and Find: A Double Series of Short Studies on the Benedicite* (London: Society for Promoting Christian Knowledge, 1879), 273.

9. Ibid. 326.

10. William Sharp, *Papers Critical and Reminiscent*, ed. Elizabeth Sharp (London: William Heinemann, 1912), 68, 70.

11. On gardens, see Dinah Roe, 'Naturally Artificial: The Pre-Raphaelite Garden Enclosed', unpublished essay (2017).

12. Christina G. Rossetti to William Michael Rossetti, 17 September 1845, *Letters*, I, 4, and 30 July 1852, *Letters*, I, 57; Christina G. Rossetti to Amelia Barnard Heimann, 14 July 1871, *Letters*, I, 372, and November 1865, *Letters*, I, 259; Christina G. Rossetti to Dante Gabriel Rossetti, 23 December 1864, *Letters*, I, 208.

13. Christina G. Rossetti to Amelia Barnard Heimann, 9 August 1868, *Letters*, I, 313.

14. Jan Marsh, *Christina Rossetti: A Literary Biography* (London: Pimlico, 1995), 6.

15. See, for example, Cyril of Alexandria, 'Third Epistle to Nestorius', in Bryan D. Spinks, *Do This in Remembrance of Me: The Eucharist from the Early Church to the Present Day* (London: SCM Press, 2013), 116.

16. Christina G. Rossetti to Frederick Shields, 24 October 1881, *Letters*, II, 307.

17. See Diane D'Amico and David A. Kent, 'Christina Rossetti's Notes on Genesis and Exodus', *The Journal of Pre-Raphaelite Studies*, 13 (2004), 49–98 (51).

18. Christina G. Rossetti to Anne Burrows Gilchrist, Autumn 1865, *Letters*, I, 254.

19. Christina G. Rossetti, *Time Flies: A Reading Diary* (London: Society for Promoting Christian Knowledge, 1885), 168–9.

20. S. T. Coleridge, *Biographia Literaria* (1815–17), in H. J. Jackson, ed., *The Major Works* (Oxford: Oxford University Press, 2008), 313.

21. See William Michael Rossetti, 'Animal-Design and Landscape: Aspects of their Contemporary Treatment', *Macmillan's Magazine*, 8 (May–October 1863), 116–23.

22. Alison Chapman and Joanna Meacock, *A Rossetti Family Chronology* (New York: Palgrave Macmillan, 2007), 398.

23. Giorgio Agamben, *The Highest Poverty: Monastic Rules and Form-of-Life*, trans. Adam Kotsko (Stanford: Stanford University Press, 2013), 111 ff.

24. Francis of Assisi, 'The Second Version of the Letter to the Faithful', in Regis J. Armstrong and Ignatius C. Brady, trans., *Francis and Clare: The Complete Works* (Mahwah, NJ: Paulist Press, 1982), 66–76 (71); and 'The Canticle of Brother Sun', ibid. 37–9.

25. Bonaventure, *Commentaria in Quatuor Libros Sententiarum Magistri Petri Lombardi*, quoted in Timothy J. Johnson, 'Francis and Creation', in

Michael J. P. Robson, ed., *The Cambridge Companion to Francis of Assisi* (Cambridge: Cambridge University Press, 2012), 143–58 (152).

26. John Hart, *Sacramental Commons: Christian Ecological Ethics* (Lanham: Rowman & Littlefield, 2006), 23.

27. Beverly Seaton, *The Language of Flowers: A History* (Charlottesville and London: University Press of Virginia, 1995), 14; Dominic Janes, '"The Catholic Florist": Flowers and Deviance in the Mid-Nineteenth-Century Church of England', *Visual Culture in Britain*, 12.1 (2011), 77–96 (78). On flower missions see 'Flower Services in Churches', *The Garden* 2 (June 1877), 463–4; Constance O'Brien, 'History of a Flower Mission', *The Garden*, 10 (March 1877), 199–203; and F. S. Stowell, 'Flower Missions and Their Work', *Demorest's Magazine*, 18 (August 1892), 381–9.

28. William J. E. Bennett, *The Principles of the Book of Common Prayer Considered: A Series of Lecture Sermons* (1845; London: W. J. Cleaver, 1848), 188, 230, 302.

29. Gisela Hönnighausen, 'Emblematic Tendencies in the Works of Christina Rossetti', *Victorian Poetry*, 10.1 (1972), 1–15 (15); Marsh, *Rossetti*, 451.

30. See Donna Haraway, *The Companion Species Manifesto: Dogs, People, and Significant Otherness* (Chicago: Prickly Paradigm Press, 2003).

31. William Michael Rossetti, *Some Reminiscences of William Michael Rossetti*, 2 vols (New York: Charles Scribner's, 1906), I, 5; William Michael Rossetti, ed., *The Poetical Works of Christina Georgina Rossetti, with Memoir and Notes* (London: Macmillan, 1904), p. ix.

32. William Sharp, *Papers Critical and Reminiscent* (London: William Heinemann, 1912), 75; Mackenzie Bell, *Christina Rossetti: A Biographical and Critical Study* (Boston: Roberts Brothers, 1989), 30.

33. Ibid. 43.

34. Elisabeth Cary, *The Rossettis: Dante Gabriel and Christina* (New York and London: G. P. Putnam's, 1900), 15–16; Thomas Burnett Swann, *Wonder and Whimsy: The Fantastic World of Christina Rossetti* (Francestown, NH: Marshall Jones, 1960), 32.

35. See, for example, Kathryn Burlinson, '"Frogs and Fat Toads": Christina Rossetti and the Significance of the Nonhuman', in Mary Arseneau, Antony H. Harrison, and Lorraine Janzen Kooistra, eds., *The Culture of Christina Rossetti: Female Poetics and Victorian Contexts* (Athens: Ohio University Press, 1999), 170–93 (177); Edward Bouverie Pusey, *The Presence of Christ in the Holy Eucharist: A Sermon, Preached before the University, in the Cathedral Church of Christ, in Oxford, on the Second Sunday after Epiphany, 1853* (Oxford and London: John Henry Parker, 1853), 21–2.

36. Theodore Watts-Dunton, 'Reminiscences of Christina Rossetti', *The Nineteenth Century: A Monthly Review*, 37.216 (February 1895), 355–66 (362–3).

37. Rossetti, *Time Flies*, 36.

38. Ibid. 62.

39. Ibid. 203.
40. Ibid.
41. 'Contemptuous of his home beyond', ibid. 129–30; published in Rossetti, ed., *Poetical Works*, 414–15.
42. Rossetti, *Time Flies*, 53, 174, 184, 170, 207.
43. Ibid. 148–9.
44. Ibid. 204–5.
45. Ibid. 198.
46. Christina G. Rossetti to Anne Burrows Gilchrist, Autumn 1865, *Letters*, I, 254; Rossetti's itinerary included numerous Italian towns, Pavia, Brescia, Verona, Lecco, as well as Paris, Basle, Freiberg, and Strasburg; see Rossetti, *Time Flies*, 113–14.
47. Christina G. Rossetti to Anne Burrows Gilchrist, 14 June 1866, *Letters*, I, 275; Christina G. Rossetti to Alice Boyd, 8 May 1870, *Letters*, I, 353; Christina G. Rossetti to Sophia May Eckley, 2 August 1869, *Letters*, I, 328.
48. Christina G. Rossetti to Lucy Madox Brown, August 1867, *Letters*, I, 301.
49. Catherine Keller, *Cloud of the Impossible: Negative Theology and Planetary Entanglement* (New York: Columbia University Press, 2014), 132.
50. Ibid. 132; Werner Heisenberg, in Paul Davies, *God and the New Physics* (New York: Simon and Schuster, 1983), 112.
51. Rossetti, *Seek and Find*, 260.
52. Keller, *Cloud*, 143, 145.
53. William Michael Rossetti, *Rossetti Papers 1862–1870* (London: Sands and Co., 1903), 120.
54. Andre Vauchez, *Francis of Assisi: The Life and Afterlife of a Medieval Saint*, trans. Michael F. Cusato (New Haven and London: Yale University Press, 2012), 233.
55. Dante Alighieri, *The Divine Comedy 3: Paradiso*, trans. Robin Kirkpatrick (London: Penguin, 2007), canto XI, 49, canto XXXII, 90; Maria Francesca Rossetti, *A Shadow of Dante: Being an Essay Towards Studying Himself, His World and His Pilgrimage* (London, Oxford, and Cambridge: Rivingtons, 1871), 232, 205.
56. Odette Bornard, ed., *The Diary of W. M. Rossetti 1870–73* (Oxford: Oxford University Press, 1977), 75; Christina G. Rossetti to Amelia Barnard Heimann, 16 August 1871, *Letters*, I, 377.
57. William Holman Hunt, *Pre-Raphaelitism and the Pre-Raphaelite Brotherhood*, 2 vols (London: Macmillan and Co., 1905), I, 488; Sr. M. Catherine Frederic, 'The Franciscan Spirit as Revealed in the Literary Contributions of Francis Thompson', *Franciscan Studies*, 11.1 (1951), 21–39.
58. John Henry Newman, 'Tract 75: On the Roman Breviary as Embodying the Substance of the Devotional Services of the Church Catholic' (1836), in *Tracts for the Times by Members of the University of Oxford*, 6 vols (London: J. G. F. and J. Rivington; Oxford: J. H. Parker, 1840), III, 9.
59. Anon., 'Dr. Newman's Religious Autobiography', *The Saturday Review of Politics, Literature, Science and Art* (25 June 1864), 785–7 (786); Richard

Frederick Littledale, 'The Professional Studies of the English Clergy', *The Contemporary Review* (April 1879), 1–36 (31).

60. See Vauchez, *Francis of Assisi*, 234; John R. H. Moorman, *The Sources for the Life of S. Francis of Assisi* (Manchester: Manchester University Press, 1940), 8–9; Gareth Atkins, ed., *Making and Remaking Saints in Nineteenth Century Britain* (Manchester: Manchester University Press, 2016).

61. See Christina G. Rossetti to Anne Burrows Gilchrist, 21 December 1864, *Letters* I, 208; in Fiona MacCarthy, *The Last Pre-Raphaelite: Edward Burne-Jones and the Victorian Imagination* (Cambridge, MA: Harvard University Press, 2012), 24, 233.

62. R. J. Armstrong, J. A. W. Hellman, and W. J. Short, eds., *Francis of Assisi: Early Documents*, 4 vols (New York: New City Press, 1999–2002), quoted in Johnson, 'Francis and Creation', 145.

63. Anna Jameson, *Legends of the Monastic Orders* (London: Longman, Brown, Green, and Longmans, 1852), 261; Mrs Oliphant, *Francis of Assisi* (London: Macmillan, 1882), 122, 128.

64. Johnson, 'Francis and Creation', 147–50; Michael Robson, *St Francis of Assisi: The Legend and the Life* (London and New York: Continuum, 1997), 241–3; Vauchez, *Francis*, 276.

65. Christina G. Rossetti, *Annus Domini: A Prayer for Each Day of the Year, Founded on a Text of Holy Scripture* (Oxford and London: James Parker, 1874), 58.

66. Ibid. 95.

67. Ibid. 98, 101.

68. Ibid. 321; GNIPE, 'Splendid Aliens', *The Speaker: The Liberal Review*, 15.372 (17 November 1906), 211.

69. In a section devoted to the Passion, Rossetti's 'Good Friday' is preceded by Archer Gurney's 'Good Friday', which invokes the *Stabat Mater Dolorosa*, in fact composed by the Franciscan Jacopone da Todi; see also Elizabeth Ludlow, *Christina Rossetti and the Bible: Waiting with the Saints* (New York and London: Bloomsbury, 2014), 110.

70. Orby Shipley, ed., *Lyra Messianica: Hymns and Verses on the Life of Christ, Ancient and Modern* (London: Longman, Green, Longman, Roberts, and Green, 1864), 236–7; the other 'Lyra' volumes, printed with the same publisher, are *Lyra Eucharistica: Hymns and Verses on the Holy Communion* (1863) and *Lyra Mystica: Hymns and Verses on Sacred Subjects, Ancient and Modern* (1865).

71. Rossetti, *Annus Domini*, 107.

72. Christina G. Rossetti, 'Notes on Genesis and Exodus', reprinted in D'Amico and Kent, 'Notes', 73.

73. Rossetti, *Time Flies*, 163–4.

74. Ibid. 165.

75. Ibid. 163, 165; see the chapter on 'Nests' in Gaston Bachelard, *The Poetics of Space*, trans. Maria Jolas (Boston: Beacon Press, 1994), 90–104.

76. Rossetti, 'Genesis and Exodus', 75; Rossetti, *Seek and Find*, 84–5.

77. Rossetti, 'Genesis and Exodus', 73–5.

78. Christina G. Rossetti to Amelia Barnard Heimann, 29 August 1872, *Letters*, I, 402; 'Brother Bruin' appeared in Christina G. Rossetti, *Poems* (Boston: Roberts Brothers, 1888).

79. Rossetti, *Reminiscences*, I, 185.

80. Rossetti, *Time Flies*, 62.

81. See Todd O. Williams, 'Environmental Ethics in Christina Rossetti's *Time Flies*', *Prose Studies: History, Theory, Criticism*, 33.3 (2011), 217–29 (223).

82. Christina G. Rossetti to Amelia Barnard Heiman, 29 August 1872, *Letters*, I, 402.

83. John Ruskin, from a report of a meeting on vivisection, 9 December 1884, in E. T. Cook and Alexander Wedderburn, eds., *The Works of John Ruskin*, 39 vols (London: George Allen, 1903–12), XXXIV, 643.

84. John Henry Newman, 'Sermon X: The Crucifixion' (1842), in *Parochial and Plain Sermons in Eight Volumes* (London, Oxford, and Cambridge: Rivingtons, 1875), VII, 136.

85. Henry Edward Manning, Speech, 21 June 1882, in Robert H. Perks, *Why I Condemn Vivisection* (Paignton: The Order of the Golden Age, 1905), 18.

86. Basil Wilberforce, Speech, 9 May 1899, ibid.; and 'Paradise', in *Sermons Preached in Westminster Abbey* (London: Elliot Stock, 1898), 158.

87. J. B. Atlay, *Sir Henry Wentworth Acland, Bart. K.C.B., F. R. S. Regius Professor of Medicine in the University of Oxford: A Memoir* (London: Smith, Elder and Co., 1903), 426–7.

88. Edward King, 'Who is my Neighbour?' (1883), in B. W. Randolph, ed., *The Love and Wisdom of God: Being a Collection of Sermons by Edward King* (London: Longmans, Green and Co., 1910), 108; Henry Parry Liddon, 'The Work of the Holy Spirit' (1890), *Sermons by H. P. Liddon* (New York: Thomas Whittaker, 1891), 79.

89. Henry William Burrows, 'The Intensity of the Divine Nature', in *Lenten and Other Sermons* (London: William Wells Gardner, 1880), 159–67; Elizabeth Wordsworth, *Henry William Burrows: Memorials* (London: Kegan Paul, Trench, Trübner, and Co., 1894), 154.

90. Christina G. Rossetti to William Michael Rossetti, 25 October 1861, *Letters*, I, 151.

91. Christina G. Rossetti to Dante Gabriel Rossetti, 30 August 1875, *Letters*, II, 56.

92. Christina G. Rossetti to Dante Gabriel Rossetti, 10 September 1875, *Letters*, II, 56.

93. Christina G. Rossetti to Violet Hunt, February 1884, *Letters*, III, 178; Christina G. Rossetti to Frederic James Shields, 15 September 1889, *Letters*, IV, 159.

94. Christina G. Rossetti to Edmund McClure, 24 October 1893, *Letters*, IV, 352, and 21 March 1894, *Letters*, IV, 373.

95. The undated 'A Word for the Dumb' was first published in Christina G. Rossetti, *New Poems, Hitherto Unpublished or Uncollected*, ed. William Michael Rossetti (London and New York: Macmillan and Co., 1896);

Christina G. Rossetti to Mary Minto Ruxton, October 1886, *Letters*,
III, 342–3; Christina G. Rossetti to Amelia Barnard Heimann,
27 April 1883, *Letters*, III, 113; Christina G. Rossetti to Dante Gabriel
Rossetti, January 1879, *Letters*, II, 196.

96. Chapman and Meacock, *Family Chronology*, 44, 97; Christina G. Rossetti
to Amelia Barnard Heimann, 13 July 1853, *Letters*, I, 72.
97. Rossetti, *Reminiscences*, II, 539.
98. Christina G. Rossetti to Amelia Barnard Heimann, 17 May 1867, *Letters*,
I, 293; *Animal World: An Advocate of Humanity*, 10 (1879), 178.
99. Christina G. Rossetti to William Michael Rossetti, 25 August 1849,
Letters, I, 18.
100. Christina G. Rossetti to Lady Pauline Trevelyan, 3 July 1858, *Letters*, I, 118;
Christina G. Rossetti to Letitia Norquoy Scott, 24 June 1858, *Letters*, I, 116;
Christina G. Rossetti to George Gordon Hake, 27 April 1876, *Letters*, II, 86.
101. Christina G. Rossetti to Dante Gabriel Rossetti, 3 January 1876, *Letters*,
II, 78, and 18 July 1873, *Letters*, I, 435 n. 1.
102. Christina G. Rossetti to George Gordon Hake, October 1874, *Letters*, II,
27, and 27 April 1876, *Letters*, II, 86.
103. Christina G. Rossetti to Dizzy, 26 February 1876, *Letters*, II, 83.
104. Christina G. Rossetti to George Gordon Hake, 25 May 1876, *Letters*, II,
87; and April 1876, *Letters*, II, 85.
105. Haraway, *Companion Species*, 9.
106. Chapman and Meacock, *Family Chronology*, 123; Gilbert White, *The
Natural History and Antiquities of Selborne* (1789; London: Penguin, 1987),
letter xxxv, 196; Edward Bouverie Pusey, 'Tract 67: Scriptural Views of
Holy Baptism' (1835), in *Tracts for the Times*, II, 389–90.
107. Marsh, *Rossetti*, 443; Christina G. Rossetti to William Michael Rossetti,
21 July 1879, *Letters*, II, 204.
108. Christina G. Rossetti to Amelia Barnard Heimann, 15 August 1859,
Letters, I, 125; Christina G. Rossetti to Caroline Maria Gemmer, 5
December 1872, *Letters*, I, 415.
109. Christina G. Rossetti to William Michael Rossetti, 18 August 1858,
Letters, I, 120.
110. Frances Mary Lavinia Polidori, *Commonplace Book*, quoted by kind permission of the Angeli-Dennis Collection, University of British Columbia
Special Collections Division, Box 12–87, from facsimile in Bodleian
Libraries, Oxford, MS Facs.d.286; *The Mirror of Literature, Amusement,
and Instruction*, 20.574 (3 November 1832).
111. E. T. Cook, *The Life of John Ruskin*, 2 vols (1911; New York: Haskell
House, 1968), I, 501.
112. Rossetti, ed., *Rossetti Papers 1862–1870*, 222–3.
113. Rossetti, *Annus Domini*, 169.
114. Chapman and Meacock, *Family Chronology*, 222.
115. Christina G. Rossetti to Amelia Barnard Heimann, 20 July 1864, *Letters*,
I, 200.

116. Thomas à Kempis, *The Imitation of Christ* (Grand Rapids, MI: Christian Classics, 1940), 26, 91; Rossetti, *Seek and Find*, 113.

117. Christina G. Rossetti, *Letter and Spirit: Notes on the Commandments* (London: Society for Promoting Christian Knowledge, 1883), 130.

118. Ibid. 131.

119. Ibid. 131–2.

120. Rossetti, *Seek and Find*, 125, 113.

121. Thomas Nagel, 'What Is It Like to Be a Bat?' *The Philosophical Review*, 83.4 (1974), 435–50; Rossetti, *Seek and Find*, 36.

122. Ibid. 20, 22.

123. For example, Algernon Charles Swinburne, 'Mr Arnold's New Poems', *Fortnightly Review*, 2.10 (1867), 414–45 and William Sharp, 'The Rossettis', *Fortnightly Review*, 39.231 (1886), 414–29; John Coleridge, 'The Nineteenth-Century Defenders of Vivisection', *Fortnightly Review*, 38.182 (1882), 225–36 (236).

124. Ibid. 236.

125. Richard Bauckham, 'Reading the Sermon on the Mount in an Age of Ecological Catastrophe', *Studies in Christian Ethics*, 22.1 (2009), 76–88 (81).

126. Ibid. 83.

127. Christina G. Rossetti, *The Face of the Deep: A Devotional Commentary on the Apocalypse* (London: Society for Promoting Christian Knowledge, 1892), 474.

128. Rossetti, *Seek and Find*, 3; Christina G. Rossetti to the Reverend Charles Gutch, January 1879, *Letters*, II, 191–4, published as 'A Harmony on First Corinthians XIII', *New and Old*, 7 (January 1879), 34–9; Ludlow, *Rossetti*, 8.

129. Lynda Palazzo, *Christina Rossetti's Feminist Theology* (Basingstoke: Palgrave, 2002), 69.

130. Rossetti, *Seek and Find*, 177.

131. Palazzo, *Rossetti*, 71.

132. Rossetti, *Seek and Find*, 260.

133. Ibid. 287–8.

134. Ibid. 288.

135. Ibid. 15.

136. Christina G. Rossetti to Anne Burrows Gilchrist, December 1862, *Letters*, IV, 413; and see Alexander Gilchrist, 'Inventions to the Book of Job', in *The Life of William Blake* (London: John Lane, 1907), 301–10.

137. Rossetti, *Seek and Find*, 87, 89, 36–7.

138. Ibid. 34, 277.

139. Ibid. 114–15.

140. Ibid. 112.

141. Ibid. 115.

142. Ibid. 116.

143. Rossetti, *Time Flies*, 129.

144. Linda E. Marshall, 'Astronomy of the Invisible: Contexts for Christina Rossetti's Heavenly Parables', *Women's Writing*, 2.2 (1995), 167–81; Anna Henchman, 'Outer Space: Physical Science', in Matthew Bevis, ed., *The Oxford Handbook of Victorian Poetry* (Oxford: Oxford University Press, 2013), 690–708 (697).

145. Thomas Aquinas, *Summa Theologica* (Ohio: Benziger, 1947), 1492.

146. Rossetti, *Letter and Spirit*, 52.

147. See Michael Marder, *Plant-Thinking: A Philosophy of Vegetal Life* (New York: Columbia University Press, 2013).

148. Rossetti, *Seek and Find*, 261–2.

149. M. M. Mahood, *The Poet as Botanist* (Cambridge: Cambridge University Press, 2008), 3.

150. Rossetti, *Seek and Find*, 261.

151. See Sharon Ruston, *Shelley and Vitality* (Basingstoke: Palgrave, 2005).

152. Christina G. Rossetti to Alice Boyd, 7 July 1870, *Letters*, I, 358; Christina G. Rossetti to Amelia Barnard Heimann, 28 August 1882, *Letters*, III, 60; Christina G. Rossetti to William Michael Rossetti, 6 August 1883, *Letters*, III, 142.

153. Christina G. Rossetti to Olivia Narney Singleton, 11 May 1894, *Letters*, IV, 383; Edmund Gosse, *Critical Kit-Kats* (New York: Dodd, Mead and Co., 1896), 161; Christina G. Rossetti to William Michael Rossetti, 11 August 1875, *Letters* II, 51.

154. Christina G. Rossetti to Caroline Maria Gemmer, 3 March 1883, *Letters*, III, 103.

155. Christina G. Rossetti to Amelia Barnard Heimann, 20 July 1852, *Letters*, I, 54, and, 29 July 1852, *Letters*, I, 55.

156. Marsh, *Rossetti*, 2010.

157. Atlay, *Henry Wentworth*, 214.

158. See, for example, the extensive entry on 'Plants' in Pusey's first edition copy of *Encylopædia Britannica; or a Dictionary of Arts, Sciences and Miscellaneous Literature*, 3 vols (Edinburgh, 1768–71); and the card catalogue entry for Lancelot Andrewes' *The Devotions of Bishops Andrewes* (Oxford: John Henry Parker, 1846), which includes the line 'With Dr Pusey's dried flowers', both in Pusey House, Oxford.

159. C. A. Johns, *The Forest Trees of Britain*, 2 vols (London: Society for Promoting Christian Knowledge, 1869), I, p. ix; and see Bernard Lightman, *Victorian Popularizers of Science: Designing Nature for New Audiences* (Chicago and London: University of Chicago Press, 2007), 56.

160. George Henslow, *The Theory of Evolution of Living Things and the Application of the Principles of Evolution to Religion Considered as Illustrative of the 'Wisdom and Beneficence of the Almighty'* (London: Macmillan, 1873), pp. x–xi.

161. Richard Phillips, *The Young Botanists; in Thirteen Dialogues, with Twelve Coloured Engravings* (London: Richard Phillips, 1810); Peter Parley, *Tales About Plants, with Numerous Engravings* (London: Thomas Tegg, 1839);

John Lindley's *Elements of Botany: Structural, Physiological, Systematical, and Medical* (London: Bradbury and Evans, 1849); Carl Linnæus, *Systema Naturae per regna tria naturæ*, 3 vols (Lugduni: J. F. Gmelin and J. B. Delamolliere, 1789–96); John Hutton Balfour, *Phyto-theology; or, Botanical Sketches intended to illustrate the works of God in the structure, functions, and general distribution of plants* (London and Edinburgh: Johnstone and Hunter, 1851); Charles Kingsley, *Madam How and Lady Why; or, First Lessons in Earth Lore for Children* (London: Bell and Daldy, 1870); Margaret Plues, 'Botanical Rambles', *The Churchman's Shilling Magazine*, 2 (November 1867), 279–86. On the Rossettis' copies of these books, see the auction catalogues of T. G. Wharton, J. and L. M. Tregaskis, and Henry Sotheran and Co.

162. Phillips, *Young Botanists*, pp. iv–v, 59.

163. Ibid. 14, 48, 49.

164. Benedict Read, 'Was there Pre-Raphaelite Sculpture?', in Leslie Parris, ed., *Pre-Raphaelite Papers* (London: The Tate Gallery, 1984), 97–110.

165. Theresa M. Kelley, *Clandestine Marriage: Botany and Romantic Culture* (Baltimore: Johns Hopkins University Press, 2012), 1, 4.

166. Balfour, *Phyto-theology*, pp. x, 208.

167. John Keats to J. H. Reynolds, 19 February 1818, in Robert Gittings, ed., *Letters of John Keats* (Oxford: Oxford University Press, 1970), 65–7 (66).

168. Elizabeth Kent, *Flora Domestica, or The Portable Flower-Garden, with Directions for the Treatment of Plants in Pots, and Illustrations from the Works of the Poets* (London: Taylor and Hessey, 1823), pp. xxi–xxii, xxv; Christina G. Rossetti to William Michael Rossetti, 1 October 1874, *Letters*, II, 28.

169. Elaine P. Miller, *The Vegetal Soul: From Philosophy of Nature to Subjectivity in the Feminine* (New York: State University of New York Press, 2002), 186.

170. See Seaton, *Language of Flowers*; Rossetti also knew Elizabeth Steele Perkins's *Elements of Drawing and Flower Painting: In Opaque and Transparent Water-Colours* (London: Thomas Hurst, 1834), which she shared with Maria.

171. Henry Christmas, 'Of the Furniture and Ornaments of Churches', in James Cottle, ed., *Some Account of the Church of St Mary Magdalene, Taunton, and the Restoration Thereof: Together with Several Notices on Ecclesiastical Matters* (London: Vizetelly Brothers and Co., 1845), 119–28 (119).

172. Ibid. 120.

173. James F. White, *The Cambridge Movement: The Ecclesiologists and the Gothic Revival* (Cambridge: Cambridge University Press, 1962).

174. Janes, 'Catholic Florist', 83; William Pettit Griffith, *Architectural Botany; Setting Forth the Geometrical Distribution of Foliage, Flowers, Fruit, etc.* (London: Gilbert and Rivington, 1852).

175. Augustus Welby Pugin, *Floriated Ornament: A Series of Thirty-One Designs* (London: Henry G. Bohn 1849), 2.

176. Ibid. 3–5.

177. John Ruskin, *The Seven Lamps of Architecture* (1849), Cook and Wedderburn, eds., *Works*, VIII, 246, 102.

178. Stanley A. Shepherd, *The Stained Glass of A. W. N. Pugin* (Reading: Spire Books, 2009), 359; and see Henry William Burrows, *The Half-Century of Christ Church, Albany Street, St Pancras* (London: Skeffington & Son, 1887).

179. Frederick Oakeley, *The Catholic Florist: A Guide to the Cultivation of Flowers for the Altar* (London: Richardson, 1851).

180. Anon., 'The Western Luminary, June 2', *Christian Remembrancer*, 14 (1847), 113–23 (121), reprinted from *The Western Luminary*, 2 June 1847; Robert Liddell, *The Services and Furniture of St Paul's, Knightsbridge: A Letter to the…Bishop of London…in reply to a Protest from one of the Churchwardens* [C. Westerton] (London, 1854), 10; John Purchas, *'Directorium Anglicanum'; Being a Manual of Directions for the Right Celebration of the Holy Communion, for the Saying of Matins and Evensong, and for the Performance of other Rights and Ceremonies of the Church, According to the Ancient Uses of the Church of England* (London: Joseph Masters, 1858), 204–5.

181. Janes, 'Catholic Florist', 84; Agnes Lambert, 'The Ceremonial Use of Flowers: A Sequel', *The Nineteenth Century: A Monthly Review*, 7.39 (1880), 808–27 (815).

182. C. M. Jackson-Houlston, '"Queen Lilies"? The Interpretation of Scientific, Religious and Gender Discourses in Victorian Representations of Plants', *Journal of Victorian Culture*, 11.1 (2006), 84–110; and see also Ann B. Shteir, *Cultivating Women, Cultivating Science: Flora's Daughters and Botany in England 1760–1860* (Baltimore: Johns Hopkins University Press, 1996).

183. William Alexander Barrett, *Flowers and Festivals; or Directions for Floral Decoration of Churches* (London, Oxford, and Cambridge: Rivingtons, 1868), 5, 6, 13–14.

184. Christina G. Rossetti to Dante Gabriel Rossetti, October 1874, *Letters*, II, 25 and 26 n. 2; Christina G. Rossetti to Caroline Maria Gemmer, 3 March 1883, *Letters*, III, 103.

185. Christina G. Rossetti, *Called to Be Saints: The Minor Festivals Devotionally Studied* (London: Society for Promoting Christian Knowledge, 1881), p. xiii.

186. See Rossetti, *Letter and Spirit*, 13.

187. Rossetti, *Called to Be Saints*, 431.

188. Ibid. 436.

189. Ibid. 436, 446.

190. Ibid. 446–8.

191. Ibid. 448.

192. Ibid. 449.

193. Ibid. 43.

194. Ibid. 59–60.

195. Ibid. 107–8.

196. Ibid. 148–9.
197. Ibid. 90.
198. Ibid. 335.
199. Aquinas, *Summa Theologica*, 136, 271, 497; Thomas Petri, OP, *Aquinas and the Theology of the Body: The Thomistic Foundations of John Paul II's Anthropology* (Washington, DC: The Catholic University of America Press, 2016), 236 ff.
200. Pusey, 'Tract 67', 24; Christina G. Rossetti to Dante Gabriel Rossetti, 11 March 1865, *Letters*, I, 232.
201. Plato, *Timaeus and Ceritias*, trans. Robin Waterfield (Oxford: Oxford University Press, 2008), 78.
202. See Peter Larkin, *Wordsworth and Coleridge: Promising Losses* (New York: Palgrave Macmillan, 2012), 84 ff.
203. Ludlow, *Rossetti*, 156–7; see also Catherine Musello Cantalupo, 'Christina Rossetti: The Devotional Poet and the Rejection of Romantic Nature', in David A. Kent, ed., *The Achievement of Christina Rossetti* (Ithaca: Cornell University Press, 1987), 301–21.
204. Linda M. Lewis, *Elizabeth Barrett Browning's Spiritual Progress: Face to Face with God* (Columbia and London: University of Missouri Press, 1998), 232.
205. Susan Mumm, *All Saints Sisters of the Poor: An Anglican Sisterhood in the Nineteenth Century* (Woodbridge: Boydell, 2004), 32; Chapman and Meacock, *Family Chronology*, 287.
206. Christina G. Rossetti to Lady Georgiana Mount-Temple, 9 April 1886, *Letters*, III, 309.

4

Green Grace and the End of Time, 1885–1894

In the last decades of her life, Rossetti developed her ecological reading of grace into a loving eschatology in which she envisioned the apocalypse as reparative and restorative. The circumstances surrounding this deepening of her vision go beyond the deaths of so many close family members and friends into a period of grave ill health (she developed cancer in 1891, three years before her death), and a millennial meditation on the century's end. Her late writings, especially *Time Flies: A Reading Diary* (1885), *The Face of the Deep: A Devotional Commentary on the Apocalypse* (1892), and her popular cycle of poems, *Verses* (1893), are fixated on New Testament eschatology, and characterized by what she called a 'habit of attention' to the experience of its message.[1] The resonance of Revelation as a prophecy of destruction, mutation, and drought leading to a burnt-out world in which there is 'no more sea' (21. 1) was powerful for Rossetti, for whom the horrors of vivisection, poverty, and environmental collapse were immediate. But she read John's vision as a promise that God would enter into creation in order to renew it from within, not as a resigned acceptance of the end of the world. All that was required of creation was that it be prepared to become the new kingdom of God through a loving communion with itself. As the only species that considered the rest of creation subservient to it, the human threatened to break this communion, she wrote, by 'rehearsing and forestalling on a minor scale the last awful days', and in doing so delaying the joy and grace of the Second Advent.[2] By reimagining the teachings of Revelation in prose forms that combined poetry, scripture, journal entries, exegesis, and commentary, Rossetti sought to guide her reader back into a shared creation through which God could enter the world. In this new creation

God would pitch his tent 'with men' in a habitat that she described as both urban, 'for Londoners, for Parisians, for citizens of all cities', and organic, adorned with violets, snowdrops, lilies, honeysuckle, and thorns.[3] The city of God would not transcend materialism as either a fetishized and Edenic pastoral or a mechanized metropolis. Rather, Rossetti argued, God's kingdom was of earth, revealed as a New Jerusalem in which all things participate equally. Renewed and restored, the new creation, she wrote, would promote 'Absolute unanimity amongst all creatures', and evolve a 'love of kindred' for the 'whole human family' into an all-inclusive 'fellow-creaturely sympathy'.[4]

Rossetti rejected the idea of the end of time as a schism in which the saved were raptured into another time and space. For her the apocalypse opened creation to a new and expanded way of thinking and being driven through the indwelling of God in the whole of creation. She believed the process by which God re-enters the world to initiate it into new life was driven by grace: only 'by grace', she wrote, can human life 'expand' from its 'concentrated' being into a state of 'delighted welcome' of diverse and emergent others.[5] Like Aquinas, Rossetti understood grace as 'prevenient' because she believed it 'came before' creation and so brought something from nothing, generating the universe from its first outward rush, and then animating all beings and substances in it.[6] In its prevenient form, grace was both the deep from which all things are generated eternally without beginning or end, and also the expression of God's dynamic and perichoretic gathering of creation's diversity into his being. As Rossetti wrote in *The Face of the Deep*, the 'more we think over these diversities', the more 'we may discern something common underlying all that is individual', a grace that is regenerated by the interaction of the human, nonhuman, and divine.[7] But as the expression of a God who empties himself into his creation, grace also frees things of their subjective needs and desires to join them in love for each other, especially in moments of suffering ('For we know that the whole creation groaneth and travaileth in pain together', Romans 8. 22). In Rossetti's writing, this chapter suggests, grace becomes kenōtic and weak, the basis of a new kind of post-apocalyptic being integrated into the Trinity. Rossetti thus greens grace by identifying it as the dynamism by which all things are moved into interconnection with God and in which the old creation becomes the new.

This final chapter focuses on the relationship between this green grace and the end of time through Rossetti's later life exegesis of Revelation. It reveals Revelation as a text that, for Rossetti, unmasks the status quo to uncover and reveal a way of voicing a 'more excellent way' (1 Corinthians 12. 31) for the world that can be materially worked towards, rather than simply anticipated.[8] As she confirmed in *Seek and Find: A Double Series of Short Studies on the Benedicite* (1879), 'all things work together for good to them that love God'; grace is an equally shared gift that dissolves distinctions between created beings and outlaws the abusive logic of those things to which she was so opposed—cruelty, war, slavery, and vivisection.[9] Her vision in these late writings finds a visual analogy in William Blake's 'The Reunion of the Soul & the Body', engraved for an 1808 edition of Robert Blair's *The Grave* (1743), in which two bodies entwine against the backdrop of a burning cemetery. In *Time Flies*, Rossetti described the design as a rapturous reunion of 'the descending soul and the arising body rushing together in an indissoluble embrace', and compared it to a passage in *The Divine Comedy* that 'describes a company of the blessed yearning for the Resurrection'.[10] She used Charles Cayley's English translation of Dante to imagine the body 'rebuilding' itself after death in a process that renews 'beloved ties' across creation and restores its members in the New Jerusalem as saints.[11] As she wrote in 'All Saints', also published in *Time Flies*:

> As grains of sand, as stars, as drops of dew,
>   Numbered and treasured by the Almighty Hand,
>   The Saints triumphant throng that holy land
> Where all things and Jerusalem are new.   (ll. 1–4)

Rossetti privileges the nonhuman members of the Communion of Saints here as those who never wander from grace. As she warned throughout her writing, only the human was capable of experiencing itself as outside or cut off from grace, either willingly through unbelief, or reluctantly, considering particular actions too sinful to be forgiven. But for Rossetti, sin is always forgiven because of grace: every creature in its specificity and distinction is part of God's creation, his divine body, and so becomes 'perfect' in the new creation where all is renewed and 'rebuilt'.

The first section of this chapter examines the relationship between grace and baptism, that which Rossetti described as a 'primeval call of order and life out of chaos'.[12] As an Anglo-Catholic sacrament, baptism secures the transmission and reception of grace for all things through the element of water. In Rossetti's theology, the nonhuman is graced from the beginning of time through its closeness to oceans and rivers, rainfall and storms, and so exemplifies the experience of grace for the human. Rossetti's dependence on the sea in particular, as an image both of grace and medicinal restoration, is addressed in the second section through John's apocalyptic prediction that there will be 'no more sea' in the new creation. This line becomes a lens through which to discuss Rossetti's reading of the 'new' creation not as néos ('what was not there before'), but rather as kainós ('what is new and distinctive').[13] For Rossetti understood the phrase 'no more sea' to mean the disappearance of material distinctions and barriers between things in a newly restored and sustainable earth. She explored the covenant God made to sustain life in another aquatic image, the rainbow, one that appears not only in Genesis, but also in Revelation. The fragility of the rainbow is also a way of understanding the dissolution of linear time in the aeonic or cyclical eternity of the new creation. As the second section claims, Rossetti proposed cyclical time, repetition, and rhythm—manifest in nonhuman life, and in human-made art—to help her reader imagine the infinity that follows the end of time. The final section of the chapter, and of this book, argues that her ecological reading of Revelation is dependent on a theology of kenōsis and weakness, one in which the human and nonhuman are gentled into a preparatory anticipation of the Second Advent. With reference to both the Anglo-Catholic revival of kenōsis, and contemporary theories of weak thinking, Rossetti's eschatology addresses end things only in their renewal through tenderness, kindness, and love. The culmination of her life and vision is thus an explicit rejection of a strong, egoic thinking of the end of time through which apocalyptic fantasies of destruction and terror are replaced by a practical and hopeful fellowship between things moved into God by grace.

The 'grace of baptism'

Rossetti's radical reading of grace as an apocalyptic as well as loving energy is founded in her Anglo-Catholic reading of the term, one that did not obviously accord with conventional Protestant or Catholic definitions. Traditionally, Protestantism defended a view of grace as a cloak or covering of original sin that makes the believer acceptable or 'justified' before God. By faith alone (*sola fide*) can this one-time moment of being 'born again' (John 3. 3) be triggered through grace, and while good works can make humans holy, they do not add anything to their justification. In Catholicism, however, grace is received by the believer through the sacraments and participation in the life of God through the Church. Driven by faith and good works, grace cleanses the believer continually from within and so effects a 'little apocalypse': 'if any man be in Christ, he is a new creature: old things are passed away; behold, all things are become new' (2 Corinthians 5. 17). Open and free, rather than conferred on some and not others, grace reveals the world to any being that accepts it through 'the love of God, and the communion of the Holy Ghost' (2 Corinthians 13. 14). As Paul discovered on his way to Damascus, grace reconciles beings with God and allows them to see as he does, lovingly and inclusively, and through divine co-operation. Pusey wrote that this co-operation is like an ever-present feeling through which the believer can register the dwelling of God as that which 'at all times awaits, forecomes, accompanies, follows, encompasses us. It is within us, and without us.' As such, grace 'comes to us' not only 'through ordinances' but also 'without them', that is, through attention to its circulation in the world as an energy that sustains relationships between things in this time as well as the next.[14] Pusey's understanding of grace as at once doctrinal and phenomenological helped shape Rossetti's sense that the things of creation are kept in grace by attending to its movement in others.

How to sustain grace through relationship was an urgent question for nineteenth-century Anglo-Catholics, whose belief in the sacramental theory of grace through baptism (or baptismal regeneration) was threatened in the nineteenth century by a series of events known as the Gorham Controversy. In 1847, the Bishop of Exeter, Henry Phillpotts, refused to appoint George Cornelius Gorham to a clerical post in his diocese because of his denial of baptismal regeneration. Gorham protested, and while his appeal was initially rejected by the ecclesiastical Court of Arches, it was later accepted by the secular Judicial Committee of the Privy Council. The judgment shocked many Anglicans as well as Anglo-Catholics, who considered it an attack on the Church of England's 'spiritual rights'.[15] The Tractarian reaction was pronounced, and many churches displayed the Nicene Creed, in which 'one Baptism for the remission of sins' is acknowledged, in churches and on baptismal fonts.[16] The controversy was a significant one for Rossetti, not least because Gorham's success triggered the departure of William Dodsworth from Christ Church, Albany Street, for Roman Catholicism. As noted in Chapter 1, Dodsworth's fierce belief in an imminent Second Coming to mark the beginning of the Millennium moved Rossetti, and she listened to his sermons on the signs of the times amidst the events of the Gorham Controversy. His replacement, Henry William Burrows, sought to calm his congregation by repositioning the font (the site of baptism in the church) opposite the altar to remind them of the significance of sacramental baptism. In 1868, he started a campaign supported by the Rossetti family to redesign the font 'to express honour and reverence for Holy Baptism', and hired William Butterfield to encase it in 'richer marbles' with a 'large red cross inlaid on the inside of its bowl'.[17] The emphasis on the font helped to establish baptism, not just as a symbolic entry point into the church, but as a 'real' moment of spiritual regeneration that, Pusey wrote, went back 'fifteen centuries'.[18] Newman shared Pusey's belief in baptism's early Church significance, and argued it was foundational to life, 'colourless, like air or water; it is but the medium through which the soul sees Christ'.[19] His elemental conception of baptism as 'like air or water' envisioned it as both matter and energy, and so able to provide a spiritual birth 'of water and the Spirit' to shape the human as at once material and divine.[20]

Baptism was thus essential to the transmission and reception of grace. Rossetti's mother went to great lengths to retrieve documentation proving her own baptism, and was quick to christen all of her children—Maria and Gabriel at All Souls Church, Langham Place, and William and Christina at Trinity Church, Marylebone.[21] While William and his wife Lucy insisted that they attached no 'importance, whether spiritual or temporal, to the baptismal ceremony', Rossetti urged them to christen their children.[22] When her 18-month-old nephew, Michael Ford, contracted meningitis in January 1883, Rossetti sat with the family during his last hours and baptized him herself shortly after his death.[23] She later wrote to Lucy that she could not consider her '"happy" children' really to be *'happy'* unless through 'the sole door' of baptism 'whereby entrance is promised into the happiness which eye has not seen nor ear heard'.[24] An insensitive letter in any circumstances, it nevertheless underlined her belief in the 'grace of Baptism' as that into which the believer is guided by the 'practical' 'Call' of the 'Divine'.[25] She inherited the notion of a 'call' into grace from Augustine, who claimed that the faithful are 'reached by some calling' sounded through the experience of 'those things' that 'delight us'. In acknowledging grace through delight, the faithful are transformed internally and set on a path 'towards God' on which they undergo a process of perfection realized finally at the end of time.[26] For Augustine, grace rehabilitates human beings from within, healing them from their state of original sin, and so deeming them dependent completely on God: without grace, humans die into damnation. Grace is still prevenient and originary in this theology, but, having been extinguished by original sin, needs to be re-given into the world as an unmerited gift available only to those God elects to receive it. Rossetti nuanced this rather bleak view of the human as an inherently sinful being with reference to Aquinas, who considered grace a new nature. The recipient is changed internally by the process, transformed from an independent entity into a communal being. Grace is thus 'super' natural because it adds to and divinizes the natural so that it can participate in God.

Like Gregory of Nyssa, who conceived of a world that is saved repeatedly by a synergizing grace that brings all things together in a mystical union, Aquinas defined grace as the means by which God moves beings into action and faith through him and each other.[27] In Aquinas's connected reality, or the 'unity of the world', all things derive 'from God' and are 'ordered to others' and 'to God' through relationship.[28] This created and collective world might be hierarchal, with God and angels at the top and vegetation at the bottom, but it is still an interconnected one that allows for the transmission of grace through and to all things. It is a model in which grace not only circulates around things to keep them in relationship, but also intervenes to 'perfect' the world when it becomes disordered or broken. Rossetti worried that such disorder had become heightened in the nineteenth century, the human pursuit of 'knowledge by avenues of cruelty or impurity', she wrote, rupturing an interconnection based on grace.[29] For her, humans justified their mistreatment of creation via war, slavery, industrialism, child labour, and vivisection by conceiving of themselves outside the creation of which they are part. But she also feared that its abusive relationship to the nonhuman was evidence of the human's unpreparedness for the apocalypse. God was not the cause of Dodsworth's signs of the times, then, but humans, who sought to evade blame by propagating a misreading of the apocalypse as catastrophic and terminal. As Ailise Bulfin argues, late Victorian culture was crowded with catastrophe texts eager to imagine the apocalypse through a 'myriad of entropic images of total war, natural disaster, the fall of civilization, and the death of the sun'.[30] This newly secular eschatology was obsessed with a dying world in which waning suns and stars cast the earth into a suffocating darkness. Popularized by writers like H. G. Wells, the 'apocalypse' soon signified alien invasions, global wars, and biological decline, as well as meteorological and geological disasters.

Rossetti was genuinely alarmed by the prospect of natural disasters. She described the 1887 earthquake and floods off the Mediterranean coast of southern France and northern Italy as an 'awful awestriking experience', especially because she knew William and his family were on their way to San Remo during the quake.[31] But such events had little to do with the Second Advent, and attributing natural or human-made cataclysms to God served only to obscure Revelation's ultimate message that the new creation would transform life, not destroy it. John's vision of a new creation free of death, sorrow, tears, and pain would be secured, Rossetti thought, only through the renewal of grace in the present through fellowship between things. She thus worked to sustain the flow of grace in her apocalyptic writings by convincing her reader of the baptismal connection of human, nonhuman, and divine. As she wrote in *Seek and Find*, the Christian pilgrim 'starts from a well, the blessed water of Baptism: refreshment as of water goes along with him, the copious dews and showers of grace: his own tears for sorrow and (alas!) for sin help to fill the pools'.[32] Baptism into grace was thus a material and spiritual process, as Jesus declared in John 3. 5: 'Except a man be born of water and of the Spirit, he cannot enter into the kingdom of God'. Influenced by Pusey, Rossetti also conceived of baptism has having two phases or 'volumes', the first a 'Register of Baptism for this world', and the second a 'Register of Final Perseverance for the next'.[33] In this double baptism, she asserted that the second birth is dependent on the first to bring it into being. In this she differed from Pusey, whose description of 'two births, the natural and the baptismal' presented the first birth as 'accompanied by' a 'second birth' that restores 'our decayed natures'.[34] Rossetti did not negate childbirth as incomplete and imperfect, but considered the two inter-dependent even if they belonged to different orders and times. As she wrote in *The Face of the Deep*, the 'waters of Baptism' are both 'under' and 'above' the 'firmament', of earth and heaven, a connected and continuously flowing 'river of Divine pleasures' in which the old and new creation is cognate.[35]

As usual, Rossetti presented the nonhuman's relationship with baptismal grace as an exemplar for the human to follow. In her poem, '"Before the Throne, and before the Lamb"', published in *The Face of the Deep*, the element of water models a nonhuman expres-sion of grace through which the saints can connect to it. They can only 'sing as one' by looking to the natural world to score their communal chorus as an imitation of the voice of 'many waters' and their 'unclouded thundering' (ll. 1–2). Always open to the elements, the nonhuman is baptized automatically into grace through the rain, sea, rivers, and springs, part of a cycle from which the human seeks shelter. As Rossetti explored in 'Thy lilies drink the dew' in *Time Flies*, non-humans like lilies and lambs are 'types' of Jesus precisely because they flourish in a state of constant receptivity to the baptismal waters of dew and streams:

> Thy lilies drink the dew,
> Thy lambs the rill, and I will drink them too;
>   For those in purity
> And innocence are types, dear Lord, of Thee.
>   The fragrant lily flower
> Bows and fulfils Thy Will its lifelong hour;
>   The lamb at rest and play
> Fulfils Thy Will in gladness all the day;
>   They leave tomorrow's cares
> Until the morrow, what it brings it bears.
>   And I, Lord, would be such;
> Not high or great or anxious overmuch,
>   But pure and temperate,
> Earnest to do Thy Will betimes and late,
>   Fragrant with love and praise
> And innocence thro' all my appointed days;
>   Thy lily I would be,
> Spotless and sweet, Thy lamb to follow Thee.

Grace is conjured immediately in the poem's circularity here, which begins and ends with the image of the lily, lamb, and narrator joined in the divine body. The sequence of dropped lines also creates a series of pauses in which the reader is encouraged to breathe in and share with the things of the poem the same invisible breath through which God created the earth and will re-create it at the end of time.[36] This formal orchestration of breath also corresponds to the poem's baptismal experience of water through relationship, the lilies revived by the dew, the lambs by the stream, and the narrator through her encounter with them. Like the saints who sing with the voice of the waters in '"Before the Throne"', the narrator here becomes the lily—'Thy lily I would be'—joined with the nonhuman through grace to enact Paul's words 'every one members one of another' (Romans 12. 5).

The lily and lamb of 'Thy lilies drink the dew' invite the narrator, and also the reader, to 'consider' them as models of being-in-grace with others, both 'betimes and late', that is, before and after the new creation. They share a connection through water that Rossetti continued into the next entry in *Time Flies*, a short prose passage on 'cudweed', a plant that thrives in water and 'puts forth a blossom which in its turn puts forth around itself other blossoms'.[37] Like Ruskin, who remarked that leaves grow in families that embrace each other, Rossetti also imagined the blossoms of the cudweed entwined.[38] But for Rossetti, the family unit is not strong enough to sustain grace outside of its divine connection with creation. For the things of the world can only experience grace in kinship with each other, not simply through biological connection, an idea she explored further in *Time Flies* in three Easter poems, 'Easter Day', 'Easter Monday', and 'Easter Tuesday'.[39] Each poem maps the 'marriage' of human and nonhuman through Christ's resurrection as a symbol of the new creation. 'Easter Day', for example, establishes an earth in which the return of Christ triggers a rebirth in which speech is replaced by song, and earth wakes its birds, flowers, and lambkins to build a bower in which the human is given to grace in a 'spousal day':

> Earth wakes her song birds,
>   Puts on her flowers,
> Leads out her lambkins,
>   Builds up her bowers:
> This is man's spousal day,
>   Christ's day and ours.   (ll. 13–18)

The kinship between things creates the conditions for this marriage, one that looks forward to the union between the holy city and the messiah in the new creation (Revelation 21. 2). But the poem's last line, 'Christ's day and ours', identifies the 'ours' as inclusive of birds, flowers, and lambkins that signpost the new creation for the human, and so connect all things into one grace that carries the world into the apocalypse. In the prose entry on 'Easter Monday' Rossetti proposed the water lily as another signpost, a 'type of the Resurrection' that folds 'beneath the water' at night and resurfaces in 'the morning' to renew the day.[40] Together, the water lily, like the birds, flowers, and lambkins, circulates baptismal grace in a way that keeps things in a state of flux and vitality. As the narrator of 'Easter Tuesday' declares, 'Out in the rain a world is growing green', a description of a movement towards a green grace into which all things will 'wake without a sigh' (ll. 1, 12).

'No more sea'

If rainfall, showers, dew, and tears sustained the flow of baptismal grace for Rossetti, then the origin of this grace was the sea. In 'Lord, we are rivers running to Thy sea', part of her reading of Revelation 3. 21–2, she imagined the Christian as a river that runs back to its source in God and is restored in the 'sweetness' of his waters.[41] In fluvial form, Rossetti wrote, the Christian also douses God's 'consuming fire' (Deuteronomy 4. 24) and so becomes 'Immutable amid mutability, permanent amid permanence'.[42] Anticipating the at once tranquil and formidable 'oceanic feeling' Freud later elucidated, Rossetti considered the sea restorative and healthful as well as indicative of God's vastness and depths.[43] Like many Victorians, she travelled to the coast in search of a pelagic remedy for illnesses caused by London's climate, and claimed that the sea made a 'world of difference' to her emotional and physical wellbeing.[44] She considered Hastings a 'lovely place' that was 'good for London eyes'; Seaford a retreat where 'The air is good, & the sea is good'; and Torquay a place that 'greatly revived' her.[45] Sea-creatures also appealed to her because of their hybridic being as water and matter, and she referred to sea-mice and sea-ferns as 'marine relative[s]' of things on the land.[46] Rossetti also collected pebbles and shells, but, ever respectful of the rights of her fellow beings, did not take living creatures away from the sea, and bemoaned

William's aquatic collection of 'bottled monsters'. Writing to him about his 'smelly' acquisitions, she wryly reported that 'my investigations are carried on from a campstool pitched some way from the water's edge,—so are by no means exhaustive. Shingle I see: & I think I have heard of sand.'[47]

Of all the sea creatures she encountered, Rossetti had a particularly vivid response to an octopus she viewed in Brighton aquarium in 1886. She was sent to Brighton in August with her niece Olivia to recover from the shock of her mother's death. While the family were long aware of the grave state of Frances's health, Rossetti, who had always lived with her mother and was her carer for much of this time, was left particularly stunned by the bereavement.[48] Rossetti remembered that she and Olivia 'haunted the aquarium' together, and were transfixed by a creature that appeared to them to be directly out of John's vision.[49] As she wrote in *The Face of the Deep*, 'of all living creatures' the octopus most approaches 'Satanic suggestion':

> Inert as it often appeared, it bred and tickled a perpetual suspense: will it do something? will it emerge from the background of its water den? I have seen it swallow its live prey in an eyewink, change from a stony colour to an appalling lividness, elongate unequal feelers and set them flickering like a flame, sit still with air of immemorial old age amongst the lifeless refuse of its once living meals. I had to remind myself that this vivid figure of wickedness was not in truth itself wickedness.[50]

The octopus symbolized 'wickedness' for Rossetti not only because it consumed its prey with such disregard, but also because of its own mistreatment, an incarcerated creature for whom the aquarium served as a prison.[51] As John stated, God will not only judge the living and the dead, but 'destroy them which destroy the earth' (Revelation 11. 18). The octopus is not truly wicked for Rossetti because, torn from its aquatic home, it is caught within a human logic of abuse and cruelty only the new creation could obliterate.

Many readers of Revelation feared the sea itself would be obliterated, and took literally the prediction that following the passing of 'the first heaven and the first earth' there would be 'no more sea' (Revelation 21. 1). As Rossetti wrote in *Seek and Find*: 'At first reading "there was no more sea," our heart sinks at foresight of the familiar sea expunged from earth and heaven; that sea to us so long and so inexhaustibly a field of wonder and delight'.[52] But she answered this anxiety with a reference to the prophet Habakkuk, who after questioning God is 'spoken' to by him through the natural world (Habakkuk 1. 3). While God is 'the chief singer on my stringed instruments' (3. 19), his voice embodied in the environment, Habakkuk also suggests that his word or melody only signifies through enquiry and exposition. Rossetti is interested especially in Habakkuk 3. 8 and 3. 10, wherein the prophet suggests that God removes willingly any obstacles that impede his people—sea, mountain, sun or moon—and then transforms these phenomena into things through which he can communicate. She follows her reading of Habakkuk by rethinking the line 'no more sea' as meaning that the sea does not vanish, but rather becomes one with God. Inseparable and alike, the sea and God become one entity, a message to the human to treat the natural world as she would the divine. As Rossetti claimed, Revelation and Habakkuk were both written 'for our instruction as regards ourselves, and consequently as regards the visible creation in reference to ourselves'.[53] In her reading, John prophesies not the disappearance of water from the earth, but the passing away of those who refuse to perceive the sea as God, and so demean it as a commodity or resource.

In Rossetti's vision of the new creation, the sea remains in its crystalline form as a 'sea of glass' (Revelation 4. 6), as well as 'mingled with fire' (14. 2). At once transparent and consuming, the sea dissipates distinctions between the sea and land, nonhuman and human, rural and urban, divine and material, as things are reconciled to each other in a renewed creation. As Rossetti wrote in *Seek and Find*: 'Thus we shall not lose the translucent purity of ocean, nor yet a glory as of its myriad waves tipped by sunshine . . . What shall we lose? A barrier of separation.'[54] In her narrative, the unfolding of the new creation negates the idea of the cosmos as an assembly of delimited physical parts outside of the mind, and reveals it as a non-physical realm of energies in which things appear through their faithful experience of them. If there is 'no more sea', there is no more 'unrest, of spurning at limits, of advance only to recede'; in its place appears a baptismal, regenerating body of water in the New Jerusalem's 'pure river of water of life, clear as crystal' (Revelation 22. 1).[55] Her poem '"And

there was no more sea"' replaces the disaster language of catastrophe
literature with an expression of God's love, one that brings together
the multiple ways in which the world is voiced and experienced in a
'oneness of contentment'.[56] In prioritizing the inclusivity of God's love
for and as all things, Rossetti placed the poem deliberately in *The Face
of the Deep*, not with her commentary on 'no more sea' in Revelation
21. 1, but in her reading of 5. 13.[57] Here John states that 'every
creature which is in heaven, and on the earth, and under the earth,
and such as are in the sea, and all that are in them' sing blessings to the
lamb on the throne:

> Voices from above and from beneath,
>   Voices of creation near and far,
> Voices out of life and out of death,
>   Out of measureless space,
>   Sun, moon, star,
>   In oneness of contentment offering praise.
>
> Heaven and earth and sea jubilant,
>   Jubilant all things that dwell therein;
> Filled to fullest overflow they chant,
>   Still roll onward, swell,
>   Still begin,
>   Never flagging praise interminable.
>
> Thou who must fall silent in a while,
>   Chant thy sweetest, gladdest, best, at once;
> Sun thyself today, keep peace and smile;
>   By love upward send
>   Orisons,
>   Accounting love thy lot and love thine end.

At the start of this poem, the narrator presents a world in which things
still perceive themselves to be separate from each other, their voices
numerous and split spatially between a multiplicity of origin points
invisible and visible: 'Heaven and earth and sea'. But by the end of the
first stanza, this multiplicity has become multiplex, as the voices are
channelled into one single offer of praise. Heaven, earth, and sea
express no anxiety at the prospect of their forewarned demise because
they are converged seamlessly in a 'jubilant' union saturated by grace,
'Filled to fullest overflow'. As they 'swell' together, they collectively

send their love 'upward', not to a distinct or transcendent realm above them, but rather into 'Orisons', a word Rossetti plays on as both 'prayer' and 'horizon'. By granting the word its own line suspended between effusive expressions of love in lines 16 and 18, 'orisons' becomes both an expression of devotion to God, and the limit at which the earth and sky meet before they embrace to forge the new creation. Rossetti might have visualized the love of creation moving upwards towards God, but she imagined the dead—'Thou who must fall silent'—participating in God in a new time that defied spatiality. Reborn into a God that permeates it 'all in all' (1 Corinthians 15. 28), creation becomes part of what Pierre Teilhard de Chardin called an 'environment of union', a gathering-together of things that mutually grow in grace.[58]

God's promise that the apocalypse would usher in transformation rather than destruction is sealed in Revelation by the appearance of a rainbow, another baptismal image as well as sign of a covenant repeated from Genesis 9. 13 and Ezekiel 1. 28. In Revelation, however, the rainbow extends its bow to circle around the throne of the lamb, and waves out from a centre through expanding circles of praise from angels, the Elders, and the four beasts. For Rossetti, the rainbow was also an incarnation of Christ in the last moments of time. She wrote in *The Face of the Deep* that in his being in the Trinity, Christ glitters like the 'jasper' and 'sardine stone' and so summons a rainbow of 'dazzling brilliancy, permeated by pure light', the stones radiating both an iridescent opacity and a 'blood-red translucen[ce]'.[59] As the 'chief rainbow', he commands the resurrected to 'train' behind him in a 'fainter, less perfect' second rainbow, the two bows forming a hoop, or 'glory', an optical phenomenon in which the light of the sun or moon reflects off water droplets in the atmosphere to form kaleido-scopic rings of light.[60] While the optical theory of the glory was not theorized until the late twentieth century, the word glory was used from at least the fifteenth century to mean a circle of light (an aureole or halo) or revelation of celestial light from heaven. This combination of water and light, grace and God created a baptismal image for Rossetti, one that 'proceeds from a centre' to create a '*completely revealed circle*'.[61] Invisible to the human eye, for whom the horizon blocks the full-circle rainbow, the complete vision of light is nevertheless available, an image of the actuality of what remains unseen and promise of its full revelation in a world of changed vision. Like the multi-coloured hoop Holman Hunt painted around his risen Christ in his 1847 *Christ and the Two Marys*, Rossetti's rainbow anticipates the new creation by ringing around creation and holding it buoyant within the light of grace.

As a sign of grace and continuity, the rainbow was further confirmation that the earth would be restored and rebuilt rather than destroyed at the end of time. It was necessarily a reserved sign, only partially available to the observer for whom its 'light which viewed directly would blind'.[62] Its fractional display was also a reminder that the fulfilment of the experience of earth-bound existence was itself not yet fully revealed or available. Rossetti stressed that the believer must retain this uncomfortable, dislocated sense of life as 'a portion only, not the whole' in order to understand it as a precursor for the unity of the next world. The next world was not a replacement for the old, but rather a restoration of it, an idea that required the believer to participate in this world attentively and lovingly. She argued that only those willing to engage and identify with the brokenness of creation are able to recognize that they are part of a 'whole which we see not: the part declares the unbroken, continuous, unvaried whole'.[63] This process by which the unseen reveals the seen is manifested in the rainbow, Rossetti suggested, its invisible and 'colourless light' the very basis of its incarnation in things such as the 'rainbow shell' of 'A Birthday' (l. 5) or the dew-dropped spider's web in *Time Flies*.[64] At once a 'compendium of colour' as well as an 'absence of tints', the shell and the web appear through an imperceptible 'celestial whiteness' in which 'all colour' is latent. While in the old creation distinctions between colours are preserved to maintain earthly diversity, in the new creation 'all tints' are resolved into a 'perfectly balanced harmony', the rainbow made whole and complete.[65]

Rossetti's focus on baptismal images like the rainbow, the sea, rivers, and tears helped her to conceptualize this transition from the old to the new creation, especially in relation to time. In a poem she wrote to conclude the 'All Saints' section of *Called to Be Saints: The Minor Festivals Devotionally Studied* (1881), she envisioned time as a 'rainbow-coloured bubble', flimsy, fragile and defined by sorrow, death, pain, and greed (l. 11).[66] She called this temporal time a 'bubble-life tumultuous' that creates pain because the human strives to mark its passing by the accumulation of wealth and things that are incompatible with an existence that is essentially volatile and breakable (l. 12). Whatever is 'heaped-up measure beyond measure' in the old creation, her narrator observes, has no meaning in the new time, destined as it is for an eternal 'quietness' in which distinctions between rich and poor, excess and scarcity are dissolved (ll. 7–8). The pilgrimage into the new time is communal and companionable for Rossetti, and she renamed the poem '"Whither the Tribes go up, even the Tribes of the Lord"' for *Verses* (1893), a reference to Psalms 122's emphasis on a fellowship shared with 'brethren and companions' (122. 8). Her sense of the old creation as a 'continuous Advent season' did not diminish the importance of lived time, but rather emphasized that the things of creation must await the apocalypse in kinship with each other.[67] Any disruption to this harmony threatened to delay or even collapse the coming of the reign of God. As Rossetti argued in her commentary on Revelation 21. 4, breaking this fellowship through the exercise of power over another erodes devotional intent. Only those willing to be 'carried in kind arms out into the reviving sunshine' she wrote, 'laid down in a pleasant spot to inhale the sweet free air, learning gradually to assimilate a renewed hope, joy, peace' could enter into the altered time of the new creation, not those who act 'like giants rejoicing at the goal'.[68] By focusing on the feeling of 'hope, joy, peace' in the present, the believer prepares herself, as if in a 'period of probation', for the passing of chronological time into the new aeonic time, the eternity of God in which there is no beginning or end, before or after.[69] As temporal becomes eternal, and spatial becomes omnipresent, both the chronological time of earth and the everlasting time experienced by the angels and saints enter mutually into the timelessness of God.

Rossetti argued that believers could comprehend the difficult concept of timelessness through the analogous idea of rhythmic or cyclical time. Cyclical time is available obliquely to the human in the rotation of light and dark, the tidal forces of the moon and sun, patterns of sleep, the biorhythms of plants, the water cycle, and the succession of the seasons. While these rhythms are inherent to the structure and experience of nonhuman life, Rossetti recognized that the human required additional assistance comprehending these rhythms in art. In *Time Flies*, she suggested that art could illustrate how to understand time by giving it a voice and face:

> Heaven and earth alike are chronometers.
>
> Heaven marks time in light, by the motion of luminaries.
>
> Earth marks time in darkness, by the variation of shadows.
>
> To these chronometers of nature art adds clocks with faces easily decipherable and voices insistently audible.
>
> Nature and art combine to keep time for us: and yet we wander out of time![70]

Rossetti presents heaven and earth here as 'chronometers' of nature that mark time through light and darkness. Art does not merely reveal this process, but adds to it clock faces and voices, both forms and expressions of the workings of heaven and earth that the human finds more accessible. Rossetti is anxious that her reader might 'wander out of time' because in doing so she might lose touch with a rhythmic movement towards the new creation. She worked to keep her reader 'in time' through the repeated cadences of her poetry, which she believed could train and familiarize the human with the rhythmic movement of cyclical time. This was especially important in a period obsessed with the linear progression of time and its public keeping by local clocks administered centrally by the newly constructed 'Big Ben', built in 1859.[71]

The public time created by Big Ben imposed discipline on labour, transport, and the mail system. Through the shift from seasonal time to an accelerated industrial time, public time also initiated a double experience in which humans felt in control of time by mapping its passing, but also regulated by its strictures. This was problematic for Rossetti because industrial and consumer time constituted a refusal to live in the cyclical time of divine creation, and consequently a failure to keep time at all: 'We misappropriate time, we lose time, we waste time, we kill time', she wrote, 'We do anything and everything with time, except redeem the time'.[72] In these lines, Rossetti argued for the redemption or regaining of time by re-experiencing it through its repetition in art and memory as a way of sustaining it into the new time. As a repetition and transformation of the old, the new creation is a theotic recycling of what has gone before, the material world not destroyed, but divinized. As she wrote in her poem for *Time Flies*, ' "But Thy commandment is exceeding broad" ', a reference to Psalm 119. 96 in which the believer is encouraged to follow God's law and time, the laughter and joy of the 'new creation' is a repetition of that experienced in the old world:

> Sow and reap: for while these moments creep,
>   Time and earth and life are on the wane:
> Now, in tears; to-morrow, laugh and reap
>   Once again.   (ll. 9–12).

While the 'now' of line 11 is a veil of tears to be passed through into the new creation, the laughter and gifts of 'to-morrow' are given 'Once again', and so derive from a time prior to the new creation. For even though the old creation is shaped by a longing for the new, it remains a time into which Jesus was given, a time of joy as well as sorrow. It is this cyclical movement between joy and sorrow, life and death, and ultimately between the old and new creation that Jesus was sent to communicate to the human.

As Jesus's allusions to lilies and sparrows attest, only the human required instruction on how to live in cyclical time. It is in a human form, then, that God sends himself originally to prepare creation for entry into the new time by revealing how to live in grace within a time that 'ends' in 'eternal life' (1 John 1. 2). His Second Advent, Rossetti thought, would also renew the world, one in which the human appeared not only to have misunderstood cyclical time, but to be involved actively in damaging its continued operation and fulfilment in the new time. Christ's multiple nature as divine, human, animal, plant, grain, rock, light, and water allows him to embody grace, but it is a process blocked by the human's refusal to enter fellowship with other things. She quoted Jesus's words in Luke 12. 50 in *The Face of the Deep* to make her point: ' "But I have a baptism to be baptized with; and how am I straitened till it be accomplished!" ' While in *Time Flies*, Rossetti called Jesus's relationship with creation an 'indissoluble union' and 'blessing', by *The Face of the Deep* she turned to Jesus as a 'shelter' from an environmental collapse and the process that would renew it.[73] For while she worked and prayed for the readiness of creation to enter the New Jerusalem, she was troubled by the possible consequences of a premature Advent for which creation was not prepared. This is especially apparent in her dystopian short story 'A Safe Investment', in which she envisioned Jesus's return to a dark and aphotic earth whose inhabitants are ruled by consumerism and fear.[74] The story opens on a 'moonless' and 'utterly starless' night, the sky smothered by a smog-filled 'blot of blackness' not seen 'since the world was' at its beginnings.[75] The darkness is only broken by the 'dim glare of shops' and 'flickering gas-lamps', symbols of consumerism and excess into which a 'solitary traveller' rides on a 'white horse'.[76] When a gas-lamp explodes suddenly, it casts a hellish 'red light' through which the traveller glimpses briefly the town and its inhabitants.[77] But as a Jesus figure who embodies all creatures, he sees into the 'deepened darkness' with 'owl's eyes' to witness a series of 'signs of the times'.[78] The sea is 'deep boiled like a pot of ointment' and littered with abandoned cargo and the bodies of sailors; the county bank has been ruined by unfair trade; and neighbours are set against each other in 'the panic of accumulated losses'.[79]

The traveller reads these 'signs', not as punitive tokens of God's power, but as the consequence of a town in which individualized material loss is valued over communal empathy. A mother bemoans the death of her soldier son because she has lost his salary; an old man scrabbles for coins from his broken 'strong-box'; and an investor grieves his now obsolete outlay on a new water reservoir.[80] Mired in monetary woes, everyone the traveller meets appears affectively dead and unwilling to remove the barrier of material greed to connect with others. None welcomes the traveller or even notices his presence, and the town is drowned by a hostility Rossetti deliberately figures in environmental terms as a flood: 'They had no eyes, no thought, no sympathy, save each man for himself; none stretched a helping hand to his neighbour, or spoke a word of comfort, or cared who sank or who swam in this desolation which had come like a flood'.[81] Relief from this climatic murkiness and disaster comes in the form of a brightly lit hill cottage, in which a 'calm, cheerful-looking woman' welcomes both the traveller and his horse.[82] Joyful in 'that night of ruin', the woman confesses that as a young child she was instructed by a divine figure called 'One' to send all her wealth to the hill cottage 'where a light shines to lighten every one that goeth into the house'.[83] She now redistributes this wealth to orphans, widows, the sick, and strangers, and embodies Rossetti's 'moral': 'being mindful to entertain strangers' is to 'have entertained angels unawares'.[84] An echo of scriptural scenes of hospitality like Abraham and Sarah's warm reception of three men in Genesis 18 or Solomon's embrace of a stranger bride in the Song of Solomon 1. 5, this final line serves as a response to the story's dystopia. But Rossetti also reminded her reader that the safest investment is God, the word 'investment' a play on the act of putting on clerical robes or vestments. Like the Tractarian priest, with responsibility for the social as well as spiritual welfare of his parish, her reader must also embrace others and so redress the devastating results of inhospitality.

Rossetti's story constitutes a warning that the society which opts to value 'idols of gold' (Revelation 9. 20) over the living things that comprise it will be destroyed ultimately by its avarice, luxury, and self-obsession. But she also wrote about the consequences for individuals who neglect the poor, the vulnerable, and the disadvantaged. In 'Despised and Rejected' (1864), for example, the narrator experiences paranoia, panic, and isolation only after he ignores the cries of a stranger who arrives at his door. The narrator is a last-man figure, lonely and friendless, and imprisoned in 'darkness as a dead man out of sight' in a sunless and hostile 'bitter night' where 'none remains' (ll. 1–5). Yet the poem shows that the phrase 'none remains', like the negation 'no more sea', is meaningless to God, who is ever-present despite the narrator's refusal to open the door to the stranger, or even look at his bleeding body. Even though it is the stranger's wounded cry that rings through the poem, the real terror of the scene lies in the narrator's rejection of grace when it is available to him:

> 'Open, lest I should pass thee by, and thou
> One day entreat My Face
> And howl for grace,
> And I be deaf as thou art now.
> Open to Me.'   (ll. 25–9)

Implicit in the stranger's repeated cry to 'open thy door' is the notion of the loving voice that greets those who knock in Song of Solomon 5. 2 and Revelation 3. 20. While the narrator might be bound to 'howl for grace', the last three lines of the poem confirm its eternal openness to him. For when the narrator finally opens his door, he discovers it covered in the now lost stranger's blood, a reference to the Passover act of daubing lamb's blood on households spared by God (Exodus 12. 7).

The promise of grace is continual and eternal, then, but only in relationship to others. Rossetti stressed that failure to sanctify grace through hospitality or forgiveness leads to despondency and fragmentation, wherein a refusal to participate in creation constitutes a refusal to participate in the life of God. In this context, the prospect of 'no more sea' becomes a broader comment on a human unwillingness to engage with the oceans and those who reside therein as part of one creation and divine body. As she argued in *The Face of the Deep*:

> What is there, is there anything, from which Christ would exclude us? He so identifies His own with Himself that we must stand or fall according to this word: 'Inasmuch as ye have done it unto one of the least of these My brethren, ye have done it unto Me . . . Inasmuch as ye did it not to one of the least of these, ye did it not to Me.' He shares with us His Name, He makes us partakers of the Divine Nature.[85]

She repeated this reference to Matthew 25. 40 in *Called to Be Saints* and *Time Flies*, describing it as a 'Beatitude' or graced blessing that 'stands open to all' and works as a 'seal' to 'stamp the end rather than the beginning'.[86] While baptism 'initiates' things into grace, she wrote, participation with it in the divine life seals or stamps things within an eternal grace beyond time. Grace is not a transitive action that intervenes into time to secure particular outcomes, then, but rather an ongoing and immanent force in which things are always (preveniently) perfect.[87] As the last section suggests, things sustain such perfection in God only in a weakened state, a kenōsis experienced instinctively by the nonhuman, but that the human must learn to embrace to prevent ecological collapse and welcome the new creation.

Kenōsis and the Weakening of Creation

By the end of her life, Rossetti was perceived by the public as something of a recluse. Visitors to her residence on Torrington Square recorded witnessing a mystical but resigned figure, a portrait much publicized by William, who declared that the loss of their mother was 'the practical close' of his sister's life.[88] William Sharp too considered her 'last years' as a 'sad and lonely' period in which she produced a poetry 'of impassioned mysticism' and 'haunted' cadences; and George Gissing only had to remind his reader that his character, Henrietta Winters, was an admirer of Rossetti's writing to justify her 'morbid' and 'mystical views'.[89] One British newspaper even declared that 'our most eminent poetess, Miss Christina Rossetti' has 'for years' 'shut herself out from all society and lived in absolutely monastic retirement in a quiet Bloomsbury square'.[90] Written in the last year of her life, the report was misleading, although Rossetti had been very ill with breast cancer, which she developed in 1892. She survived a successful mastectomy, but a heart condition precluded further surgery when the cancer returned the following year. Rossetti's death on 29 December 1894 was attributed to scirrhus and cardiac failure, one for which William declared she had prepared herself 'with calmness and fortitude, and even (I am sure) a large under-current of satisfaction'. The note of slight disdain with which the agnostic William recounted his sister's readiness for death is also apparent in his account of his sister's 'vein of sprightliness': he was disconcerted by the moments of joy her 'deeply devotional nature' ensured, and was keen to present a woman writer 'settled' into a 'current' of 'self-suppression and self-seclusion'. His final depiction cast Rossetti as an ascetic devoid of 'cheerfulness' and tormented by her 'own deservings and undeservings', finally 'weighed' down by her devotion to Christ.[91]

These accounts had little to do with the reality of Rossetti's life even towards its end. As William's own memory betrayed, Rossetti spent much of her late life feeling contented and vivacious; she read her poems aloud, prayed silently, and received visitors, clergy and friends alike. She also made a will in which she divided her little wealth between family, charities, and religious bequests, and worried mainly about the fates of her cats, Muff and Carrots.[92] The details William uses to describe her final weeks in his histories of the family do not add up to his broad-brush image of a dispossessed Christian, and it is unlikely that a poet for whom death promised a transition into a newly transformed earth would have so violently agonized through her last days. She no doubt suffered pain during this period, but Rossetti was not especially reclusive or despairing, and remained faithful to what Evelyn Underhill calls a 'practical mysticism' in which the believer turns to 'ordinary contemplation' of reality by exercising the spiritual practices of prayer and attention.[93] She continued to direct this ordinary contemplation to plants and animals, as well as God, and considered the connection between all things to be a 'practical' phenomenon made available through the 'practice' of prayer and litany.[94] Her practical approach to faith was not dogmatic, however, but rather vulnerable and yielding, even 'weak'. As she wrote in her commentary on Revelation 1. 8, God deliberately 'formed us weak' through his 'preventing' (prevenient) 'grace' through which all things come into being gently and weakly.[95] In welcoming this weakness, Rossetti sought to become like Christ by letting go of a strong individual identity to enter into theotic relationship with God.

Theosis, or the divinization of creation, was dependent on kenōsis, the self-emptying of Christ into the world, and both served to counter the secular sovereignties of imperialism, nationalism, and consumerism. While lilies and birds help the human to consider what it means to prepare for the reception of Christ, the believer can only achieve unity with Christ and enter the new creation through the renunciation of power, authority, and transcendence through the (ecological) love command. Weakened by kenōsis, the human opens herself to a thinking of the world already given in the communal being of the nonhuman, one in which things work together and ultimately transform into new species and genera, rather than defend selfishly their own being to erase competition from others.[96] Even priests, Rossetti declared in *Seek and Find*, should follow the example of Peter and Paul in following 2 Corinthians 12. 9: 'My grace is sufficient for thee: for My strength is made perfect in weakness'.[97] If baptism initiated and then sealed the believer into grace, and the Eucharist nourished and renewed it, then kenōsis ensured the full participation of all things within God's reign of peace. This cosmic transformation in which all things 'are changed into the same image' (2 Corinthians 3. 18) relies on things to become 'partakers of the Divine Nature', Rossetti wrote, a process which is dependent on Christ's Incarnation.[98] As the believer is incorporated into Christ through baptism, so Christ becomes part of creation by emptying himself into the world and so divinizing it: 'Let this mind be in you, which was also in Christ Jesus: Who, being in the form of God, thought it not robbery to be equal with God: But made himself of no reputation, and took upon him the form of a servant, and was made in the likeness of men' (Philippians 2. 5–7).

Philippians 2 is the scriptural basis for kenōsis and kenōtic being, and Rossetti quoted it in both *Seek and Find* and *The Face of the Deep* as a way of exploring the relationship between kenōsis and theosis as terms revived recently in Anglo-Catholicism's return to early Christian tradition. Kenōtic models of the Incarnation became increasingly popular in the nineteenth century as a way to reconcile the historical Jesus with his being in the Trinity, especially in relation to contemporary theories of evolution.[99] Legatees of Tractarian theology such as Charles Gore and John Richardson Illingworth argued that evolution was evidence that grace was required to 'complete' species 'perpetually undergoing transmutation'. In completing or perfecting the human in the image of God, grace enabled the self-emptying movement of kenōsis to soften its ego and individualism and so introduce 'a new species into the world— a Divine Man transcending past humanity'.[100] For Rossetti, the emergence of this divine human through kenōsis enabled a deification of all things that levelled creation in a subversion of hierarchical taxonomies. Through Christ's adoption of the 'form of a servant', she wrote in *Seek and Find*, the things of creation are redeemed from an outsider status 'as aliens' to become 'members of the sacred household', in which 'happiness consists now as of yore in choosing, doing, suffering, God's will'. Only by 'following in the steps of that Divine Son Who for our sakes, took upon Him the form of a servant (Phil. ii. 7)', she noted, is the believer predisposed to await the new creation alongside others from all denominations as part of one 'Catholic' or universal Church.[101]

Catholic universalism was a direct rejection of nineteenth-century Christianized visions of British imperialism and power for Rossetti. As Josh King argues, late works like *Verses* promoted a 'profoundly eschatological and anti-nationalist perspective' for an international Christian community.[102] But Rossetti also understood this perspective to include all things, as the section headers for *Verses* confirm. Divided into an eight-part arrangement based on the Anglican liturgy for Holy Communion, *Verses* offered 'Songs for Strangers and Pilgrims' and the 'New Jerusalem and its Citizens', as well as residents of other dimensions ('Divers Worlds: Time and Eternity') and those caught in anthropocenic ruination ('The World: Self-Destruction').[103] Even those whose souls do not make it into Paradise, and instead wait for the new creation in the suffering of Hades, remain part of creation and are redeemable in the new time. While Rossetti's vision is unusually comprehensive, if not cosmic, it was still Anglo-Catholic and Trinitarian.[104] She did not, for example, favour the broad-church Christianity promoted by Sara Coleridge, whose *Memoirs and Letters* she read 'aloud to Mamma' just before her mother died.[105] While Coleridge's theological insight engaged the Rossetti women, her 'broad' reading of grace was distinctively 'stronger' than Rossetti's because it engaged the ego and will. For Coleridge, grace cannot transform the receiver unless she willingly co-operates with its influence. She worried that without active engagement, grace threatens to make faith and individual conscience redundant.[106] In an endorsement of a personal relationship with God, Coleridge wrote: 'it seems to be a point with the Oxford writers' to 'represent, not children only, but men, as the *passive* un-co-operating subject (or rather, in one sense, *object*) of divine operation' and refuse the notion of 'grace as an *influence*' or 'co-agent of the human will'. The 'operations' of grace are 'not our concern, any more than the way in which God created the earth', a subject she could not 'believe that God ever meant us to understand'. Grace is regenerative, Coleridge declared, but not mystically so: it does not exist 'in unconscious subjects, as in infants', she wrote, challenging baptismal regeneration, especially as some of those baptized in infancy will go onto to become the 'worst of men'.[107]

For Rossetti, however, the encompassing reach of grace extended above all to the 'worst of men', a redemptive energy that kept life in movement towards the new creation. Without grace, the world stands 'aloof', she wrote in *Seek and Find*, a rigid and unloving 'type of stability'; with grace, the 'atmosphere' sparkles with 'currents and commotions...overarching and embosoming not earth and sea only, but clouds and meteors, planets and stars'.[108] Within this cosmic vision 'all moves, waxes, wanes, while itself changes not', a reading that substitutes Coleridge's model of conversion, in which the believer strives for 'goodness and power', with a dynamic model of weakness, in which grace is given freely to all.[109] Rossetti removed grace from any association with power, and she identified in Christ's kenōsis a way of bringing together Christian and non-Christian alike as part of what she called a 'plenitude of perfection'. This is achievable, she wrote, only if creation learns to 'tread the same steps' as the kenōtic Christ by negating the binaries through which the world is divided from itself. Kenōsis thus nullifies that strong thinking in which things are ordered and classified and so, she claimed, 'reverses the world's judgment' about what holds value.[110] As she declared in a paraphrase of 1 Corinthians 1. 27: 'God hath chosen the foolish things of the world to confound the wise; and God hath chosen the weak things of the world to confound the things which are mighty'.[111] Even as creation evolves and doubles 'again and again', it exists 'in God's hand', not as a mass of disparate beings struggling for acceptance, but as part of a union granted by kenōsis.[112] Rossetti's weak thinking of creation thus undermines the dualisms that atomize the world from within, as she explained in *The Face of the Deep*:

> God the Son once of free will assumed the form of a servant, therefore and for evermore is He worthy of power,—once for our sakes He became poor, therefore of riches,—once He thought as a child, therefore of wisdom,—once He was slain through weakness, therefore of strength,— once He endured the Cross, therefore of glory,—once, yea many times He was contradicted, reviled, blasphemed, therefore of blessing.[113]

Rossetti's list of dualisms here does not replace one side of the contrary with another, but rather undermines the oppositional reasoning on which they are based. Servitude can only turn to power, poverty to wealth, the child's view to wisdom, suffering to glory, and abuse to blessing, through a willingness to disavow objective judgements about who might enter the kingdom of God. As John Caputo argues in *The Weakness of God*, the new creation is not for the 'insiders', but the 'outsiders', those 'who have no papers to present, who cannot prove that they are card-carrying members of the religions of the Book... for "all whom they found, both good and bad" (Matthew 22. 10)'.[114]

One of Rossetti's most often used images of kenōsis was the 'lowest' or 'last' place, founded on the scriptural hope that the 'forsaken' will 'inherit everlasting life' through vulnerability: 'But many that are first shall be last; and the last shall be first' (Matthew 19. 30). In assessing her preference for the lowest place, some readers might accuse Rossetti of obscuring an ethic of submission already imposed on women under the guise of theological sacrifice. But her poem 'The Lowest Place'

(1863) almost immediately retracts the request for surrender in the narrator's remark that she should not 'dare' to even ask for it, followed by an appeal to be raised to the same place as God:

> Give me the lowest place: not that I dare
>   Ask for that lowest place, but Thou hast died
> That I might live and share
>   Thy glory by Thy side.
>
> Give me the lowest place: or if for me
>   That lowest place too high, make one more low
> Where I may sit and see
>   My God and love Thee so.

The poem only makes sense as an expression of self-abnegation outside of its theological frame. As a statement of faith, it becomes a prayer for weakness in anticipation of meeting God face to face in the apocalypse (Revelation 22. 4). For God is neither first or last but rather both, 'Alpha and Omega' (1. 11), and a renunciation of duality that, like kenōsis, 'reverses' the strong thinking that delays the coming of the new creation. As Charles Gore argued, kenōsis requires an empathetic identification with the powerless, which, in Sarah Coakley's words, necessitates a 'blueprint' for an ideal 'human moral response' that reveals the 'nature' of divinity to be '"humble" and "non-grasping"'.[115] A direct challenge to '*machismo*' and 'worldly power', kenōsis impels an ontological change in which 'strength is made perfect in weakness' (2 Corinthians 12. 9) and all things are emptied of egoic status to harmonize human and nonhuman into co-inherence with God.[116] At the same time, kenōsis is a direct request for a specifically *human* vulnerability for Rossetti, in part because the plant and animal already know how to love God without toil or spin, but also because the human is the one species willing to turn away from grace because of a reluctance to become weak.

Rossetti employed 'weak' forms like contemplation, prayer, and poetry to expose her readers to the unexpected and perplexing mysteries Sara Coleridge found so objectionable. Submission to grace was the route, not to self-annihilation and torment, but to a joyful self-disclosure before God that created the means for approaching what she called 'a sacred Inscrutability of Mystery' in the form of the 'Ever Blessed Trinity'.[117] Her belief in the Trinity was practical in that it described her experience of the interconnectedness of creation with the divine achieved through weakness. While some branches of

Protestantism sought to move beyond the 'tangled Trinities' debated by the Fathers, Rossetti embraced this entanglement precisely because it modelled a cosmos in which things emerge through interaction with other things.[118] By emptying themselves into each other in kenōtic relationship, things are entangled in Christ, the 'manifestation of the Unapproachable Trinity', and so become ontologically inseparable.[119] Rossetti gave an example of kenōsis in *Time Flies* in the story of St Perpetua and St Felicitas, third-century Christian martyrs whose account of the events leading up to their martyrdom was believed to have been recorded by Perpetua in her prison diary.[120] A married noblewoman and mother, Perpetua finds herself imprisoned alongside a pregnant slave called Felicity, both sentenced to death for their Christian faith. While Perpetua's father secures her freedom on the condition she disavow God, the noblewoman chooses to stay with the vulnerable and powerless Felicity, and both suffer horrific deaths in a series of Roman military games.[121] Rossetti does not highlight the women's devotion to God amidst their public slaughter but rather their loyalty to each other through God. Both equally 'noble' in her retelling, the women mirror Christ's kenōsis by 'enduring' with each other as they reject the possibility of worldly salvation for a shared grace in God.[122] Their actions move them beyond the time of the old creation and into the new, Rossetti concludes, '"where there is neither . . . bond nor free; but Christ is all, and in all"', a paraphrase of Colossians 3. 11. For Rossetti, this subversion of the dualistic and egotistic affirms God as a 'simplicity' available to those who 'seek Him' in 'simplicity of heart'.[123]

Many of the poems Rossetti wrote in the last ten years of her life seek to gentle the reader into a preparatory weakness through which to receive Christ, enter the Trinity, and welcome the new creation. In a prayer for grace in *The Face of the Deep*, for example, she asked God to ready her for what is to come:

> In this age of probation prepare Thou generation after generation for the eternal ages of perfected sanctity; until the knowledge of Thy glory shall fill the earth as the waters cover the sea, and all saints shall be co-extensive with all nations. Father, Son, Holy Spirit, Co-Eternal Trinity in Unity, we plead the Merits of Jesus Christ. Amen.[124]

The homily requests that the Christian engage with 'knowledge' of God and creation to perceive a glory already present in all things and 'all nations'. Rossetti's implication is that the new creation is the old creation discerned through different eyes. She encouraged her reader to pray her way into such discernment, not because it would help save her soul in the future, but because it revealed a joyful and dynamic way of being with others in this time that would bring on the new creation. The new creation is not an 'afterlife', but a confirmation of this life lived in faith and love, as she illustrated in a short poem for *The Face of the Deep*, 'Love builds a nest on earth and waits for rest'. The poem comes towards the end of her reading of Revelation, and follows Rossetti's commentary on 21. 23 wherein John states that the New Jerusalem, illuminated by God and the Lamb, has 'no need' of sun or moonlight.[125] In the commentary, Rossetti commented that the reader might expect the Christian confronted with John's prophecy to turn to the 'strong faith' of the 'king' and 'freeman'.[126] But the poem counters this will to power with a gentle language of love, rest, and warmth: 'Love sends to heaven the warm heart from its breast, | Looks to be blest and is already blest' (ll. 2–3). It is a language that resists the history of 'crimes' and 'unrighteousness' with which Rossetti associated kingship in her commentary, a position in which it is almost impossible to connect to God. If a 'rich man' finds it hard to 'enter into the kingdom of heaven', she wrote, how much more difficult for 'royal rich men to whom tribute, custom, fear, honour, are due'.[127]

Rossetti rejected the 'strong' status of kings for the 'weak' status of Jesus. She followed her critique of male power with a description of Jesus that refers directly to the kenōtic lines of Philippians 2: 'O Perfect Lord Jesus, Who being the Creator wert pleased to abase Thyself to become a Creature, and amongst creatures a dutiful Son' and 'a submissive Subject'.[128] Through weakness, Jesus perfectly incarnates affection and love. But Rossetti also offered the reader a second archetype of weakness in the figure of Mary Magdalene. Quoting John 20. 14, 'Make us as Mary when she turned and said Rabboni', at the end of her reading of Revelation 21. 24, she elevated Mary as an embodiment of kenōsis.[129] Recognizable to her Victorian readership as a fallen woman, Mary is precisely the kind of weakened outsider Caputo argues is central to the kingdom of God. In her weakness, she perceives the risen Jesus as a gardener, an intimate part of the nonhuman world, before he reveals himself to her as the Christ, at once human and divine. In Rossetti's reading, the moment of recognition between Jesus and Mary is a kenōtic one in which different orders of being are poured into each other through discernment. She confirms this by concluding her commentary on Mary with her poem, 'Bring me to see, Lord, bring me yet to see', in which all things—from 'nations', 'priests', 'kings', 'patriarchs', and 'mothers' (ll. 2, 7–9) to 'holy little ones', 'hermits', 'life-losers', and the 'blessed hungry and athirst' (ll. 10, 14, 16–17)—become one with Christ through the cross. Reprinted in *Verses* under the title 'The General Assembly and Church of the Firstborn', a reference to Paul's description of the 'heavenly Jerusalem' in Hebrews 12. 23, the poem closes with an image of all things moving into kenōsis through the crucifixion: 'All who bore crosses round the Holy Rood, | Friends, brethren, sisters, of Lord Jesus Christ' (ll. 18–19).

Rossetti had already envisioned the cross as a symbol of emptying in a series of Easter poems for *Time Flies*. In the poems, she presented the process from Jesus's descent from equality with God to his Incarnation in human form and finally to a barbarous death by crucifixion to be one of unequivocal kenōsis. In 'Monday in Holy Week', for example, she portrayed Jesus listing his sacrifices for the reader only to suggest that they result in an offer of emptiness: 'Bitter death I bore for thee, | Bore My cross to carry thee, | And wilt thou have nought of Me?' (ll. 6–8).[130] While in 'One step more, and the race is ended' (retitled 'Septuagesima' in *Verses*), she linked the carrying of the cross directly to the setting of the sun (l. 12), a 'figure of Christ', she wrote in *The Face of the Deep*, that dies with him at the crucifixion to signal the end of the old creation.[131] Jesus's weak posture 'grown faint upon the Cross' in 'Good Friday' even weakens creation itself, as heaven and earth shake in anticipation of their transformation (l. 1).[132] The kenōsis of the cross is further transformed in *The Face of the Deep* into a sacramental symbol of an earth broken by industry and technology, but renewable through a weak commitment to its diversity through the demotion of human power. Her prayer on Revelation 2. 23, for example, displaces and empties human subjectivity through the repetition of the word 'All' in which everything becomes graced: 'O Jesus, All Holy, All Just, All Merciful, deliver us from our perverse selves, and no other enemy can ruin us'.[133] As the poem that follows, 'Lord, carry me', relates, emptied of the self the human can receive Jesus's weakness on the cross as 'Power' (l. 4), or what Caputo calls the 'power of powerlessness, the power of the call, the power of protest that rises up from innocent suffering and calls out against it'.[134]

Like the practical call of the divine Rossetti heard from God through Augustine, the weak power of the vulnerable is voiced by the nonhuman as well as the human. As a tree, the cross is both an embodiment of Jesus's brokenness, and an image of vegetal inter-dependence, reaching both horizontally and vertically to embrace all things. The cross is also a 'type' of the 'tree of life' that John promises will grow next to the 'river of water of life' (Revelation 22. 1–2), and so reveals creation as a branching network of energies comprising 'all nations, and kindreds, and people, and tongues' (Revelation 7. 9). In her reading of this line, Rossetti observed that these things are connected, and so made divine, through difference in 'harmony' with each other rather than sameness in 'unison'. Where 'Babel dissolved the primitive unison into discord', she claimed, 'Pentecost reduced the prevalent discord to contingent harmony' in order to 'keep time and tune'.[135] As the spirit descends on creation, it moves things into relation with each other, not as thinking and doing beings concerned with individual desires, but as interconnected aspects of one encounter with the divine. Rossetti does not seek a prelapsarian status for the natural world here, but rather imagined creation's diversity dying into this encounter. All things are included in this weak cruciferous embrace from plants whose petals grow crosswise to those who suffer emotional or physical distress. As she wrote in the concluding poem to her reading of Revelation 7. 9: 'Thy Cross cruciferous doth flower in all | And every cross, dear Lord, assigned to us: | Ours lowly-statured crosses' (ll. 1–3). In this cross-shattered state, creation is drawn into a divine life defined by forgiveness and redemption and sustained within it through an inclusive grace.[136]

Rossetti's final vision was one of kenōtic, self-less, power-less love for other things able to resist the egoic pull of ambition, greed, privilege, and supremacy. Her reading of Revelation, like her reading of Christianity, concluded that the yearning of the 'I' was only fulfilled when it was dissipated across the persons of the Trinity and reasserted in a cruciform plurality. In this form, all things are both one and multiple, 'changed into the same image' but only by a 'Spirit' that is internally triadic (2 Corinthians 3. 18). In a poem published in *The Face of the Deep* and retitled 'Passiontide' for *Verses*, Rossetti imagined

God's love as a way of perceiving the human as an embodiment of diversity—creaturely, plant-like, elemental, and divine—who is called to God through grace (she notably changed the phrasing of this call from 'To deck heaven's bowers' in *The Face of the Deep* to 'To grace Heaven's bowers' in the later *Verses*).[137] The last lines of the poem capture the dizzying confusion of becoming multiple, the Trinity of 'I's here caught amidst a series of dashes, brackets, and indents:

> 'Come thou who waiting seekest Me'—'Come thou for
> whom I seek and wait'—
> (Why will we die?)—
> 'Come and repent: come and amend: come joy the joys
> unsatiate'—
> —(Christ passeth by . . .)—
> Lord, pass not by—I come—and I—and I.
> Amen.   (ll. 13–18)

While the lines are unsettled lyrically by their uncertain rhythm, they situate the reader in an antiphonal dialogue that splits into three in the penultimate line. But Rossetti's use of the dash here, usually regarded as the provenance of Emily Dickinson, is connective and relational, and models a kinship based on the 'I' as a repeating, multiple, and shared mode of being. The dash signifies both the thoughtful silence of the believer confronted by God's voice and her connection to it. While Dickinson's dash might be read as part of a similarly nondual grammar, Rossetti found her verse 'wonderfully Blakean' but compromised by 'a startling recklessness of poetic ways and means'—visionary perhaps, but formally and spiritually audacious.[138] By the end of her life, Rossetti had little interest in the self-assertion of the individual self, and sought to embed her writing not only in the writings of Christian tradition, but in a fellowship of creatures and things joined in the divine body. From her focus on the natural world to her anti-vivisectionist politics and final reimagining of Revelation, she argued that creation was held and moved by a green grace in which all things imaged and flourished in God and should be attended to as such. Her faithful rejection of the violent dogmatism of power, strength, and force to embrace the love and grace of the weak remains compelling and apposite, and establishes Rossetti as a significant voice in the ongoing study of Christianity and ecology.

Notes

1. Christina G. Rossetti, *The Face of the Deep: A Devotional Commentary on the Apocalypse* (London: Society for Promoting Christian Knowledge, 1892), 51.
2. Ibid. 349.
3. Ibid. 480–1.
4. Ibid. 189, 185, 201.
5. Ibid. 185.
6. Ibid. 547; Thomas Aquinas, *Summa Theologica* (Cincinnati: Benziger, 1947), 1519, and see Peter Groves, *Grace: The Cruciform Love of God* (Norwich: Canterbury Press, 2012), 99.
7. Rossetti, *Face of the Deep*, 118.
8. See Christopher Rowland, *The Open Heaven: A Study of Apocalyptic in Judaism* (New York: Crossroad, 1982); and *Radical Prophet: The Mystics, Subversives and Visionaries who foretold the End of the World* (London: I. B. Tauris, 2017).
9. Christina G. Rossetti, *Seek and Find: A Double Series of Short Studies on the Benedicite* (London: Society for Promoting Christian Knowledge, 1879), 79.
10. Christina G. Rossetti, *Time Flies: A Reading Diary* (London: Society for Promoting Christian Knowledge, 1885), 88.
11. Charles Cayley, *The Paradise* (London: Longman, Brown, Green, and Longmans, 1854), canto XIV, quoted in Rossetti, *Time Flies*, 88.
12. Rossetti, *Seek and Find*, 44.
13. Johannes Behm, 'Kainós', in Gerhard Kittel, *Theological Dictionary of the New Testament*, 10 vols (Grand Rapids, MI: Wm B. Eerdmans, 1965), 447–54 (447).
14. Edward Bouverie Pusey, *Sermons During the Season from Advent to Whitsuntide* (Oxford: John Henry Parker, 1848), 35–46 (35).
15. Peter Benedict Nockles, *The Oxford Movement in Context: Anglican High Churchmanship 1760–1857* (Cambridge: Cambridge University Press, 1994), 97.
16. John Shelton Reed, *Glorious Battle: The Cultural Politics of Victorian Anglo-Catholicism* (Nashville: Vanderbilt University Press, 1996), 64.
17. Henry William Burrows, *The Half Century of Christ Church, Albany Street, St Pancras* (London: Skeffington & Son, 1887), 50–1.
18. Edward Bouverie Pusey, 'Tract 67: Scriptural Views of Holy Baptism' (1835), in *Tracts for the Times by Members of the University of Oxford*, 6 vols (London: J. G. F. and J. Rivington; Oxford: J. H. Parker, 1840), II, 41.
19. John Henry Newman, *Lectures on the Doctrine of Justification* (London: Rivington, 1840), 332–7.
20. Pusey, 'Tract 67', 23.
21. Alison Chapman and Joanna Meacock, *A Rossetti Family Chronology* (Basingstoke: Palgrave Macmillan, 2007), 88.
22. William Michael Rossetti, *Some Reminiscences of William Michael Rossetti*, 2 vols (New York: Charles Scribner's, 1906), II, 446–7.

23. Jan Marsh, *Christina Rossetti: A Literary Biography* (London: Pimlico, 1995), 511.
24. Christina G. Rossetti to Lucy Madox Brown Rossetti, Summer 1887, in Anthony H. Harrison, ed., *The Letters of Christina Rossetti: Volume 1 1843–1873; Volume II 1874–1881; Volume III 1882–1886; Volume IV 1887–1894* (Charlottesville and London: The University Press of Virginia, 1997, 1999, 2000, 2004), IV, 51; further references are abbreviated to *Letters*.
25. Rossetti, *Face of the Deep*, 83, 547.
26. Augustine, 'To Simplician—On Various Questions', I, ques. 2, vii, 21 in John H. S. Burleigh, trans., *Augustine: Earlier Writings* (Philadelphia: Westminster Press, 1953), 405.
27. Ekkehard Mühlenberg, 'Synergism in Gregory of Nyssa', *Zeitschrift für die alttestamentliche Wissenschaft*, 68 (1977), 93–4; Morwenna Ludlow, *Gregory of Nyssa, Ancient and (Post)modern* (Oxford: Oxford University Press, 2007), 119.
28. Aquinas, *Summa*, 329.
29. Rossetti, *Face of the Deep*, 158.
30. Ailise Bulfin, '"The End of Time": M. P. Shiel and the "Apocalyptic Imaginary"', in Trish Ferguson, ed., *Victorian Time: Technologies, Standardizations, Catastrophes* (Basingstoke: Palgrave Macmillan, 2013), 153–77 (155).
31. Christina Rossetti to William Michael Rossetti, 28 February 1887, *Letters*, IV, 17.
32. Rossetti, *Seek and Find*, 105.
33. Rossetti, *Face of the Deep*, 99.
34. Pusey, 'Tract 67', 44 n. 1.
35. Rossetti, *Face of the Deep*, 239.
36. See Jean-Louis Chrétien, *Pour reprendre et perdre haleine: dix brèves meditations* (Montrouge Cedex: Bayard Éditions, 2009).
37. Rossetti, *Time Flies*, 53.
38. See John Ruskin, 'Of Leaf Beauty', *Modern Painters: Volume V*, in E. T. Cook and Alexander Wedderburn, eds., *The Works of John Ruskin*, 39 vols (London: George Allen, 1903–12), VII, 25.
39. Composition dates unknown except for 'Easter Monday' (1864), all published in Rossetti, *Time Flies*, 264–6.
40. Rossetti, *Time Flies*, 265.
41. Rossetti, *Face of the Deep*, 144.
42. Ibid. 144.
43. On the phrase 'oceanic feeling', see Sigmund Freud, *Civilization and its Discontents*, trans. James Strachey (New York and London: W. W. Norton, 2010).
44. Christina G. Rossetti to Anne Burrows Gilchrist, 14 June 1868, *Letters*, I, 311.
45. Christina G. Rossetti to Amelia Barnard Heimann, 6 May 1873, *Letters*, I, 425; Christina G. Rossetti to DGR, 17 July 1879, *Letters*, II, 203;

Christina G. Rossetti to Lucy Madox Brown Rossetti, 21 March 1887, *Letters*, IV, 26.

46. Christina G. Rossetti to Miss Newsham, 21 August 1889, *Letters*, IV, 154.
47. Christina G. Rossetti to William Michael Rossetti, 21 July 1879, *Letters*, II, 204.
48. Marsh, *Rossetti*, 541.
49. Christina G. Rossetti to Rose Donne Hake, 27 September 1886, *Letters*, III, 341.
50. Rossetti, *Face of the Deep*, 470–1.
51. See Marsh, *Rossetti*, 541–2.
52. Rossetti, *Seek and Find*, 107.
53. Ibid. 107.
54. Ibid. 108.
55. Ibid. 109.
56. Rossetti, *Face of the Deep*, 189–91.
57. Ibid. 191.
58. Pierre Teilhard de Chardin, *The Future of Man*, trans. Norman Denny (New York: Harper & Row, 1964), 192.
59. Rossetti, *Face of the Deep*, 151.
60. Ibid. 550.
61. Ibid. 152.
62. Ibid.
63. Ibid.
64. Ibid. 99; 'A Birthday' (1857); Rossetti, *Time Flies*, 82.
65. Rossetti, *Face of the Deep*, 99.
66. Christina G. Rossetti, *Called to Be Saints: The Minor Festivals Devotionally Studied* (London: Society for Promoting Christian Knowledge, 1881), 518–19.
67. Rossetti, *Face of the Deep*, 289.
68. Ibid. 485.
69. Rossetti, *Time Flies*, 181; see Jürgen Moltmann, *The Coming of God: Christian Eschatology*, trans. Margaret Kohl (London: SCM Press, 1996), 282.
70. Rossetti, *Time Flies*, 180.
71. Trish Ferguson, 'Introduction', in Ferguson, ed., *Victorian Time*, 1–15 (1).
72. Rossetti, *Time Flies*, 180.
73. Ibid. 110; Rossetti, *Face of the Deep*, 245–6.
74. The story was originally published in the *Churchman's Shilling Magazine*, 2 (November 1867), 287–92; and in *Commonplace and other Short Stories* (London: F. S. Ellis, 1870), 239–53; references are to *Commonplace*.
75. Rossetti, 'Investment', 241.
76. Ibid. 242.
77. Ibid.
78. Ibid. 241, 243–4.
79. Ibid. 244, 245.
80. Ibid. 249.

81. Ibid. 249–50.
82. Ibid. 251.
83. Ibid. 251, 252.
84. Ibid. 253.
85. Rossetti, *Face of the Deep*, 107.
86. Rossetti, *Time Flies*, 2; Rossetti, *Called to Be Saints*, 54; Rossetti, *Face of the Deep*, 224.
87. See Aquinas, *Summa*, 2552.
88. Rossetti, *Reminiscences*, II, 526.
89. William Sharp, *Papers Critical and Reminiscent*, ed. Elizabeth Sharp (London: William Heinemann, 1912), 95, 96, 98; George Gissing, *The Whirlpool* (London: Lawrence and Bullen, 1897), 396.
90. Clipping of unattributed newspaper, Rossetti–Heimann Collection, Princeton University, in Chapman and Meacock, *Family Chronology*, 403.
91. See ibid. 387, 393, 404; Rossetti, *Reminiscences*, II, 531–4.
92. Ibid. 539.
93. Evelyn Underhill, *Practical Mysticism* (New York: E. P. Dutton, 1915).
94. Rossetti, *Face of the Deep*, 59.
95. Ibid. 25.
96. See Holmes Rolston, III, 'Kenosis and Nature', in John Polkinghorne, ed., *The Work of Love: Creation as Kenosis* (Grand Rapids, MI: Eerdmans, 2001), 43–65.
97. Rossetti, *Seek and Find*, 309.
98. Rossetti, *Face of the Deep*, 107.
99. See David Brown, *Divine Humanity: Kenosis Explored and Defended* (London: SCM Press, 2011).
100. J. R. Illingworth, 'The Incarnation in Relation to Development', in Charles Gore, ed., *Lux Mundi: A Series of Studies in the Religion of the Incarnation* (London: John Murray, 1890), 179–214 (195, 207).
101. Rossetti, *Seek and Find*, 146–7.
102. Josh King, *Imagined Spiritual Communities in Britain's Age of Print* (Columbus: Ohio State University Press, 2015), 248–9.
103. Ibid. 234; Karen Dieleman, *Religious Imaginaries: The Liturgical and Poetic Practices of Elizabeth Barrett Browning, Christina Rossetti, and Adelaide Procter* (Athens: Ohio University Press, 2012), 153–4.
104. Rossetti, *Face of the Deep*, 206.
105. Christina G. Rossetti to Lucy Madox Brown Rossetti, 11 January 1886, in *Letters*, III, 294; the *Memoirs* were edited by Sara's daughter, Edith, with whom Rossetti had attended Christ Church, Albany Street, as a child, and met again in 1887 in Torquay with Mrs Swynfen Jervis, widow of the fern hunter with whom she had stayed in the 1850s.
106. See Jeffrey W. Barbeau, *Sara Coleridge: Her Life and Thought* (New York: Palgrave Macmillan, 2014); and Robin Schofield, *The Vocation of Sara Coleridge: Authorship and Religion* (New York: Palgrave Macmillan, 2018).

107. Sara Coleridge to Henry Nelson Coleridge, 23 September 1837, in Edith Coleridge, ed., *Memoirs and Letters of Sara Coleridge*, 2 vols (London: Henry S. King, 1873), I, 184–6, 187.

108. Rossetti, *Seek and Find*, 24.

109. Ibid. 24; Coleridge, *Memoirs*, 187.

110. Rossetti, *Face of the Deep*, 189.

111. Rossetti, *Called to Be Saints*, 175.

112. Ibid.

113. Rossetti, *Face of the Deep*, 189.

114. John Caputo, *The Weakness of God: A Theology of the Event* (Bloomington and Indianapolis: Indiana University Press, 2006), 278.

115. Charles Gore, *The Incarnation of the Son of God* (London: J. Murray, 1891), 159–62; Sarah Coakley, *Powers and Submissions: Spirituality, Philosophy and Gender* (Oxford: Blackwell, 2002), 10, 21.

116. Ibid. 10.

117. Rossetti, *Face of the Deep*, 126.

118. Horton Davies, *Worship and Theology in England: From Watts and Wesley to Martineau, 1690–1900*, 6 vols (Michigan and Cambridge: Wm B. Eerdmans, 1996), IV, 194.

119. Rossetti, *Face of the Deep*, 151.

120. Rossetti, *Time Flies*, 47–8.

121. Thomas J. Heffernan, *The Passion of Perpetua and Felicity* (Oxford: Oxford University Press, 2012), 69.

122. Rossetti, *Time Flies*, 48.

123. Rossetti, *Face of the Deep*, 295, 307.

124. Ibid. 374.

125. Ibid. 512.

126. Ibid. 513.

127. Ibid. 514.

128. Ibid. 515.

129. Ibid.

130. Rossetti, *Time Flies*, 260.

131. Ibid. 165; Rossetti, *Face of the Deep*, 215.

132. Rossetti, *Time Flies*, 263.

133. Rossetti, *Face of the Deep*, 79.

134. Caputo, *Weakness*, 43.

135. Rossetti, *Face of the Deep*, 231.

136. See Stanley Hauerwas, *Cross-Shattered Christ: Meditations on the Seven Last Words* (Grand Rapids, MI: Brazos Press, 2004).

137. Rossetti, *Face of the Deep*, 523.

138. Christina G. Rossetti to William Michael Rossetti, 6 December 1890, in *Letters*, IV, 222.

Select Bibliography

Manuscripts

Anon., 'The Principal Clergy of London: Classified According to their opinions on the Great Church questions of the day', 1844, Bodleian Libraries, University of Oxford, MS Add.c.290.

Frances Mary Lavinia Polidori, *Commonplace Book*, Angeli-Dennis Collection, University of British Columbia Special Collections Division, Box 12–87; facsimile in Bodleian Libraries, Oxford, MS Facs.d.286.

Frances Mary Lavinia Polidori, 'Diaries of Frances Mary Lavinia Rossetti', 131 leaves, entries for 18–26 January 1881, Angeli-Dennis Collection, University of British Columbia Special Collections Division, Box 6–16, 12–17; facsimile in Bodleian Libraries, Oxford, MS Facs.c.96.

Christina G. Rossetti, 'Memoranda for my Executor', Angeli-Dennis Collection, University of British Columbia Special Collections Division, Box 10, 10–12; facsimile in Bodleian Libraries, Oxford, MS Facs.d.285.

Christina G. Rossetti, *Sing Song: A Nursery Rhyme Book* (1868–70), British Library, London, Ashley MS 1371.

Other

Adams, Carol J., *The Sexual Politics of Meat: A Feminist-Vegetarian Critical Theory* (New York and London: Continuum, 1990).

Agamben, Giorgio, *The Highest Poverty: Monastic Rules and Form-of-Life*, trans. Adam Kotsko (Stanford: Stanford University Press, 2011).

Aquinas, Thomas, *Summa Theologica* (Cincinnati: Benziger, 1947).

Armstrong, Isobel, *Victorian Poetry: Poetry, Poetics and Politics* (London and New York: Routledge, 1993).

Armstrong, Regis J. and Ignatius C. Brady, trans., *Francis and Clare: The Complete Works* (Mahwah, NJ: Paulist Press, 1982).

Arseneau, Mary, *Recovering Christina Rossetti: Female Community and Incarnational Poetics* (New York: Palgrave Macmillan, 2004).

Arseneau, Mary, Antony H. Harrison, and Lorraine Janzen Kooistra, eds., *The Culture of Christina Rossetti: Female Poetics and Victorian Contexts* (Athens: Ohio University Press, 1999).

Atkins, Gareth, ed., *Making and Remaking Saints in Nineteenth Century Britain* (Manchester: Manchester University Press, 2016).

Barad, Karen, *Meeting the Universe Halfway: Quantum Physics and the Entanglement of Matter and Meaning* (Durham, NC: Duke University Press, 2007).

Barrett, William Alexander, *Flowers and Festivals; or Directions for Floral Decoration of Churches* (London, Oxford, and Cambridge: Rivingtons, 1868).

Barush, Kathryn R., *Art and the Sacred Journey in Britain 1790–1850* (London and New York: Routledge, 2016).

Battiscombe, Georgina, *Christina Rossetti: A Divided Life* (New York: Holt, Rinehart and Winston, 1981).

Bauckham, Richard, 'Reading the Sermon on the Mount in an Age of Ecological Catastrophe', *Studies in Christian Ethics*, 22.1 (2009), 76–88.

Bell, Mackenzie, *Christina Rossetti: A Biographical and Critical Study* (Boston: Roberts Brothers, 1989).

Bennett, Jane, *Vibrant Matter: A Political Ecology of Things* (Durham, NC: Duke University Press, 2010).

Bennett, William J. E., *The Principles of the Book of Common Prayer Considered: A Series of Lecture Sermons* (1845; London: W. J. Cleaver, 1848).

Blair, Kirstie, *Form and Faith in Victorian Poetry and Religion* (Oxford: Oxford University Press, 2012).

Bradstock, Andrew, and Christopher Rowland, *Radical Christian Writings: A Reader* (Oxford: Blackwell, 2002).

Brown, David, *Divine Humanity: Kenosis Explored and Defended* (London: SCM Press, 2011).

Brown, Kate E., 'Futurity and Postponement: Christina Rossetti and the Yearning for Advent', *Intertexts*, 8.1 (2003), 15–21.

Brown, Stewart J., and Peter B. Nockles, eds., *The Oxford Movement: Europe and the Wider World 1830–1930* (Cambridge: Cambridge University Press, 2012).

Brown, Stewart J., Peter B. Nockles, and James Pereiro, eds., *The Oxford Handbook of the Oxford Movement* (Oxford: Oxford University Press, 2017).

Burrows, Henry William, *The Half-Century of Christ Church, Albany Street, St. Pancras* (London: Skeffington & Son, 1887).

Caputo, John, *The Weakness of God: A Theology of the Event* (Bloomington and Indianapolis: Indiana University Press, 2006).

Chapman, Alison, and Joanna Meacock, *A Rossetti Family Chronology* (New York: Palgrave Macmillan, 2007).

Chardin, Pierre Teilhard de, *The Future of Man*, trans. Norman Denny (New York: Harper & Row, 1964).

Christie, Douglas E., *The Blue Sapphire of the Mind: Notes for a Contemplative Ecology* (Oxford: Oxford University Press, 2013).

Coakley, Sarah, *Powers and Submissions: Spirituality, Philosophy and Gender* (Oxford: Blackwell, 2002).

Coakley, Sarah, *God, Sexuality, and the Self: An Essay on the Trinity* (Cambridge: Cambridge University Press, 2013).

Coleridge, Edith, ed., *Memoirs and Letters of Sara Coleridge*, 2 vols (London: Henry S. King, 1873).

Cook, E. T., and Alexander Wedderburn, eds., *The Works of John Ruskin*, 39 vols (London: George Allen, 1905).

Crump, Rebecca, ed., *The Complete Poems of Christina Rossetti: A Variorum Edition*, 3 vols (Baton Rouge and London: Louisiana State University Press, 1979, 1986, 1990).

D'Amico, Diane, 'Christina Rossetti's *Later Life*: The Neglected Sonnet Sequence', *Victorians Institute Journal*, 9 (1980–1), 21–8.

D'Amico, Diane, *Christina Rossetti: Faith, Gender, and Time* (Baton Rouge: Louisiana State University Press, 1999).

D'Amico, Diane, 'The House of Christina Rossetti: Domestic and Poetic Spaces', *The Journal of Pre-Raphaelite Studies*, 19 (2010), 31–54.

D'Amico, Diane, and David A. Kent, 'Christina Rossetti's Notes on Genesis and Exodus', *The Journal of Pre-Raphaelite Studies*, 13 (2004), 49–98.

Dieleman, Karen, *Religious Imaginaries: The Liturgical and Poetic Practices of Elizabeth Barrett Browning, Christina Rossetti, and Adelaide Procter* (Athens: Ohio University Press, 2012).

Dodsworth, William, *The Signs of the Times: Sermons Preached in Advent 1848* (London: Joseph Masters, 1849).

Douglas, Brian, *The Eucharistic Theology of Edward Bouverie Pusey: Sources, Context and Doctrine within the Oxford Movement and Beyond* (Leiden and Boston: Brill, 2015).

Edwards, Denis, *Jesus the Wisdom of God: An Ecological Theory* (Eugene, OR: Wipf and Stock, 2005).

Evans, C. Stephen, *Exploring Kenotic Christology: The Self-Emptying of God* (Oxford: Oxford University Press, 2006).

Ferguson, Trish, ed., *Victorian Time: Technologies, Standardizations, Catastrophes* (Basingstoke: Palgrave Macmillan, 2013).

Fredeman, William E., *The P. R. B. Journal: William Michael Rossetti's Diary of the Pre-Raphaelite Brotherhood 1849–1853* (Oxford: Clarendon Press, 1975).

Fredeman, William E., ed., *The Correspondence of Dante Gabriel Rossetti, The Formative Years: Charlotte Street to Cheyne Walk (1835–1862)*, 2 vols (Cambridge: D. S. Brewer, 2002).

Furnish, Victor Paul, *The Love Command in the New Testament* (Nashville and New York: Abington Press, 1972).

Gaard, Greta, ed., *Ecofeminism: Women, Animals, Nature* (Philadelphia: Temple University Press, 1993).

Giebelhausen, Michaela, *Painting the Bible: Representation and Belief in Mid-Victorian Britain* (Aldershot: Ashgate, 2005).

Gosse, Edmund, *Critical Kit-Kats* (New York: Dodd, Mead and Co., 1896).

Gottlieb, Roger S., *This Sacred Earth: Religion, Nature, Environment* (New York: Routledge, 2004).

Gottlieb, Roger S., ed., *The Oxford Handbook of Religion and Ecology* (Oxford: Oxford University Press, 2006).

Grass, Sean C., 'Nature's Perilous Variety in Rossetti's "Goblin Market"', *Nineteenth-Century Literature*, 51.3 (1996), 356–76.

Groves, Peter, *Grace: The Cruciform Love of God* (Norwich: Canterbury Press, 2012).

Haraway, Donna J., *The Companion Species Manifesto: Dogs, People, and Significant Otherness* (Chicago: Prickly Paradigm Press, 2003).

Haraway, Donna J., *Staying with the Trouble: Making Kin in the Chthulucene* (Durham, NC: Duke University Press, 2016).

Harrison, Anthony H., *Christina Rossetti in Context* (Chapel Hill and London: University of North Carolina Press, 1988).

Harrison, Anthony H., ed., *The Letters of Christina Rossetti: Volume 1 1843–1873; Volume II 1874–1881; Volume III 1882–1886; Volume IV 1887–1894* (Charlottesville and London: The University Press of Virginia, 1997, 1999, 2000, 2004).

Harrison, Verna, 'Perichoresis in the Greek Fathers', *St Vladimir's Theological Quarterly*, 35 (1991), 53–65.

Hart, John, *Sacramental Commons: Christian Ecological Ethics* (Lanham: Rowman & Littlefield, 2006).

Hassett, Constance, *Christina Rossetti: The Patience of Style* (Charlottesville and London: University of Virginia Press, 2005).

Heady, Chene, '"Earth has clear call of daily bells": Nature's Apocalyptic Liturgy in Christina Rossetti's *Verses*', *Religion and the Arts*, 15 (2011), 148–71.

Hensley, Nathan K., 'Christina Rossetti's Timescales of Catastrophe', *Nineteenth-Century Contexts*, 38.5 (2016), 399–415.

Hessel, Dieter T., and Rosemary Radford Ruether, eds., *Christianity and Ecology: Seeking the Well-Being of Earth and Humans* (Cambridge, MA: Harvard University Press, 2000).

Humphries, Simon, ed., *Christina Rossetti: Poems and Prose* (Oxford: Oxford University Press, 2008).

Hunt, William Holman, *Pre-Raphaelitism and the Pre-Raphaelite Brotherhood*, 2 vols (London: Macmillan and Co., 1905).

Ives, Maura, ed., *Christina Rossetti: A Descriptive Bibliography* (New Castle, DE: Oak Knoll Press, 2011).

Janes, Dominic, *Victorian Reformation: The Fight Over Idolatry in the Church of England, 1840–1860* (Oxford: Oxford University Press, 2009).

Janes, Dominic, '"The Catholic Florist": Flowers and Deviance in the Mid-Nineteenth-Century Church of England', *Visual Culture in Britain*, 12.1 (2011), 77–96.

Jenkins, Willis, *Ecologies of Grace: Environmental Ethics and Christian Theology* (Oxford: Oxford University Press, 2008).

Johnson, Elizabeth A., *She Who Is: The Mystery of God in Feminist Theological Discourse* (New York: Crossroad Publishing, 1992).

Jones, Kathleen, *Learning not to be First: The Life of Christina Rossetti* (Oxford: Oxford University Press, 1992).

Jones, Timothy Willem, and Lucinda Matthews-Jones, *Material Religion in Modern Britain: The Spirit of Things* (New York: Palgrave Macmillan, 2015).

Keble, John, *Occasional Papers and Reviews* (Oxford and London: James Parker and Co., 1877).

Keble, John, *Lectures on Poetry 1832–1841*, trans. E. K. Francis, 2 vols (Oxford: Clarendon Press, 1912).

Keller, Catherine, *Cloud of the Impossible: Negative Theology and Planetary Entanglement* (New York: Columbia University Press, 2014).

Kelley, Theresa M., *Clandestine Marriage: Botany and Romantic Culture* (Baltimore: Johns Hopkins University Press, 2012).

Kent, David A., ed., *The Achievement of Christina Rossetti* (Ithaca: Cornell University Press, 1987).

Keynes, Geoffrey, *The Note-Book of William Blake called the Rossetti Manuscript* (London: The Nonesuch Press, 1935).

King, Josh, *Imagined Spiritual Communities in Britain's Age of Print* (Columbus: Ohio State University Press, 2015).

Kooistra, Lorraine Janzen, *Christina Rossetti and Illustration: A Publishing History* (Athens: Ohio University Press, 2002).

Kooistra, Lorraine Janzen, 'Teaching Victorian Illustrated Poetry: Hands-on Material Culture', *Victorian Review*, 34.2 (2008), 43–61.

Larkin, Peter, *Wordsworth and Coleridge: Promising Losses* (Basingstoke: Palgrave Macmillan, 2012).

Larkin, Peter, *City-Trappings (Housing Heath or Wood)* (London: Veer Books, 2016).

Liddon, Henry Parry, *Life of Edward Bouverie Pusey*, 4 vols (London: Longmans, 1894).

Lightman, Bernard, *Victorian Popularizers of Science: Designing Nature for New Audiences* (Chicago and London: University of Chicago Press, 2007).

Littledale, Richard Frederick, *The North-Side of the Altar* (London, 1865).

Littledale, Richard Frederick, 'The Religious Education of Women', *The Contemporary Review*, 20 (June 1872), 1–26.

Littledale, Richard Frederick, 'The Professional Studies of the English Clergy', *The Contemporary Review* (April 1879), 1–36.

Ludlow, Elizabeth, *Christina Rossetti and the Bible: Waiting with the Saints* (London: Bloomsbury, 2014).

Ludlow, Elizabeth, 'Christina Rossetti's *Later Life*: A Double Sonnet of Sonnets (1881): Exploring the Fearfulness of Forgiveness', *Literature Compass*, 11.2 (2014), 84–93.

Ludlow, Morwenna, *Gregory of Nyssa, Ancient and (Post)modern* (Oxford: Oxford University Press, 2007).

Lysack, Krista, 'The Productions of Time: Keble, Rossetti, and Victorian Devotional Reading', *Victorian Studies*, 55.3 (2013), 451–70.

McGann, Jerome J., 'The Religious Poetry of Christina Rossetti', *Critical Inquiry*, 10.1 (1983), 127–44.

McGrath, Alister E., *The Open Secret: A New Vision for Natural Theology* (Oxford: Wiley-Blackwell, 2008).

Mahood, M. M., *The Poet as Botanist* (Cambridge: Cambridge University Press, 2008).

Marder, Michael, *Plant-Thinking: A Philosophy of Vegetal Life* (New York: Columbia University Press, 2013).

Marsh, Jan, *Christina Rossetti: A Literary Biography* (London: Pimlico, 1995).

Marsh, Jan, 'Christina Rossetti at Haigh Hall', *The Journal of Pre-Raphaelite Studies*, 17 (2008), 47–9.

Marshall, Linda E., 'What the Dead are Doing Underground: Hades and Heaven in the Writings of Christina Rossetti', *The Victorian Newsletter*, 72 (1987), 55–60.

Marshall, Linda E., 'Astronomy of the Invisible: Contexts for Christina Rossetti's Heavenly Parables', *Women's Writing*, 2.2 (1995), 167–81.

Mason, Emma, 'Christina Rossetti and the Doctrine of Reserve', *Journal of Victorian Culture*, 7.2 (2002), 196–219.

Mazel, Adam, '"You, Guess": The Enigmas of Christina Rossetti', *Victorian Literature and Culture*, 44 (2016), 511–33.

Mazzeno, Laurence W., and Ronald D. Morrison, eds., *Victorian Writers and the Environment: Ecocritical Perspectives* (London and New York: Routledge, 2017).

Members of the University of Oxford, *Tracts for the Times*, 6 vols (London: J. G. F. and J. Rivington; Oxford: J. H. Parker, 1833–41).

Meredith, SJ, Anthony, *Gregory of Nyssa* (London and New York: Routledge, 1999).

Miller, Elaine P., *The Vegetal Soul: From Philosophy of Nature to Subjectivity in the Feminine* (New York: State University of New York Press, 2002).

Moltmann, Jürgen, *God in Creation: A New Theology of Creation and the Spirit of God*, trans. Margaret Kohl (New York: Harper & Row, 1991).

Moltmann, Jürgen, *The Coming of God: Christian Eschatology*, trans. Margaret Kohl (London: SCM Press, 1996).

Moore, Stephen D., ed., *Divinanimality: Animal Theory, Creaturely Theology* (New York: Fordham University Press, 2014).

Moorman, John R. H., *The Sources for the Life of S. Francis of Assisi* (Manchester: Manchester University Press, 1940).

Morrison, Kevin A., 'Christina Rossetti's Secrets', *Philological Quarterly*, 90.1 (2011), 97–116.

Morton, Timothy, *The Ecological Thought* (Cambridge, MA: Harvard University Press, 2010).

Mumm, Susan, *Stolen Daughters, Virgin Mothers: Anglican Sisterhoods in Victorian Britain* (London and New York: Leicester University Press, 1999).

Mumm, Susan, ed., *All Saints Sisters of the Poor: An Anglican Sisterhood in the Nineteenth Century* (Woodbridge and New York: Boydell, 2001).

Neale, John Mason, and Richard Frederick Littledale, *A Commentary on the Psalms, from Primitive and Medieval Writers, and from the Various Office-books and Hymns of the Roman, Mozarabic, Ambrosian, Gallican, Greek, Coptic, Armenian, and Syriac Rites*, 4 vols (London: Joseph Masters, 1868).

Negri, Antonio, and Michael Hardt, *Empire* (Cambridge, MA: Harvard University Press, 2000).

Newman, John Henry, *Lectures on the Doctrine of Justification* (London: Rivington, 1840).

Newman, John Henry, *Parochial and Plain Sermons in Eight Volumes* (London, Oxford, and Cambridge: Rivingtons, 1875).

Newman, John Henry, *An Essay in Aid of a Grammar of Assent* (1870; New York: Image, 1955).

Newman, John Henry, *Apologia Pro Vita Sua* (1864; London: Penguin, 1994).

Nichols, Ashton, *Beyond Romantic Ecocriticism: Toward Urbanatural Roosting* (New York: Palgrave Macmillan, 2011).

Nockles, Peter Benedict, *The Oxford Movement in Context: Anglican High Churchmanship 1760–1857* (Cambridge: Cambridge University Press, 1994).

Packer, Lona Mosk, *Christina Rossetti* (Berkeley and Los Angeles: University of California Press, 1963).

Palazzo, Lynda, *Christina Rossetti's Feminist Theology* (New York: Palgrave Macmillan, 2002).

Parkins, Wendy, ed., *Victorian Sustainability in Literature and Culture* (London: Routledge, 2018).

Polkinghorne, John, ed., *The Work of Love: Creation as Kenosis* (Grand Rapids, MI: Eerdmans, 2001).

Prettejohn, Elizabeth, ed., *The Cambridge Companion to the Pre-Raphaelites* (Cambridge: Cambridge University Press, 2012).

Prevot, Andrew, *Thinking Prayer: Theology and Spirituality Amid the Crises of Modernity* (Notre Dame: University of Notre Dame Press, 2015).

Prickett, Stephen, *Romanticism and Religion: The Tradition of Coleridge and Wordsworth in the Victorian Church* (Cambridge: Cambridge University Press, 1976).

Pugin, Augustus Welby, *Floriated Ornament: A Series of Thirty-One Designs* (London: Henry G. Bohn 1849).

Pusey, Edward Bouverie, *The Articles treated on in Tract 90 reconsidered and their Interpretation vindicated in a Letter to the Rev. R. W. Jelf, D. D.* (Oxford: John Henry Parker, 1841).

Pusey, Edward Bouverie, *The Holy Eucharist a Comfort to the Penitent: A Sermon Preached Before the University in the Cathedral Church of Christ, in Oxford, on the Fourth Sunday after Easter* (New York: D. Appleton, 1843).

Pusey, Edward Bouverie, *The Entire Absolution of the Penitent* (Oxford: John Henry Parker, 1846).

Pusey, Edward Bouverie, *Sermons During the Season from Advent to Whitsuntide* (Oxford: John Henry Parker, 1848).

Pusey, Edward Bouverie, *The Presence of Christ in the Holy Eucharist: A Sermon, Preached before the University, in the Cathedral Church of Christ, in Oxford, on the Second Sunday after Epiphany, 1853* (Oxford and London: John Henry Parker, 1853).

Pusey, Edward Bouverie, *Parochial Sermons*, 2 vols (Plymouth: The Devenport Society, 1862).

Pusey, Edward Bouverie, *The Miracles of Prayer: A Sermon Preached Before the University in the Cathedral Church of Christ, in Oxford on Septuagesima Sunday, 1866* (Oxford: John Henry and James Parker, 1866).

Pusey, Edward Bouverie, *On the Clause 'And the Son', in Regard to the Eastern Church and the Bonn Conference: A Letter to the Rev. H. P. Liddon* (Oxford: James Parker, 1876).

Reed, John Shelton, *Glorious Battle: The Cultural Politics of Victorian Anglo-Catholicism* (Nashville and London: Vanderbilt University Press, 1996).

Robson, Michael, *St Francis of Assisi: The Legend and the Life* (London and New York: Continuum, 1997).

Robson, Michael, ed., *The Cambridge Companion to Francis of Assisi* (Cambridge: Cambridge University Press, 2012).

Roe, Dinah, *Christina Rossetti's Faithful Imagination: The Devotional Poetry and Prose* (Basingstoke: Palgrave Macmillan, 2006).

Roe, Dinah, *The Rossettis in Wonderland: A Victorian Family History* (London: Haus, 2011).

Rogers, Scott, 'Re-Reading Sisterhood in Christina Rossetti's "Noble Sisters" and "Sister Maude"', *Studies in English Literature 1500–1900*, 43.4 (2003), 859–75.

Rossetti, Christina G., *Verses* (London: Private Printing by Gaetano Polidori, 1847).

Rossetti, Christina G., *Goblin Market and Other Poems* (Cambridge and London: Macmillan and Co., 1862; 2nd edn, 1865).

Rossetti, Christina G., *The Prince's Progress and Other Poems* (London: Macmillan and Co., 1866).

Rossetti, Christina G., *Commonplace and Other Short Stories* (London: F. S. Ellis, 1870).

Rossetti, Christina G., *Sing-Song: A Nursery Rhyme Book* (London: George Routledge and Sons, 1872).

Rossetti, Christina G., *Annus Domini: A Prayer for Each Day of the Year, Founded on a Text of Holy Scripture* (Oxford and London: James Parker, 1874).

Rossetti, Christina G., *Speaking Likenesses, with Pictures thereof by Arthur Hughes* (London: Macmillan and Co., 1874).

Rossetti, Christina G., *Goblin Market, The Prince's Progress, and Other Poems* (London: Macmillan and Co., 1875).

Rossetti, Christina G., *Seek and Find: A Double Series of Short Studies on the Benedicite* (London: Society for Promoting Christian Knowledge, 1879).

Rossetti, Christina G., *A Pageant and Other Poems* (London: Macmillan, 1880).

Rossetti, Christina G., *Called to Be Saints: The Minor Festivals Devotionally Studied* (London: Society for Promoting Christian Knowledge, 1881).

Rossetti, Christina G., *Letter and Spirit: Notes on the Commandments* (London: Society for Promoting Christian Knowledge, 1883).

Rossetti, Christina G., *Time Flies: A Reading Diary* (London: Society for Promoting Christian Knowledge, 1885).

Rossetti, Christina G., *Poems* (Boston: Roberts Brothers, 1888).

Rossetti, Christina G., *The Face of the Deep: A Devotional Commentary on the Apocalypse* (London: Society for Promoting Christian Knowledge, 1892).

Rossetti, Christina G., *Verses: Reprinted from 'Called to Be Saints', 'Time Flies', 'The Face of the Deep'* (London and Brighton: Society for Promoting Christian Knowledge, 1893).

Rossetti, Christina G., *New Poems, Hitherto Unpublished or Uncollected*, ed. William Michael Rossetti (London and New York: Macmillan and Co., 1896).

Rossetti, Christina G., *Sing-Song: A Nursery Rhyme Book*, with one hundred and twenty illustrations by Arthur Hughes Engraved by the Brother Dalziel (London: Macmillan and Co., 1915).

Rossetti, Maria Francesca, *Exercises in Idiomatic Italian through literal translation from the English*, and *Aneddoti italiani: Italian Anecdotes selected from 'Il Compagno del Passeggio Campestre'*, 2 vols (London: Williams and Norgate, 1867).

Rossetti, Maria Francesca, *A Shadow of Dante: Being an Essay towards Studying Himself, His World and His Pilgrimage* (London, Oxford, and Cambridge: Rivingtons, 1871).

Rossetti, Maria Francesca, *Letters to my Bible Class on Thirty-Nine Sundays* (London and Oxford: Society for Promoting Christian Knowledge, 1872).

Rossetti, William Michael, ed., *The Poetical Works of Christina Georgina Rossetti, with Memoir and Notes* (London: Macmillan, 1904).

Rossetti, William Michael, *Some Reminiscences of William Michael Rossetti*, 2 vols (New York: Charles Scribner's, 1906).

Rossetti, William Michael, ed., *The Works of Dante Gabriel Rossetti* (London: Ellis, 1911).

Rossetti, William Michael, ed., *Dante Gabriel Rossetti: His Family Letters with a Memoir* [1895], 2 vols (London: AMS Press, 1970).

Rowell, Geoffrey, *The Vision Glorious: Themes and Personalities of the Catholic Revival in Anglicanism* (Oxford: Clarendon Press, 1991).

Rowland, Christopher, *The Open Heaven: A Study of Apocalyptic in Judaism* (New York: Crossroad, 1982).

Rowland, Christopher, *Radical Prophet: The Mystics, Subversives and Visionaries who foretold the End of the World* (London: I. B. Tauris, 2017).

Scheid, Daniel P., *The Cosmic Common Good: Religious Grounds for Ecological Ethics* (Oxford: Oxford University Press, 2016).

Scheinberg, Cynthia, *Women's Poetry and Religion in Victorian England: Jewish Identity and Christian Culture* (Cambridge: Cambridge University Press, 2002).

Scott, Heidi, 'Subversive Ecology in Rossetti's *Goblin Market*', *The Explicator*, 65.4 (2010), 219–22.

Scott, William Bell, *Autobiographical Notes of the Life of William Bell Scott*, 2 vols (London: Osgood, McIlvaine, 1892).

Sharp, William, *Papers Critical and Reminiscent*, ed. Elizabeth Sharp (London: William Heinemann, 1912).

Shevelow, Kathryn, *For the Love of Animals: The Rise of the Animal Protection Movement* (New York: Henry Holt, 2009).

Shipley, Orby, ed., *The Church and the World: Essay on Questions of the Day* (London, 1867).

Stramara, Daniel F., 'Gregory of Nyssa's Terminology for Trinitarian Perichoresis', *Vigiliae Christianae: A Review of Early Christian Life and Language*, 52.3 (1998), 257–63.

Strong, Rowan, and Carol Engelhardt Herringer, *Edward Bouverie Pusey and the Oxford Movement* (London: Anthem Press, 2012).

Sultzbach, Kelly, 'The Contrary Natures of Christina Rossetti's Goblin Fruits', *Green Letters: Studies in Ecocriticism*, 14.1 (2011), 39–56.

Tanner, Kathryn, *Economy of Grace* (Minneapolis: Fortress, 2005).

Tanner, Kathryn, *Christ the Key* (Cambridge: Cambridge University Press, 2010).

Taylor, Jesse Oak, 'Where is Victorian Ecocriticism?' *Victorian Literature and Culture*, 43 (2015), 877–94.

Tennyson, G. B., *Victorian Devotional Poetry: The Tractarian Mode* (Cambridge, MA: Harvard University, 1981).

Thomas, Frances, *Christina Rossetti: A Biography* (London: Virago, 1994).

Tudge, Colin, *Why Genes are Not Selfish and People are Nice: A Challenge to the Dangerous Ideas that Dominate Our Lives* (Edinburgh: Floris Books, 2013).

Underhill, Evelyn, *Practical Mysticism* (New York: E. P. Dutton, 1915).

Vattimo, Gianni, *Belief*, trans. Luca D'Isanto and David Webb (Stanford: Stanford University Press, 1999).

Vattimo, Gianni, and Pier Aldo Rovatti, *Weak Thought*, trans. Peter Carravetta (New York: SUNY Press, 1983).

Vauchez, Andre, *Francis of Assisi: The Life and Afterlife of a Medieval Saint*, trans. Michael F. Cusato (New Haven and London: Yale University Press, 2012).

Watts-Dunton, Theodore, 'Reminiscences of Christina Rossetti', *The Nineteenth Century: A Monthly Review*, 37.216 (February 1895), 355–66.

Wheeler, Michael, *St John and the Victorians* (Cambridge: Cambridge University Press, 2012).

White, Gilbert, *The Natural History and Antiquities of Selborne* (1789; London: Penguin, 1987).

White, Jr., Lynn, 'The Historical Roots of Our Ecological Crisis', *Science*, 155.3767 (10 March 1967), 1203–7.

Williams, Isaac, *The Cathedral, or, The Catholic and Apostolic Church in England* (Oxford: John Henry Parker, 1838).

Williams, Todd O., 'Environmental Ethics in Christina Rossetti's *Time Flies*', *Prose Studies*, 33.3 (2011), 217–29.

Woolford, John, 'The Advent of Christina Rossetti', *The Review of English Studies*, 62.256 (2011), 618–39.

Wordsworth, Elizabeth, *Henry William Burrows: Memorials* (London: Kegan Paul, Trench, Trübner, and Co., 1894).

Yates, Nigel, *Buildings, Faith and Worship: The Liturgical Arrangement of Anglican Churches 1600–1900* (Oxford: Clarendon Press, 1991).

Index